ANGEL LAUGHTER

Ralph McTell

✶

Angel Laughter

AUTOBIOGRAPHY VOLUME ONE

amber
waves

from heartland publishing limited maidstone england

First published in 2000 by Amber Waves

Amber Waves is an imprint of Heartland Publishing Ltd.,
P.O.Box 902, Sutton Valence, Maidstone, Kent ME17 3HY, England
www.heartland.co.uk

ISBN 1 902684 02 8

British Library Cataloguing-In-Publication data
A catalogue record for this book is available
from the British Library.

Book design by Jeff Horne
Typeset in Adobe Caslon 11pt

Extract from *Lunar Lullaby* ©1974 Misty River Music Ltd.
used with kind permission of the publisher.

Printed and bound in Great Britain by Biddles Ltd., Guildford
on acid-free paper manufactured from sustainable forests.

For Mum and Bruce

Above, below, worlds collide
In the before and after
Oh happy to watch the sun go down
And join the angel laughter

– Ralph McTell, *Lunar Lullaby*

CONTENTS

introduction

This writing began with my recounting of our 'picnic' on the Playnies (see page 160). I enjoyed the experience so much, and the memories were so vivid, that I decided to do more. And found I couldn't stop. Sometimes after a couple of hours at the word processor I would be completely lost in time, and the warmth of the friendships or the chill of sadness would stay with me for several hours after I'd stopped typing.

Anyone familiar with my music will see how the events that shaped my songs also shaped my life. Therefore I acknowledge all the characters in these stories for the parts they played. Above all, though, it is to my mother (Mum) that I am most indebted. Her strength and courage were, and remain, an inspiration to me. We may have been among the poorest of the poor in post-war Croydon, but my growing up was enriched by stories, songs, hymns, Saturday morning pictures and a wonderful variety of characters and friends who peopled our lives.

To all of them, and especially Mum, my thanks.

My maternal grandfather, Albert Henry Moss, was born in 1879 in the village of Charlton in Northamptonshire. He was one of eleven children. He left school at eleven years of age, and did general labouring work until he moved into service, where we believe he met my grand-

mother. Alb, as he was affectionately known, worked as a general labourer, part-time wheat thresher, bill poster, postman, and was eventually the mace bearer for Brackley Council, which is where the family lived.

My grandmother, Elizabeth Coleman, was born in Bayswater in 1886, one of nine surviving children. Her mother opened a small grocer's shop in Hammersmith and from there my grandmother went into service. Albert and Elizabeth were married in 1910 and had three children: Olive Irene in 1912, Winifred Iris (my mother) in 1916, and Raymond Vivian in 1920.

My father's father was born in Addington, near Croydon. Charles May was also a general labourer and worked as a gardener on the estate of the Archbishop of Canterbury. We believe it was the Archbishop who christened my father, Frank, who was born on 7th January 1919. At some point my grandfather had become a railwayman and had progressed to engine driver. Before he retired he was promoted to driving an electric train and regarded this as a wonderful job, as he could go to work with a clean collar and tie on every day. My father's mother, Lily, was born in Barrow-in-Furness in June 1886. Her father was a blacksmith.

Frank had a difficult upbringing as his father had not wanted another child (so Lily always told my mother). Charles worshipped his daughter Ivy, who was several years older than Frank. My father was always getting into scrapes, for which he was severely beaten by my grandfather, and this culminated in him running off and joining the army as a boy soldier by the time he was fifteen. My grandfather got him out of the army and managed to find a place for him in the service of Lord Charnwood of Eaton Square. It was here that he met my mother, and when she was nineteen and he barely sixteen and a half, they became engaged.

Life in service did not suit my father, and once again he signed up, lying about his age. By the time he was seventeen he was in Cairo serving in the Royal Horse Artillery. Whilst in Egypt the regiment was reassigned to Ethiopia, where he fought the Italians involved in the dispute with Haile Selassie; and from there he was sent to Palestine. He was still there when war broke out in 1939.

Although my mother had gained a scholarship to Brackley High School, she was still put into service, and until war broke out worked for many well-to-do families. The one she talked about most often was Hugh, Marquis of Hertford. At the start of the war she was in Banbury and

obtained a job in a local pharmacy called Fox's.

She spent the war years in constant touch with Frank, but still managed to attend a few wartime dances with friends in the neighbouring villages that were home to lots of newly posted American troops. She wanted to enlist, but was persuaded against this course of action by her parents and brother, who was a serving naval petty officer. In the end she joined the Auxiliary Fire Service and vividly remembers the Coventry bombings.

When my father returned to England in 1943 they were married. I was born on 3rd December 1944 and my brother Bruce on 1st December 1946. During these two dates my father was hospitalised with a breakdown of some sort, and on release went AWOL until captured and imprisoned, we think in Colchester.

Eventually the family settled in Croydon at 30 The Waldrons, and my father got a job in a local garage, working for a Mr. Osborne. He first left us in 1947, and although he returned from time to time, his behaviour was erratic and violent. He lived rough occasionally and was very unsettled, although living with another woman in the Brighton area. He eventually became a butcher and had a shop in a village called Laughton in Sussex. In 1957 he was accidentally killed whilst trying to repair a defrosting machine in his butcher's shop. We heard about it from a small story in the *News of the World*.

Meanwhile the three of us—my mother, my brother Bruce and myself—had to get on with our lives...

∾

PART ONE

NURSERY DAYS

egg

✿

Sunshine pours in
through the top half of
the basement windows. The
light is slightly diffused through
floral curtains. Their background colour
is a creamy yellow and swirls of flowers
grow from unnaturally green stems. Below
me is a table, dark brown in colour, and at one
end stands my mother in a long-sleeved smock-
type apron that buttons up to her neck. She leans
over a small enamel dish with a blue line around
the edge. There is no tablecloth but there are place
mats made of thick cork for things to stand on.
Making his way to the chair on the other side is my
father. He is wearing a light short-sleeved shirt, open
at the neck, and his face and arms look very brown
contrasted against it. His hair is very dark and he
is smiling slightly. He sits down, and my mother,
with surgical precision, slices open the golden
brown pastry crust and removes its
supporting structure. To my utter
amazement she fishes out...
an egg cup.

A car door opens on to a huge expanse of grass. In the distance is a thin line of trees, leaves trembling. In front of them stands a fairground in full swing; it's loud even though it is far away. I turn to reach for my mother's hand but she is getting out of the car with a bundle in her arms and does not have a hand free. I drop my arm and stare at the shawl that is wrapped around my little brother, Bruce. I look at him as if for the first time. A bigger hand takes mine, and looking over my shoulder, my mother is smiling at my father and me as we walk off toward the tents and rides.

✪

A noisy puffing steam train is standing at the station platform. As we draw near, the volume is almost deafening. I grip the hand that holds mine harder. The noise is frightening but it unaccountably makes me smile. A man leans out of the tender and pushes his leg into a huge boot that is fixed to the wall and swings out of the compartment toward the wall. He connects a large hose to the tender and there is acknowledgement between him and my father.

✪

I'm sitting watching my parents get dressed. Even though there is no fire in the grate, they still stand in front of it to put on their clothes. They both dress with their backs to me but eventually I see the bits they modestly try to keep from me. My mother's body is very white, my father's only white in parts; the rest of him is sort of yellowish-brown and his hair is very black and curly.

We have a carpet in the living room. It is old but it is between us and the floorboards under which the mice hurtle about. Sometimes we hear them scurrying along between the stud walls and overhead between our ceiling and the floor of the family upstairs. Their scampering feet drives Meemo the cat crazy because he can't get at them. Meemo is very soft and sort of a sandy colour.

✺

I'm sitting on the floor when my father comes into the room with something in his hands. He sets it down. It's a tiny puppy with black and white markings. Some words are exchanged between my parents and the puppy pees on the carpet. He's very young and just sits there. I'm intrigued but not excited as he waddles about the room.

✺

Bruce has a cot in the corner of the small room adjacent to the living room and I have a noisy bed that creaks and pings with each move I make. Bruce has bronchitis and the Valor stove has a threatening witch's kettle on it which hisses venomous breath into the room. The air is slowly being starved of oxygen by the naked paraffin heater flame. Soon I develop bronchitis too, and our mother is nearly beside herself with worry. Sometimes above our combined wheezing I can hear her crying in the next room.

I love Saturday night bedtimes the best because we have clean sheets, and they are cold and make me want to breathe on my hands to stop my teeth going on edge, but after a while they are not so cold and I draw the old army blanket, which is under the patchwork bedspread, up to my chin and rub it on the skin just below my bottom lip and feel quite safe.

✳

We are always in bed at the same time and Mum always tucks us in and kisses us goodnight. She keeps the blackout curtain at the window to "help us get to sleep." In the spring and summer months there is always a chink of tantalising light which creeps in somewhere and the sound of the other flat dwellers passing through the yard. Occasionally there is even the odd visitor who descends the steps to our front door and in so doing has to pass our window. These footsteps are exciting and scary because it might be my father come home. Usually it is Mrs. Leisk from over the road.

✳

There are no pictures on the walls of our flat. The walls in Mum's bedroom are grey; so is the hall, and the front room is yellow distemper. We do not have a kitchen but we do have a scullery which was obviously used to keep skulls in. I expect they were lined up in rows in the cupboard that we are not allowed to use. There is a single cold tap with a brass handle that hovers over a huge yellow sink at one end of the room under the window. Next to this is a gas stove and next to that is a copper boiler that does not work, then a table that Mum prepares food on. The room has a stone floor and it is always too cold to eat in there.

Once every couple of weeks my mother does a wash. It is a huge job and makes me feel sad to watch her boiling up kettle after kettle of water, then using the soap whisk to try to get a lather and the little bag of blue to make the grey colour look white. There is a mangle in the yard next to the kennel in front of the Anderson shelter. Red chapped winter hands hang out the washing and the clothes prop hoists everything above the dustbins that have a strange smell all year round that strangely I do not find offensive.

❂

Every so often Mum paints the stones in the hallway with red ochre. It is so dark that you would never know that they are red but she insists that we will keep our standards up by such disciplines. White hairy fungus grows on the walls of the hall and in the toilet that we are told is poisonous and must not eat. Naturally because it grows so plentifully I decide to try it and I can state that it tastes salty and that it is not poisonous. Once we even had toadstools growing in the lavatory above the cistern.

❂

Next door is a home for wayward girls. They walk around in grey uniforms and are rigorously kept in line. At the back of their institution are some tennis courts and often in the summer evenings we can hear the plop of tennis balls being hit across the net and occasional little cries of elation and disappointment. These only serve to remind me that there is more left to the day, and resentfully I wonder how long it will be before we can stay out until it is impossible for anyone to see to play tennis.

Mr. Fox from upstairs comes down one day to apologise for something. His voice is slurred and he is swaying about and Mum shouts at him for causing a leak and water pouring through the scullery ceiling. I think she is very brave to shout at Mr. Fox and admire her for standing up to him. I afterwards realise that Mr. Fox had been drinking and my mother does not approve of drinking. In moments of desperation she tells me that she could be playing the piano in pubs instead of looking after us. On the face of it I cannot see anything wrong with this as pubs seem to be such jolly places where people are singing and laughing. I always was attracted to them and when I was out and about on my own I would always pause outside to listen to the atmosphere within.

✵

It is so cold in our room that we can pretend to smoke cigarettes and blow smoke from our mouths except that it is steam really. Our noses are always cold in the morning but the rest of us is warm in our squeaky, pingy beds. The secret is to get up and get dressed quickly; although it does not warm up the room much, we can stand near the paraffin stove that Mum lights before we have to get out of bed. I always stand too near it and burn myself, especially on the underside of my forearms when I am pulling on my vest. This makes me jump and angry when it happens and I feel stupid and I hate the stove, but it is our only morning warmth. When it does not seem to be working, I touch the top, but it always is and it burns my fingertips and makes a nasty smell and my finger prints are all smooth for a while. Sometimes I pull a hair from my head and hold it above the stove and see how near I must bring it to the top before it begins to writhe and shrivel in a strange death dance.

Mum buttons us up against the cold and she puts little Bruce on the seat on the back of her bicycle. We trudge through the snow to the nursery about half a mile away. Each time we say goodbye to her I wonder if she will come in the evening to collect us. She always does, so each day begins with sadness and closes with joy. Sometimes Anita from across the road collects us from the nursery and stays with us till Mum comes home. She's ten years older than me and goes to the Old Palace girls' school.

❂

At the nursery in the mornings we all march round and round in the room and pretend we are a band. One of the children pretends to play a shiny flute; I long to play it too because it is so shiny but I never get a go. In the morning when we arrive we all have to have our hair combed. I don't like this because ours is already done at home and they use a very fine metal comb that is dipped in some cloudy liquid and it smells of toilets and makes your hair go hard. They try to make us eat porridge but it makes me vomit so I am excused as Mummy give us Weetabix before we leave home. I don't like Weetabix much either. Bruce can eat his with warm milk but warm milk makes me sick. I think Mum would like me to eat mine with warm milk. It seems to warm her up to see us eat warm things in the morning but I drink warm tea with sugar and milk and Bruce drinks warm milk with sugar.

We are usually the last two to be brought home from the nursery, and in the evening before the other mums collect their children we eat a quarter of a slice of bread and margarine with either a single date or a piece of cubed cheese, or sometimes a single slice of cold boiled beetroot, which makes our lips red like lipstick. It has a strange sweet taste, but not sweet like jam which Bruce loves and not savoury like cheese that I love, and I don't think that I like it very much. But at least I don't throw up.

✪

Fixed to the wall of the living room is an old dark brown wooden cabinet with shelves. In the centre of the middle shelf there is a small pot in which sits a blown goose egg. It has female features painted on it and its huge eyes have long lashes. When we eventually leave this place my mother discovers some jars of pickled onions in the back of the cupboard. The onions are as dark brown as the woodwork. She had made these for Frank, my father, because they were his favourites. We eat them and they are delicious even though they are at least ten years old.

᰾

soft

The protected enclave that was The Waldrons was a strange mixture of social conditions and classes. During the reign of Henry VIII it was occupied by Sir Henry Carew, who used it as a game reserve, and it remained a private road until the beginning of this century.

It was enclosed by a wall and accessed by two gates, one at the Duppas Hill Lane entrance and the other at the hill that ran down to Southbridge Road. For many years it was a very upmarket street and it even had its own policemen who occupied a peculiar octagonal cottage at the Duppas Hill entrance. One could imagine these private police officers in top hats chasing boys who climbed the walls or gates in search of apples from the gardens or the chestnuts that fell in profusion each autumn in the Spinney, the miniature woodland in the middle of The Waldrons.

By the time Bruce and I were growing up there the cottage was derelict, although this was not unusual in post-war Croydon, where the remains of bomb-damaged and deserted properties littered the area. In Victorian times it was still a rather grand residential street, but as wars and recessions produced housing shortages, more ordinary folk started to populate the imposing old houses, and buildings that once housed one family and their servants now provided homes for dozens of people.

As I grew up I became aware of the different types of people living

around us, from comparatively wealthy ones, who kept their houses and gardens beautifully, to the poorest underclass—what would now be called problem families. But everybody rubbed along with each other somehow. There were spats and a few drink-induced quarrels up at the top of the road, but things got patched up pretty quickly, and in spite of genuine poverty in many of the homes, everyone considered themselves better off than those who lived in the estates around the 'Old Town'.

Many of the streets on the Salem Place estate had such a reputation that I was scared to enter them. There was also an area at the side of Holloway's yard where a few really rough families lived, and I avoided this as much as possible, sometimes taking the long way round to get to the shops that served the district. Once as I hurried past on my way to the shops, one of the front doors was open. There was rubbish in the hallway and no carpet, and the walls were cracked and crumbling. It was not that different to our place except that it was above ground, but it was obvious that those living there couldn't have cared less about the state of their home.

As I glanced furtively in I could see a small kid sitting on a toilet at the end of the short corridor. His name was Raymond, and he was a horrible piece of work. Once, though, even I felt compassion for him when, to impress a couple of girls, his older brother picked him up by pressing his hands over his ears and exerting the kind of pressure you would use to pick up a line of books. The kid let out the most piercing, blood-curdling shriek I had ever heard. Tears spurted from his eyes like water jets as soon as his feet left the ground.

Just past this boy's house was Warren's, the greengrocer and general store, and next to their shop was a small newsagent. Both shops had chewing gum machines and with patience and the right degree of intuition you could sometimes arrive when the arrow on the handle faced forwards. This entitled the lucky penny spender to an extra packet of gum. Once I got there and found both machines in this position—but I only had one penny, and by the time I'd raced back to get a friend to invest, the arrows had been moved on!

Down on Southbridge Road was Bowman's the bakers, and past St. Andrew's Secondary Modern school was a post office, an antique shop, newsagent and Martin's the greengrocer, who also had stalls down at Surrey Street market. The Martin boys were a tough little bunch, and Terry, who was in my class, had the nickname Pongo. I longed to have a

nickname (but not 'Pongo').

Mr. Harris ran the newsagents; he was quite a jovial man but I didn't like the way he said things to my mother. Once he tickled her over the counter, and although she said nothing at the time I knew she didn't like it and said he was "too familiar." He twisted everything around into a double entendre and Mum found him distasteful. Mrs. Harris wore lime-green frocks and had a great goitre below her chin that wobbled like a turkey's wattle when she spoke, which frightened me a little.

But we still had to go there. I liked it best when people were paying their newspaper bills and I had to wait in the shop smelling the mixed scents of chocolate, toffee and boiled sweets stored in glass jars on shelves behind the wooden counter. These essences were blended further with tobaccos and loose cigarettes, and the smell was intoxicating. I couldn't wait to start smoking.

Our house, number 30 The Waldrons, was a huge property owned by Mrs. Cox who lived at number seven across the road. It was divided into rooms and flatlets and we were in the basement: a damp, forlorn place. Above us were the Connaughtons, and across the hall was Mrs. Williams, a retired fortune teller whose uncle wrote a book on the search for the Indian rope trick called *A Magician in Many Lands*. She loaned it to me once and one of the pictures in it showed 'before and after' poses of a man sentenced to be hacked to death, which unsettled me for a very long time. Above her lived the Miss Dickinsons, across from them was Miss Elwell, and on the floor above lived Mr. and Mrs. Clarke (she was the married sister of the Miss Dickinsons).

Meemo the cat died one Christmas Eve when he got a fish bone caught in his throat.

Tyler, the puppy, was a cross between a Labrador and a bulldog; my father got him cheap because all the other pups looked like bulldogs or Labradors but this one had a bulldog's body and a Labrador's head. The lady who sold him to us named him Tyler after the peasant revolutionary and his black and white flag.

He was a great house dog; though he was never really a friend to Bruce and me, I know he was a comfort to my mother in her dark and lonely days after my father left us. He was my mother's dog and fiercely protective of her. Once when she had left Bruce and me in the old pram outside the library at Croydon Town Hall with Tyler tied to the railings,

she came out to find that a whole line of people had been kept out of the building by our ferocious guardian, who had decided that Mum should be allowed to choose her books alone.

Tyler spent most of his days in his 'kennel' which was a crate in front of the old air raid shelter. He was firmly chained to his kennel and was quite snug inside. He let me go in once but it was a bit smelly and once was enough. His chain was long enough for him to scare the dustmen who had to walk past him to collect the bins.

If Bruce and I were in the basement when my mother came home, we would hear Tyler's tail banging out a rhythm on the side of his box like a drummer to announce her return. I don't recall Mum taking him on long walks but perhaps these took place when we were in bed.

Sometimes Mr. Douglas would call round, and Mum, pulling on her old leather jacket, would tell us that they were going for a little walk, adding, "As you can see, we're not going anywhere special." Bruce and I would have loved her to go somewhere special with Mr. Douglas, as he was someone we both liked. He smiled a lot, Mum seemed to like him and he liked her, even in her old jacket.

We wondered if they would get married, hoping that they would because we liked him better than our own dad and were glad that he made Mum happy. But she found out that he was already married, and he never came round again. All three of us were sad about it.

At first Bruce and I had a potty each but I was literally elevated to the lavatory proper once I was big enough not to fall through the seat. There we had to sit until both of us had performed, which sometimes took a long time. Mum put us together for this activity as we were both scared of this end of the flat. Whilst we waited, grunted and strained, we sang little songs to ourselves or made up quizzes. Bruce discovered that if he banged his fists on his knees it sometimes helped him go, and thereafter if we got impatient we would both sit there drumming away until we had a result.

Often to while away the time I made up stories modelled on the ones our mum told us from Beatrix Potter or Allison Uttley. Mine concerned two characters called Piggy and Goat, and these yarns meandered on and on until I had managed to perform, whereupon my story would be abruptly drawn to a close with "and they all lived happily ever after." Poor little Bruce, however, sometimes had to sit there for so long that his little bum

was stuck to the rim of the pot. Whatever he had done, my mother always said, when she looked in, "Oh my Godfather Dick!"

I was spared this declaration of approval because I could pull the chain. For a long time I wondered who our godfather Dick was, but although his name was mentioned a lot (along with Jack Robinson), we never got to meet him.

In those hard grey days after the Second World War it did not seem appropriate to show signs of affection. There was work to be done, a country to rebuild, deprivation to be dealt with stoically, and if you couldn't afford things you made do.

Everyone was more or less in the same boat, and because clothes and many other things were 'on the ration' you seldom saw anyone wearing anything new, which particularly suited our fairly dire situation. Shoes were made to last longer by cutting out the toes to make summer sandals, and clothes were adapted, lengthened, shortened or completely transformed. Old skirts became trousers for small boys, and no-one was too proud to accept hand-me-downs. Our general shabbiness was probably worse than many and our circumstances poorer, but my mother still insisted we held our heads high as a family.

When couples went out, mother and father walked arm-in-arm but seldom held hands. Courting couples lay and canoodled on the grass of Duppas Hill long after they should have caught pneumonia from the damp. Children clutched their mothers' hands on the way to school, but the goodbye kiss was administered perfunctorily at home where no-one could see it. As children, we were reassured of our parents' love by much more subtle signs: coats being buttoned up and shirts and vests being tucked into trousers; shoelaces being tied properly in double bows, in mysteries of routing that was far beyond the logic of small boys; hair being brushed or combed; sandals being buckled; and occasionally spit being administered to handkerchiefs by fastidious mothers in the street to clean our faces.

We knew these signs were love tokens and had to be content with them. At nursery school Bruce and I were separated from our mum all day and we both took comfort wherever it came from. Sometimes it was worth taking a tumble just to have someone fuss over you when you scraped your knees.

Around the nursery was a large garden, and whenever the weather

was warm enough we were taken outside to play. It was always slightly hazardous playing under the trees in late autumn, as the remains of fruit attracted wasps and sometimes a child was stung. The initial shrieking usually subsided as quickly and abruptly as it had begun. I managed to get stung by a bee right under my left ear lobe and, although it hurt unbelievably, I did not cry.

The nurses painted it with something purple and I felt brave like a wounded soldier. In fact one of them told me I was a brave soldier and that kept the tears away. I loved being comforted, and although cuddling the children was rare, there were small signs of affection from those in charge of us: a hand rubbed over our lysoled hair; a hand guiding us up the step or leading us in games or little dances.

Although we often sat close to our mum or even shared the same chair, I do not remember her cuddling us or stroking us. Our intimate moments with her were mostly as she read to us in the evening; and often while she was reading I would just look at her and think how wonderful she was not to send us away so that she could go down to the pub and play the piano for all those happy people who sat in the smoke and left their kids outside with a glass of lemonade and a bag of crisps or an arrowroot biscuit.

I did envy them the crisps and lemonade though.

The head of the nursery was called Matron and she wore a white coat. She was nice to us, but she had hair as short as a man, which confused me a little. Later I heard that she was a replacement for the old matron who was addicted to pethidine. She had asked Mum to get a prescription for her and Mum's boss had realised it was forged. When she'd been rumbled, she just moved on and there was very little scandal and no detrimental effect on the children.

One day by the heavy gate at the entrance to the nursery, I failed to notice that the gate was swinging toward me. It had an iron latch which fell shut on a clip to lock it. If only my head had been almost up to the latch instead of one inch above it, the latch would not have hit me in the forehead, making a hole right through to the bone. I do not know why it was not stitched. Perhaps there was not enough skin, or perhaps Matron would have got into trouble.

Strangely it was not the pain of the wound that upset me but the anxious faces of those who tried to stop the bleeding. The hole healed up

reluctantly, only to be reopened several years later. I was tracking the path of a stair rod that had been thrown up at a conker tree to knock down some immature horse chestnuts. Round and around it twirled as it ascended through the leafy branches. Round and around it went as it descended, finally landing in exactly the same place on my forehead as the gate latch had done. That *really* made me feel sick.

The young girls who looked after us were called nurses and they wore grey uniforms, white hats and black stockings. They were all pretty and smiled and laughed a lot. Once when Bruce was crying a little as we sat on the ledge into the back garden I told him he was a "miseryguts."

"What did you call your little brother?" asked the nurse.

"Miseryguts," I replied, and it made her laugh so much I said it again, and that made Bruce upset, but we soon comforted him and it was all right. I loved it when the pretty nurses laughed.

One day a man came to the nursery and did a Punch and Judy show. It was a bit frightening but we loved it when we could finally understand Mr. Punch's words, and we all said, "That's the way to do it!" in his nasal whiny voice. But if I said it at bedtime Bruce didn't like it so much, so even though I should not have done so and I knew it worried him, I would still say, "That's the way to do it!"

Because of the dark and other things it was always hard to close the door on the day, even after Mum had read us a little story and allowed us to talk for a while. Bruce's voice would start to get drowsy and I would dread the approaching silence. Finally, when I could keep him awake no longer for company, we would say goodnight. Even this was extended by me to make it last longer.

"Goodnight Bruce."

"Goodnight Ralph."

"See you in the morning."

"See you in the morning."

"Hope you have a good night."

"Hope you do too."

Then after a short pause, and in a nasally voice, "That's the way to do it!"

After a calming down period the whole thing would begin again. Later on this rigmarole would be even more extended by the addition of our prayers.

"Have you said your prayers yet?" I would ask Bruce, and at first we would repeat together the going home prayer from school:

"Lord keep us safe this night,
Secure from all our fears,
May angels guard us whilst we sleep,
Till morning light appears."

One night I suddenly decided to announce that I would say my own prayers and in silence in my mind. I asked God to bless everyone that I knew and liked and then everyone I didn't mind too much. This soon gave rise to anxiety, as I would wonder if I had forgotten anyone and if God would think less of me for forgetting.

My litany soon got shortened to "Bless everyone in the world except the woman who went off with Daddy." I never asked God to bless him, but I didn't ask him not to. I would finish this off with an audible "Amen" and invite Bruce to say his own prayers. For a long time we did them separately so that God would not have to de-scramble them, but this I realised was probably unnecessary as there were bound to be other children saying prayers at the same time, and he could cope.

Of course I saw angels but they afforded me scant comfort. They were yellow and dark brown in colour, the colours of twilight when the creeping night sucks the life colour from the day. They never spoke, but hung motionless in our grey bedroom near the wardrobe and communicated amongst themselves like dutiful Nannies, more out of obligation than real love. They did not trouble me and I did not trouble them, but I was glad they were there.

I saw God only once and that was in a dream. I was still at nursery school and it was a sunny afternoon near the wooden climbing frame. There were several knotty apple trees in a cluster at one end of the garden, and a couple up by where a few children sat playing on the grass. There was a clear sky with just a few traces of cloud very high up. As I gazed absently at the space between earth and sky, I became aware of a trouser leg stepping out of nothing as if on an invisible ladder. At the end of the trouser, which was very dark green in colour, was a dark sock inside a black lace-up shoe. The trouser was soon matched by another, and to this was added a body and finally a head with a pleasant but unremarkable face.

"Hello children," smiled the man, "I'm God."

"Hello God," we chorused, unfazed for the most part.

"Are you having a nice time?" asked God.

"Yes!" we shouted in the manner we all use for communicating with children's entertainers.

"I just thought I would come down and see if you were all right," said God, smiling broadly from under a small moustache. Something on his lapel was drawing my eye, and though I couldn't read, I recognised it as the identity number of a Green Line bus driver. This was corroborating evidence to the dark green uniform that he was wearing. He's not God, I thought, he's a bus driver, and although Green Line bus drivers were a superior class of driver to the regular red bus driver it still did not explain his ability to descend from the sky from an invisible ladder. I was puzzled.

"Well, I must be going," said God. "Goodbye, children."

"Goodbye God!" we all shouted back, and I watched as he reached out for an invisible rung and slowly ascended into oblivion, his body disappearing into the same emptiness between the sky and the ground. All this took place at a disappointingly low level from the grass we were sitting on. In spite of his uniform I realised that it must have been God, for how else would he have been able to appear and disappear like that. As I grew up and saw other, more traditional depictions of the supreme being, I often felt like telling people what he really looked like. Until now I have kept it to myself.

One afternoon after we had all been woken from our nap after lunchtime at the nursery, one of the pretty young nurses led several of the children in a game of chase. As we wove in and out of the apple trees chasing and laughing, we all tumbled and fell and the game became one of rough and tumble. This was unusual because normally everything was a little formal. It was fun falling down and sometimes landing on her, and up we got and round the trees we went, and falling on her and feeling her softness was all I wanted to do. After a particular fall I was the first to get up, and as she rolled with some of the other children shrieking and laughing, her dress had ridden right up her thighs and I stood and gazed at all the wondrous clips and paraphernalia that held her nurse's black stockings up. She wriggled her legs to free herself from the remaining children who were still clambering over her and I became even hotter, and a strange new feeling spread all over me and I liked the feeling but somehow knew

that I was not supposed to have it. I thought I would like to marry her and find out more about all these wonderments that ladies had under their clothes.

Once a man came with a donkey and he gave the children rides on its back, but he ran out of time and neither Bruce or I got to ride him. It was nice to look at it though, and in spite of his scruffy coat it had friendly eyes and very long ears. When it had finished giving its rides the man let him wander through the grass, and while it was nibbling, the donkey allowed its penis to emerge. I was absolutely astounded by the length of it and tried to stand in front of the animal in case one of the pretty nurses saw it and was shocked. A long time after that the same thing happened with the coalman's horse, and one of the kids tried to flick a stone at it as it dangled half way to the ground. Creeping nearer to get a better shot at it, the marksman was lucky not to get soaked by an enormous torrent of urine that suddenly splattered all over the road and seemed would never end.

Kids seemed to have all manner of diseases and skin complaints then. There would always be someone with Gentian Violet painted on their faces or their heads close-cropped to discourage nits or fleas. Some kids had perpetual snot hanging from crusty nostrils. Instead of expensive cotton handkerchiefs, I carried a ripped-up square of old bed sheet and at times of winter colds I would pull this out to wipe my nose, only when no-one else was in sight. Otherwise the dried-up piece of what felt like cardboard would remain in my pocket.

Our road was a loop with an exit at one end for pedestrians and a private road into the back of a residential hotel. Between the alley known as the Waldrons Path and the hotel entrance were a few houses divided into flats, and on the other side of the hotel rear entrance was a white house which Mum called the 'Halfway House'.

This was as poor a place as I had ever seen. It was divided up into single rooms for problem families, single mothers, deserted wives, and sometimes families with nowhere else to go. The women were expected to share a gas cooker on the landing, and two toilets supplied the whole house. I don't know if there were any bathing facilities, but few of us had bathrooms in those days anyway. Some of the families who lived there were noisy, often rowing, occasionally drunk and different to the rest of the road. They were also intriguing to me and I found several friends there.

There were three pretty Anglo-Indian girls and their mother; a family from Devon with an Italian name; and a woman who, it was rumoured, had an affair with a man of eighty. She had subsequently given birth to a severely handicapped boy whose name was Roger. At the time he was called a spastic, and the assumption was that he was an idiot. In fact he was a highly intelligent, strong and muscular boy, who in spite of his ungainly walk, dribbling and contorted features managed to roam all over Croydon, where he was admired for his determination and great sense of humour. Roger turned his disabilities to his advantage and wore short pants long after the accepted period for change had passed. He practically had a beard before his mum got him his first long pants.

There were also lots of Irish. In those early years after the war, families moved from the republic to find work and in the chronic housing shortages afterwards accepted the worst kind of accommodation. I think there was always compassion for families, but single men were resented, and I can clearly remember the adverts which persisted for years in shop windows offering rooms for rent with the by-line 'No Irish Need Apply'.

One such family lived in the halfway house with a lot of kids, the oldest being Michael, who must have been about seven or eight. He was a slight boy but tall for his age, with deep brown eyes and dark freckles. He wore a pair of plimsolls until his toes poked out of the ends, with no socks. The people in the road got him a pair of second-hand shoes, and until he had been at school a week, he wore the same pair of swimming trunks for the whole summer although we were nowhere near any water.

I never got close to him, but we all sort of played together and somehow I got to play regularly in the rambling back garden. This originally had a beautifully terraced, landscaped Victorian elegance, but was now overgrown with rhododendrons and the paths were slippery even in summer. Next door was condemned as a property and was known as the Haunted House. Our games often spilled over into this place, and when I was very brave I forced myself down into the cellar that was full of fever water and felt the presence of a ghost.

One summery evening I sat with Michael on the periphery of a group of older children. They were playing a new game about dares, truth and promises, and us younger ones were not allowed to join in. This in itself was exciting because there was something else happening, and there was an edge of danger in the softening, midge-filled shadows. The boys' laughter was deeper than usual and the girls' was more shrieking. At one point

one of the girls chased after one of the boys and kissed him on the mouth. Michael and I looked at each other and grinned.

Suddenly Wendy, one of the girls, called Michael over to where they were all sitting and I followed on curiously to see what might happen. Without any warning Wendy and another girl grabbed Michael, and while one of them tickled him the other pulled down his trunks and wiggled his willie between her thumb and forefinger for a few seconds. All of them hooted with laughter and for a second Michael giggled too. Suddenly he burst into tears and they let him go. I was terrified and ran home in a state of shock and excitement. Michael and I never spoke about this humiliation, though I wanted desperately to know what thoughts had gone through his mind while it was happening. Soon afterward Michael got trousers, and later the whole family moved away.

Old Mr. Cox, the landlady's husband, used to work at the bottom of the back garden and had made a sort of shed out of some pieces of air raid shelter. In the summer he was usually stripped down to his woollen vest and flannel trousers, and although he tried to tiptoe past Bruce in his pram, the dog would bark and wake Bruce. He would bawl and my mother would tut-tut and come out and rock him until he went back to sleep. Once Mr. Cox invited me to his shed, and poured me a cup of sweet tea from his thermos into a beautiful little china cup with a poppy printed on the side of it. I thought it was one of the best things to do, sitting in his shelter sipping tea. He spoke to me, but it was one-way conversation as he was quite deaf and could never make out what I was saying. I hoped Mr. Cox would invite me again but he never did, being too busy growing things on the patch of ground that my father had once worked. Eventually this piece of land was sold for a building plot, and I was convinced that the builder had used my swing frame for a door lintel as we watched the house rise out of the vegetable plot.

One day from the bedroom window we saw a plump red-headed boy in the back garden.

"Mummy, there's a boy with red hair in the garden," I alerted her.

"It's Mrs. Cox's grandson," she said, and turned to look at him from the window. "Look at him, the fat pig."

I was surprised at this remark and have often sought to justify it. Was it because his slight stoutness was proof that he was getting enough to

eat, when in our own lives it was a double struggle for us, first to afford the right food and secondly getting us—or me at any rate—to eat?

My mother told me that at one point after my father left us that the doctor simply said, "If you don't get this child to eat soon he will die."

I was first force fed at nursery school and the feeling of that spoon being rammed down my throat only made me vomit up what little they had managed to get down me in the first place. Sometimes I would manage to keep food down all day only to throw it up at night.

Mrs. Cox's grandson wandered aimlessly about the back garden for the next couple of days with no-one to talk to. He was a lot older than me, but mustering the courage from familiarity of surroundings, I finally went out to him where he was walking in the bushes by the reformatory next door and said hello to him.

"Hello!" he said back to me, as nice as pie.

"My mum says you're a fat pig," I told him, and immediately realised it was not the right opening thing to say.

"Does she now?" said the stout redheaded lad with a grace and aplomb that astounded me. We spent the morning getting on quite well, but the age gap between us, not to mention my opening remarks, precluded a deep friendship from burgeoning. I told my mum what I had said and her conclusion was that we would probably be thrown out on to the street.

I lost my appetite completely and hardly slept for the dread of being kicked out. In my convoluted prayers I wrestled with the concept of honesty over diplomacy. For the life of me I cannot think what possessed me to tell him her remarks. Visions of the three of us plodding round the streets, with Tyler the dog barking at everyone we spoke to, and our pathetic possessions heaped on the old twin pram, woke me sweating to find that I had peed the bed. This was a habit that took a long time to fix.

All kinds of things are written about this problem now but the truth is that I was scared to leave the safety of the bed. I believed that even if I did not have to brave the freezing unlit hallway to the bathroom and used the bedside chamber pot, I could still be pounced on by the witch (one night a witch had leaped out of the wardrobe and pinned me to my bed and breathed noxious vapours into my mouth and made my eyes run. She had cackled and laughed at my terror as I lay just a few feet from my sleeping mother and brother).

Around this time another thing began to happen. Often during the

day I would seem to hear people talking in low babbling whispers, like conversations coming from down the hall of some building. It was impossible to pick out the words, and that made it even more maddening.

I suppose I became used to hearing the voices. Indeed I may have almost encouraged myself to hear them. From my favourite hymn at school, about God calling to Samuel (*Hushed Was The Evening Hymn*), I hoped that he might call me in a voice that others could hear.

I convinced myself on more than one occasion that God had spoken to me through my mind and advised me to become a missionary to far-off lands. Whether this form of ministry had greater attraction than the regular church because of the element of travel, I cannot now say. All I do remember is that I truly believed God had spoken to me, and when I later realised that he probably hadn't and that it was wishful thinking, I was filled with horror that most of the misguided despots of the world, the causers of such misery to the human race, based the legitimacy of their actions on the conviction that God had told them it was what he wanted them to do.

I needed to believe there was a God and that he heard my prayers, and I liked praying. Sleep always came to me with difficulty, but praying helped. My worst fears were that Mum would leave us, or send us to a 'home', but I also feared for people in general and children in institutions especially; people with no-one to care for them.

I balanced all this caring with resentment at rich kids and privilege, and was quite sure that I would have the last laugh in heaven if I was good. It is a hard lesson to learn that goodness is rewarded by death in the same way as wickedness.

Our landlady, Mrs. Cox, also became a figure of hatred for taking rent off my poor mum, in order that we could live in that dismal freezing damp basement that I missed so much when I was later in hospital. Once, when I took the rent across to number seven, she opened a drawer in her kitchen that seemed to me to be full of half crowns. I nearly passed out at the sight, and certainly had never seen so much money in my life before. If she had so much, why did she need our pound per week? I later realised this old lady was quite philanthropic in her way and, amongst other small acts of comparative generosity, organised a Coronation party for all the kids in the street.

I was also angry that young soldiers died for old generals, although this did not stop me wanting to be one—I suspect it was to prove that I

could be tough and manly. Some hopes, when on most occasions the plaintive call of the *Last Post* could, and still can, reduce me to tears.

The angels around the bottom of the stairs who whispered to each other did not bother me, because I could dismiss them, but the voices I began hearing seemed much more sinister. They took the form of muttering and murmuring in tones of discontent. They sounded like the noise you might hear at the beginning of a concert on the radio before the instruments tune up.

Every now and again one voice would rise to the surface, and I would be just about to catch the words he or she was saying when it would disappear in the general hubbub of sound. This voice was the one that particularly disturbed me. I was never sure whether I was being warned, threatened, advised, or admonished. Sometimes the voices would begin at full tilt and other times they would slowly increase in volume. This mostly happened when I was on my own.

Sometimes they were talking directly to me and their message would be frustrated by my inability to catch what they were saying. Most often they were talking conspiratorially, as if they were discontented. Was it with me or the world? Were they coming to get me, or planning my rescue? I could not tell, and asked my mum what they meant. She advised me that they probably would soon disappear, and that she would ask Mr. Strong at work (the assistant dispenser). She had earlier explained my curiosity about erections as having excess acid in my body. I knew that rhubarb had acid but I liked rhubarb, so I resolved not to ask about that again, and live with my erections. This was very different. I don't remember what Mr. Strong's advice was, but the voices continued and only stopped when they were ready.

Somewhere along the road Mum had bought us an old piano from the junk shop at Reeves Corner, and I loved it. It cost about eight pounds and it was definitely for me, as Bruce had absolutely no interest in it. I would spend hours playing tunes with one hand, and sometimes the voices would stop abruptly whilst playing, and sometimes they would start whilst playing. Sometimes I tried to shout them down, or sing loudly to drown them. Later, when I began to get used to them, I tried to listen in case I could learn what they were trying to tell me.

On the whole, they frightened me and I wondered to myself if I was going crazy. We had a crazy woman who used to walk through The

Waldrons from time to time and I didn't want to end up like her. She wore a mauve hat and her stockings were all loose and she had red lipstick smudged on her mouth and she was mad and I had nightmares about her. I liked happy shows on the radio because they chased these voices away. I loved people who laughed a lot because they chased them away too. But sometimes the voices would appear in the middle of these moments as well.

The voices ended finally as I entered my teens, but at this early stage I found I could sometimes drown out the noise if I hummed to myself. My preferred method of making them go away, however, was to whistle.

Men, and to some extent women, used to whistle then and they don't now. Perhaps it is because of the constant noise pollution, or more likely because people look at you if you whistle. I was coming home one day from Duppas Hill park when I first got a sound from my pursed lips. In the beginning I could only get one note out, but by the time I got home I could manage a bit of a tune. Naturally I wanted to share my new skill with everyone and wanted all my friends to be able to do it too.

I tried to explain the trick but it is impossible to explain how to whistle. You just have to walk around pursing your lips and looking stupid blowing away, until that first reedy note emanates from inside your head, and then intuitively you can eventually call up any note or any pitch you want without even sliding up to it. Soon you develop your own tone, and the popular melodies of the day were very accessible.

The impression this gave was that I was a sublimely happy child as I wandered about the place whistling away, but the truth was sometimes a little darker. Indeed, when a song came out with the words, "I whistle a happy tune so no-one will suspect I'm afraid," I was comforted that others might be hearing these scary voices too. I whistled all the time and was particularly impressed by a performer on the radio called Ronnie Ronalde who could almost warble like a real bird. Could you, I wondered, make a living from whistling? I thought that would be marvellous, so I practised all the more.

~

frank

"You sound just like your father," my mother would say, as I whistled my way round the house or along the road from school. I liked to think that I had got something that was good from him.

The hurt that he had caused us all was immeasurable. It affected us on an almost daily basis; from the moment we were awoken to go to nursery school to being the last ones collected from it, we were reminded of his lack of commitment to our well-being. In his actions he had denied us the comfort of having a mum at home. The intimacies between us all were always strained by both my mother's exhaustion and her duty to take care of us, and we were always aware of it.

The night my father first left us I was in their room. Whether I had come in to see what the noise was about or whether I was in there when the noise started I do not know and my mother does not remember. She was sitting on the bed, crying and shouting, and my father was angry. Though I have never been able to recall the actual sound of his voice I know that it was moderate and warm, but this night it had an added intensity. As the row went on, no-one seemed to notice I was there. I stood motionless, watching these two people shout and plead and deny and assert in a tableau that I had never witnessed before.

"You dropped the letter behind my back," wept my mother. My father just stood there, pale and with thunder in his eyes, and his brown skin looked yellow in the light from the forty watt filament in the clear glass bulb that lasted for years afterwards, its curly red image of points hanging like a crown between the two terminals inside the vacuum. Suddenly he seemed to notice me for the first time, as my mother's body shook with sobbing. He turned and grabbed the door handle.

"I'm leaving!" he shouted.

"Frank!" cried my mother.

There was a mighty slam of the heavy front door before a deafening silence as we waited for a change of heart and direction. It did not come, and with a huge desperate sob my mother collapsed on to the bed and cried and cried.

Hardly able to take it all in, I crawled up on to the bed, the strange feel of the knitted spread in blue with brown and white stripes feeling comfortless to my skin as my mother seemed to be burying herself deeper and deeper into it.

I reached over her back, her feet still dangling over the side of the bed and said, "Don't worry Mummy, I'll look after you."

As I uttered the words I was surprised by the way it sounded, for as they were being said I really meant it. After they had been spoken I realised the magnitude of the statement, and it had made my mother cry even more and that in turn made me cry. Bruce slept through it all.

By the few accounts that it is possible to draw on, my father did love me. He often took me to work, and I used to sing for his work mates in the cafe. He was close to a Jewish family who were tailors in the high street, and the lady of the house made a big fuss of me too. I remember being in their place, which was very dark and shadowy but not a bit scary. Their shop was near to a chiropodist. In the window of this shop was an anatomical diagram of a foot and part of a lower leg that is imprinted on my memory.

The chiropodist was called Miss Roberts. My father was conducting an affair with her even when my mother was in hospital having Bruce, and I had been sent into the care of a Mrs. Hayes. I can only surmise by what went on that all did not run smoothly between him and his mistress even after he left us.

Often my dad would be back at our place when I got in from school.

I cannot explain how, but I always seemed to know that he would be there, and my whistling would drain away before I got to the steps to our flat. The effect of his visits was to suck the energy from our little family. It would be smiles when we got in and a little chat, they would talk, and then he would go and she would cry. Sometimes they would shout and she would cry. It was terrible, and in the end I was frightened of him, not from any threat of violence but for all the pain that would ensue when he had gone. He had begun to put on a lot of weight, and although he was under six foot tall my mum says he got up to fifteen stone.

One morning he was in the flat wearing a dark suit and in need of a shave. I guess he had fallen out with his new partner and was living rough in the woods and made his way to our place still confident in some sort of welcome. By this time he had acquired an old motor car and a shotgun; later he arrived with a black dog that had been bitten by a snake and asked my mother to fix it up for him.

I have several clear memories of him that I know are accurate, and I still have tangible proof of one of them. My mother never gave us extra pennies for sweets; we had our sixpence pocket money, and because we ran errands for the whole street we picked up a few more coins this way. What we did have was a sweet tin. My mother kept everything in jars or tins to protect them from mice or dirt or fingers, and at the end of the day she would reach for the tin and dole out a sweet each. It never occurred to me to steal one, and we looked upon the treats as confirmation that she still loved us or that we had been good. My father was home, and in a genuine effort to get to know me had taken me down to the local shop, and after picking up a packet of cigarettes had asked me if I wanted a sweet. In those days a penny could buy you a gobstopper, a packet of YZ chewing gum, two flying saucers or four blackjacks.

I was so taken aback that I did not know what to ask for, so I said, "A flying saucer please?"

"Is that all you want?" he asked me, smiling at the same time.

"Yes thank you," I replied, and he duly parted with the ha'penny required, half smiling and shaking his head disbelievingly. I crunched up the rice paper outside and frothed the sherbet inside and spoke no more words to him. He asked me if I liked school, or some other inane enquiry, and I nodded.

The next memory is of being told how to hold a cricket ball. This was

probably, on a scale of one to ten, about minus five on my list of ways to improve my knowledge. Of all the men I know who have been brought up by single mothers, I am the only one that has any interest in sport at all, and that only really began when I had children of my own. I threw like a girl, and have never had good hand to eye co-ordination. These skills, such as they are, had to be acquired by imitation, bluff and sheer bravado in my early teenage years, and I was not really found out until I played football for the pub team—and then my weaknesses were put down to my veteran status.

"You have to keep the ball behind your back until the last minute, so the batsman won't know what kind of ball you're going to bowl him," explained my dad conspiratorially in my ear as he pushed my hand firmly behind me.

"Now take your run up and swing your arm over and spin the ball," he instructed. I had only a passing interest in hitting anything with a bat and when we five-year-olds played we only threw underarm. I duly tried to please him, but the ball, instead of going toward the piece of planking that he had set up as a wicket, flew straight up in the air. My father laughed and I went red with embarrassment.

"One more," he encouraged. This time the ball shot out sideways at right angles to the intended direction, and as I got more and more flustered the situation just left me until I was close to tears. To my relief he abandoned the exercise.

It was coming up to Christmas one year, and the stores were full of the usual toys and games ready for the festive season. I had spotted a child's tool set comprising a small hammer, a saw, set square and so on, neatly arranged in a presentation packet. I decided that if I was armed with this item I could make every other toy I ever needed and proposed to ask Father Christmas for it when I sent my list up the chimney.

Halfway home from school I sensed my father would be at home, and sure enough when I got there his brightly painted old Wolseley was parked outside. After saying a resentful hello, I retreated as normal, but at some point he found me and in his effort to make conversation asked me what I wanted for Christmas. I told him I was hoping for a tool set, and he asked what I wanted that for, but I couldn't tell him as it suddenly sounded stupid. Instead I just said I wanted to be a carpenter. This seemed to meet with his approval and he told me to come with him to his car. After

rummaging about in the back, he presented me with a small picture framer's hammer with the nail lifter broken off, a hacksaw, a screwdriver and a mortise or saw gauge made from two pieces of wood.

"There you are," he said, "now you've got your tool set." I looked down at my collection of scrap instruments, and wondered how far I would get with my plan to make everything we ever needed with such items. I think I knew even then that what I really wanted was the pleasure of unwrapping the tools rather than using them. I still have the broken hammer!

I do not feel able to press my mother on their relationship during these years. They were estranged and he was living with someone else. Although there are strong indications that she would have willingly taken him back, it was not to be and hopefully he enjoyed seeing Bruce and I from time to time.

Once he came to see us and took my mother to school where they both watched me leave the school gate and go dancing a 'happy to be going home' sort of dance, which resembled the Morecambe and Wise jig. I had become convinced that I had almost discovered the secret of flight at this time and may have actually been in experimental mode. My mother told me that my dad wondered if I was the 'full shilling' at the time.

On another occasion he joined us for tea, and as Bruce and I sat eating our bread and jam he flew into a rage because Bruce had his elbows on the table, and he tied his arms to the chair with the straps from our recently acquired bus conductor's outfit. This was a terrifying experience for us both, as we had seldom seen a man in real anger before. My father's temper was dreadful and years later my mother tried to rationalise it by telling us of his war experiences, but at the time it must have been hard to cope with even when they were happy together.

She told me once how he had mistaken one of his friends sitting next to her in a car for someone else and punched the guy out through the car windscreen. He had lost his sergeant's stripes twice, for fighting and for attacking an officer. There was also violence against my mother and according to his mistress he tried on more than one occasion to strangle her. I am in no doubt that had he really wanted to, he would have done so. I can only take it that reason and compassion were also part of his character. In spite of his imprisonment and subsequent hospitalisation

after the war, he was utterly fearless and with good reason. He was a good athlete and regimental heavyweight boxing champion.

He was also an above average cricketer, and was invited to play for the MCC, which he derided by saying, "I'll hit them if they get someone else to run for me."

As a result of a boxing injury when he collided with the corner post he could only blow smoke from one nostril. He told my mother that he only wanted one kid, although once Bruce had arrived it was he who named him, as he did with me. When he was on the move we were always getting letters asking for bills to paid, as he chose to give our address to avoid ever being caught up with. I believe he did the odd bit of time for minor street trading offences and I also have a memory of a suitcase full of lions made from pipe cleaners. Our neighbours across the road remember him getting their two girls to sew up some material in the shape of animals, that were then stuffed elsewhere and sold from suitcases on street corners. At one point he even acquired an electric motor and fixed it to their old treadle machine to speed up the operation.

After he left us Bruce and I never had a single birthday card or present from him, and I know that he never gave my mother a penny towards our keep. She would never lie about such a thing. The penultimate time that I saw my father was in 1951, when he arrived one day out of the blue to take me in his car to see the Festival of Britain, the great exhibition on the south bank of the Thames. The only trouble was that it was not yet built, and as we wandered round what was a giant building site I wondered if he was planning to take us on all the magical rides and amusements that would one day be in place. On the way back home he took me to a café where he bought me fish and chips. I could barely manage the knife and fork, and when he dropped me off he had a go at Mum about my table manners, which forged another quarrel and my voices came back again and I wished he would just leave us alone.

The last time I saw my father he was sitting opposite my mother by the wall. The old table had been moved across the room and now occupied the wall area next to the condemned room which was the bedroom I shared with Bruce. Now under the window was an older styled 'put-u-up' or sofa-bed with wooden arms and covered in a pink material with a thirties type pattern on it. I sat there listening to the conversation as if I was not there and once again it turned to Frank coming back to us and

got more heated. The voices in my head got louder and louder and still I could not hear what they were saying. Suddenly I burst out with a string of invective that stopped both my parents in their tracks, and they just turned and stared at me.

"Why don't you just go and leave us alone?" I shouted, my voice trembling. "You only make Mummy cry and that makes us all cry. You're no good! None of the Mays are any good! Why don't you go away and leave us alone?"

My speech went on for much longer than this but these are words that I clearly recall. Perhaps this is hardly surprising. All the time that my unbroken string of tormented sadness was being transformed into words that had been unrehearsed, other voices were encouraging me, all of them talking at once. It wasn't just my own voice I could hear as I spoke but lots of voices, and though I could not hear the actual words they seemed to be saying *Go on, tell him all those thoughts and feelings*.

The words flew out from my lips and my temperature was rising and a dark redness becoming black was enveloping me. I was frightening myself.

Where were these words coming from?

Why had I chosen this moment to let it all go?

Why weren't either of them saying anything to me?

Why are these tears falling out of my eyes and splashing on my bare knees?

Where is all this snot coming from?

For a few seconds the two of them sat there staring at me as the tears of rage and anger burnt down my hot cheeks.

My father turned to my mother and said quietly, "Did you tell him to say that?"

"No of course not!" she answered.

"No-one told me to say it!" I sobbed. "You just make us cry and we don't want you and we don't need you!"

I shook the words out of myself and sat with uncontrollable anger and sadness pouring out of me.

"I think you'd better go outside now, Ralph," said my mother. I left the room and found the piece of old bed sheet in the pocket of my jacket and blew my nose and wiped away some of the tears. Soon afterwards I heard the front door slam and my mother starting to cry, and I knew that

I would never see my father again.

In our darkest days when Mum was too ill to work, she finally went to an interview with the National Assistance Board. I found her back at home. She had been crying and was still in her best frock from the interview.

"They said, 'Go and find your husband, Mrs. May'," was all she managed to tell me.

What could I do except try to be good? I was still unable to eat much with any relish; although Bruce was becoming well built I was always a bit on the skinny side. Mum eventually found work as a charlady and scrubbed doorsteps and skivvied for some people, so once again we were self-supporting, although the struggle was hard and joyless.

Thank goodness for the radio, where you could hear people laughing at comedians who told jokes that I could not really understand, and music that made you feel good. *Take It From Here*, *Ray's a Laugh*, *Variety Playhouse*, *The Al Read Show*—I listened to them all.

I loved *Children's Hour*, and the recollection of the dramatisation of *Winnie the Pooh* still gives me a warm feeling. I can remember the sound of the actors' voices though the memory of my father's has gone forever. David Davis sang the Pooh songs, Norman Shelley played Pooh, and Wilfred Babbage played Piglet. Babbage also played the schoolmaster in *Jennings at School*, and his exasperation at Jennings' mistakes and his catchphrase, "You silly little boy!" made me laugh out loud.

At that time I thought I would have loved to have gone to boarding school and find a stupid friend like Jennings' friend Darbyshire, but I was soon to find just what being away from those I loved was really like.

❧

Part Two

Families and Friends

accident

St. Peter's Primary School was no more than a rather large house, so the transition from the nursery school I'd attended up to then, which was just up the road, was not too traumatic. To get there I only had to cross one road with very light traffic on it. Nevertheless I still managed to walk in front of an ambulance one day.

Fortunately the driver had seen me from a long way off, ambling across the road looking in the opposite direction, and timed our meeting just before I reached the other kerb before giving me the slightest toot on the horn to let me know how foolish I had been. My face was still red when I got through my front door.

My first teachers were kind and I soon learned my numbers and letters. In fact I still think of my letters and numbers in terms of the colours in which they were printed on the walls of our first year's class with Miss Gun.

The whole of the basement area doubled as the school dining room and it was here that I had to wrestle with the problem of school dinners. I found it impossible to keep the food down even if I managed to get it past my lips, and became quite adept at shoving food on to my neighbour's plate when they weren't looking.

Once this ruse had been tumbled, I began trying to hide various foods

under mashed potato or even hollowed-out boiled potatoes, but this too was discovered. My next plot came to grief when the paper bag in my pocket containing the mash and carrots burst during playtime, making me smell like a pig bucket for the afternoon. Next I tried to swap places to where the tables joined and for almost a week I was successful at dropping my food through the crack between the tables and on to the floor. Eventually by elimination the phantom food flicker was traced back to me and I was summoned to see the headmistress, Miss Clifford.

"Hello Ralph, have you been throwing your food on to the floor?" she asked me very gently. She was a sweet lady with dark hair and a slightly hooked nose.

As the realisation hit me that I had been caught almost red-handed my face responded in sympathy. My body began to ignite somewhere above my navel and rose upward like ink across blotting paper. As it reached my neck and drove quickly over my chin and up my face, the sudden evacuation of blood from my lower body began to cause a trembling in my legs, and my hands assumed the temperature of school milk bottles in January covered with a light dew.

I looked straight into her kind eyes, holding on to her desk with my wet cold hand and hardly able to stand or control my legs. My eyes, their lids throbbing, had now involuntarily filled with water and were about to overflow. My voice had all but dried up, and when it did come I hardly recognised the hoarse croak that emerged from my glowing head.

"No Miss," I managed. It was my first lie.

"All right Ralph," she said, "it must have been someone else."

I couldn't believe it. Of course she knew it was me, but I think she also knew that I had suffered enough and that I would never do it again. I don't know how I got my legs to walk out of that room, and I didn't eat school dinners again until I went to John Ruskin Grammar School. In fact it was walking home to cook myself my sausage with peas and potato that I nearly got hit by the ambulance.

In February 1950 Mrs. Leisk, Mum's cherished neighbour and confidante, was looking after me during the early half-term holiday. Mum was at work and Bruce was in nursery school. I had turned five in the previous December and had been at St. Peter's for the first few weeks of the new year.

Mrs. Leisk was a tiny woman. She had been deserted by her husband

and was as joyless as the grey basement flat she occupied with her two daughters, Valerie and Anita. Both girls were older than me and very pretty, and went to different schools. Anita, the elder, sometimes used to collect Bruce and me from the nursery, and occasionally acted as baby-sitter.

Mrs. Leisk prepared her food with a great deal of care and originality for the times, and tried to persuade me to eat dishes like stuffed tomatoes. It was hopeless though, and after managing her potatoes there was little more I could force down.

There was nothing for me to do all day except look at books, which were mostly for girls. I was not allowed to play in the garden. There was a box of old birthday cards; one in particular had a drawing of a man having a drink, and when you tilted the card his glass appeared to empty (it was a small plastic holder full of orange sand), which amused me for a little while.

This particular Saturday Mrs. Leisk took Valerie and me into Croydon to look at the shops. It was raining, and as we walked down Crown Hill we paused to peer into a sweetshop window. It was an old-fashioned confectioner's, and I was still holding on to the belief that if you looked pleadingly enough through the glass, a kind person would stop and buy you some sweets.

We were there for some minutes when I was aware of a loud revving of an engine followed by a crash and a blow to the small of my back. Someone—Valerie, I think—screamed, and as I looked round for her I was aware that the whole pane of glass in front of the shop had come loose and was about to fall out of its frame. I couldn't move, as something huge was pressed up behind me, and the pane of glass crashed down on my legs.

Because of the angle at which I was standing, the glass acted like a guillotine and sliced down the inside of my thigh, slashing straight through my overcoat and short trousers and into my leg. I don't remember the pain at this point, I just remember seeing a great flap of skin hanging down from my leg, and the flesh beneath it that was so shocked it had not yet begun to bleed.

I was very frightened and took a step backward before falling on to the shards of glass behind me. I could see that Valerie had become wedged at the knee between the two shops and was crying loudly. People were running about, and two or three of them came to help me. One man laid

the torn piece of flesh back over my leg, then they lifted me into the sweet shop and laid me on the floor.

A lorry owned by a firm called Crippen had pulled out from the store across the road and turned left to go up Crown Hill, but had misjudged the turn. It had then mounted the pavement, hitting Valerie first and then the shop front and me almost at the same time. As the glass had fallen out on to me the lorry had moved back, enabling me to stagger a few steps backward before I fell over. The driver had been drinking.

At about four fifteen that day, Anita was leaving her school at the Old Palace. She decided to go home via Surrey Street and saw the huge crowd that had gathered to gawp at the incident. She realised there must have been an accident, but cycled on home, unaware that it involved her mother, sister and me.

While I was being comforted by those in the shop and the ambulance was making its way to the scene, blood continued to pour from another unseen wound in the back of my other leg. I lay there quite still, and the familiar smell of chocolate and tobacco mixed with lemon drops and toffee were as loud to me as the voices that attempted to stop my tears and assuage my fear. Shortly after the ambulance arrived from the nearby Croydon General Hospital I passed out.

I'd lost a lot of blood, and as I came to in a lift going to my recovery ward the two orderlies were talking to each other, assuming that I was unconscious. One of them asked the other if he thought I would make it. The other orderly just shook his head.

The injuries needed over fifty stitches, and a draining tube was fitted. I woke up in a children's ward with a protective crate over my legs and some kid screaming up at the end of the ward. The next few days are lost to me, but I do remember that on awakening all I wanted was to see my mother. My legs were both swathed in bandages and I don't recall any pain. The nurses told me not to move my legs, and I tried to stay as still as I could for as long as I could. I suppose that being used to nursery made me adapt quickly to the nurses on the ward.

There were two sisters on the ward, who were very strict. The night sister was the gentler of the two, but all the nurses were wonderfully kind and compassionate toward their charges, who ranged from about four years old to thirteen. My bed was against the wall facing the window which looked out on to the car park a couple of storeys below.

None of us were allowed visitors in those days and for the life of me the only reason that I can think of is that it may have upset us to see our loved ones. For me and my already insecure nature it was a very unkind rule and I was desperate. Each evening I asked for my mum, and although they explained that all the children were in the same situation, I was not the only one who cried himself to sleep for several weeks.

My right leg, which had received the worst injury, had become infected and when I first saw the wound I nearly passed out with shock. Somehow the stitches had not held, reopening the cut, and a huge scab measuring about an inch wide had formed. It was decided not to restitch the wound and nature was left to take its course. A drain had been inserted and each day when they changed the dressings the nurse would pull a little more of the tube from my leg and cut it off.

At first I was sure that this tube was part of me and hoped to impress the nurse by my bravery. I think what really impressed them was my putting up without complaint the amount of penicillin I had to be injected with to disperse the infection. My behind must have looked like the top of a pepper pot.

Slowly I grew accustomed to the routine of hospital. There was no TV or radio and time hung heavy. I longed to get up and walk, but the nurses all said I must wait. Being so young friendships were not struck up and conversation was very limited. Children came in and out for tonsils or adenoids or appendectomies and occasionally for road accidents.

I only remember three patients clearly: the little boy in the bed on my right and the two older boys at the end of the ward. These two were both accomplished artists in my mind. They whiled away the hours drawing, one of them specialising in drawing various parts of ladies' anatomy, which he held up to us little kids to see our reactions. He also drew hands, usually with a cigarette burning between the fingers.

I admired his talent greatly, and would loved to have become his friend if I had been able to walk down to his bed. But he decided that he could have more fun tormenting the smaller kids by telling us that the men in white coats were going to take us away to the lunatic asylum. I had no idea what this meant, but it terrified me, and because I showed it he did it all the more.

Eventually I hardly slept for fear of capture, and on top of this there was the warm milk incident. As if the food was not horrible enough (sago, rice, semolina and tapioca pudding being a speciality of Croydon

General), the evening's close was announced by the delivery of a glass of warm milk.

I could not even manage my mother's milk puddings, so the hospital had no chance. For a while the nurses tried to force feed me but they finally abandoned this and I was allowed to pick at whatever I could manage to swallow. But warm milk at the end of the day was too much— and they only collected the cups when they were empty.

The little boy in the bed next to me was called Stephen; I may have felt badly off, but this lad didn't even have a teddy bear, or any interest in one. On his locker he had some *Picture Post* magazines, but no toys or anything else to occupy him. It didn't seem to bother him; perhaps he was very ill, but he hardly spoke and just lay there looking at the walls all day.

After throwing up my milk a couple of times and still not being excused taking it, I hit on a plan. When Stephen turned to drink his milk I slipped mine into the top shelf of his locker, and in the business of cup collection afterwards, its disappearance was not noticed. This simple deception went on for almost two weeks, by which time his top shelf was full and I had begun to use the bottom shelf as well. The only trouble was that each time I opened the door a terrible smell emanated from within.

With several kids incontinent on the ward there was always a strong smell of some description and this one went by largely unnoticed. Of course it was bound to be discovered eventually, and one morning when the nurses were tidying all our beds for matron's inspection the contents of Stephen's locker were revealed.

"Stephen, what on earth have you been doing?" asked the horrified nurse as the discovery was followed by the stench of rancid milk.

"Nothing, miss," said the poor little chap, his eyes widening in astonishment as beakers of different colours containing stinking milk in various states of decay continued to appear from within like tricks from a clown's pocket. I lay on my side pretending to be asleep, though somehow my pounding heart seemed to be connected to my eyelids and I was unable to stop them fluttering; at the same time my temperature was rising and my colour changing.

"It wasn't me, honest miss," came the plaintive cry from the next bed. Finally I could stand it no longer.

"It was me," I suddenly blurted, with tears and sweat pouring from

my crimson face. The two nurses looked at me, but it was no use rebuking me as I was clearly suffering enough.

"Never mind Ralph," they said kindly. "It's a good job we found it before matron did." With that they hurried off to get a bucket and clean up the odd spilt one. Stephen looked at me with a puzzled look on his face and one of the two older boys who had gleefully been watching the whole incident said in a loud voice, "Now they're definitely coming to take you away."

I was utterly miserable but managed one small heroic act when Matron asked Stephen what the terrible smell was.

"It was me," I whimpered guiltily.

"Well, next time you ask for a bedpan a bit quicker." Then turning to the nurse, she added quietly, "You can see to him after I've finished..."

My terror of the two older boys had become so marked that even the nurses noticed it, and I was moved to a smaller ward with only two other children. The days passed slowly, and once the older boys had been discharged I was moved back in to the main ward.

Mum had got me some books I could read, and I already had my shawl, a bedraggled piece of pink blanket that would have needed plastic surgery to separate me from, but for some reason all I really wanted was a fountain pen, which I used to ask for all the time.

Miraculously one arrived, but without any ink. The nurse who looked after me said that my mum was going to send it down the phone to me, and as she took it from me it fell on the floor and the top broke. She returned it to me with a piece of plaster round the cracked part with 'Ralph' written on it, and the whole thing had ink in it and I was happy for a while, although I knew that you could not send ink down the phone.

One day they wheeled my bed to the window, and there in the car park below stood my mum with Bruce, and they waved to me and I waved back. It was the first time I had seen them for six weeks, and it was too much for me and I started to cry and had to be consoled. I cried myself to sleep again for the next few days.

The infection eventually cleared and a nurse was instructed to remove the huge scab from my wounded right leg. I had to be quite brave, I was told, as it would hurt for a little while. It actually hurt quite a lot and underneath looked pretty horrible too. As it was prised off it stuck to the soft tissue underneath and pulled apart like someone pulling apart a Mars

bar. I was nearly sick, but as a reward the nurse pulled out the last of the drain tube and told me that I could soon try to walk.

Later on that day two nurses lifted me from my bed. I had only a light covering over my right leg, and apart from the constant itching as the scar healed there was no more pain. I tried a few steps but was unable to support myself; it was a scary feeling. I could move my legs but there was no strength in them. The nurses sensed my anxiety and laughed gently. They told me I'd soon be going home when I could walk a little better, and over the next few days I did improve. When I'd completed a few steps I was trembling and exhausted, but excited too as I knew that I'd soon be home with Mummy and Bruce and Tyler and Timmy the new cat.

You never say goodbye properly to those who care for you in hospital. For you it is a unique moment. They have helped you get well and now you must go. For the staff however it is just another day. Your sense of occasion is seldom theirs.

I was discharged from hospital on 13th April 1950. Seeing my mother again with Bruce's old green pushchair was wonderful. I couldn't walk and had to be pushed. It was all so unreal as we wheeled out into the spring sunshine. As we moved out of the car park, however, the noise of the buses and trams became almost unbearable. Everything was bigger and louder than I remembered it. For fifteen weeks I had been isolated from the world and to re-enter was terrifying. By the time I got home I was shaking, and for many weeks afterwards I was scared of the traffic. At one point when I was being pushed to the shops I even got scared of old 'Maida' the milkman's horse, and I was told not to be silly by Mum. I remember thinking that perhaps I was milking the situation a little, and from that moment I began to get better. I had a fairly bad limp and turned my foot inward a bit, but I had some boots that were not unlike the support boots I'd worn when I was younger and slowly my confidence returned.

I had not been home more than a few days when Mum mentioned that I was going to be sent to the seaside to something called a 'convalescent home'. The word 'home' filled me with dread and I began to shake with fear.

"Why have I got to go?" I wondered.

"So that you will get well quicker in the sea air," said my mother.

"Will you be coming?" I asked with more hope than expectation.

"No, of course not, Ralph—who would go to work and look after Bruce?"

An old brown suitcase was slowly being filled up with clothes and shoes wrapped in newspaper and all my garments were marked in Indian ink with my name in block capitals: R. MAY. I was terrified that if I went I may never be allowed to come home, and although I would have loved to go to the seaside the prospect of going alone with another bunch of strangers just filled me with morbid dread.

Luckily my tonsils became poisoned! I also developed a chest infection, and because of the amount of penicillin that I had ingested it was considered wise to let me beat it off by natural means. This meant that regretfully I would not be allowed to go. For a limping, frightened, infected boy, I think I was never so happy in my life.

Recently the correspondence that took place between my mother and her solicitor Mr. Barnes, concerning the accident and its consequences, came to light. With no telephone, their letters were exchanged at one a week, and I now have them all. At the end of it I was awarded three hundred pounds, whilst the driver was fined forty pounds and had his licence endorsed. My mother received ten shillings and sixpence to cover the cost of her fare to the court and loss of earnings. At that time she earned two pounds nine shillings a week and our rent on the basement was one pound!

∾

night duty

Her desk lamp throws a pool of light
That travels halfway up the door
Her face above its shade in shadow
Lights her hands, spills on the floor

And as she moves the faintest breeze
Not strong enough to move a leaf
Yet rustles through her dress and leaves
The lightest touch upon my cheek

In the half light from her desk lamp
I see the clock upon the wall
Its hands are moving, time is passing
Like an injured snail's crawl

Children's sleeping cries and whimpers
Not enough to make her look
The maintenance of steady breathing
Keeps head and pen poised over book

In the half light she stands up
Glides over to the infant's cot
Reaches in and feels his forehead
To find that it is slightly hot

Thumb and finger on his wrist
Shoes more silent than her dress
Reads thermometer and twists
The watch that's pinned upon her breast

Holds the top from off her pen
Between her teeth and slowly writes
"Temperature is slightly up
Seems to be more quiet tonight"

Hangs the clipboard on the hook
On silent shoes and whispering dress
Around the ward takes one more look
Before returning to her desk

I knew it wrong but could not help
But wish that I was ill as he
And that it was my brow that felt
Her finger's touch so tenderly.

That heard the whisper of that dress
As she leaned across the bed
A measure more like a caress
That touched that tiny sleeping head.

∾

magic

My full recovery was very slow and my voices persisted, but soon I had another helper to drive them away. At the age of seven, just before the inevitable dawned upon me that Father Christmas might not exist, I paid a visit to his grotto in Kennard's department store in Croydon.

Admission was sixpence each, and I was given a plastic four note harmonica. I was always aware of extra expenses that my mother incurred on Bruce and I after we had our pocket money, but that wasn't why I set about getting a tune out of it. I just played the squawky thing all the time for the love of it, and eventually a tune arrived. I can still recall the thrill of getting *Hot Cross Buns* out of the thing, and it was not long before all I could think about was getting a real shiny metal harmonica. The one I craved was made by Hohner in Germany, and several of the boys at school had mouth organs made by them.

I had seen one in Surrey Street market on a toy stall which was an Aladdin's cave out on the street for small boys. The chap who ran it was called Charlie and he spoke in a high pitched nasal monotone and wore a very thin moustache. His toys ranged in price from sixpence to about two pounds. These more expensive items were on sale in his shop and not on the stall. He had some saucy novelties like the Mannequin Pis statue that embarrassed the hell out of me because you could see the little

boy's willie. You filled the little doll with water and pressed his rubber hat and he peed for you.

The stall also sold some erotic dolls that if you pressed them their swimming tops came down and their breasts inflated, which I thought was quite exciting. Inside the shop amongst the comics and toys nestled glamour magazines such as *Spick* and *Span* and the naturist periodical *Health and Efficiency*. Once Bruce and I found one of these mags out in the park and pored over the carefully airbrushed photos of naked ladies playing tennis and volleyball. Of course Mum found some of these pictures in the back pocket of Bruce's trousers and we were asked why we wanted to look at pictures of naked ladies, a question to which it is impossible to find the right response.

After Saturday morning pictures I often hung around the stall daydreaming and watching nasal Charlie occasionally demonstrating his wares. Along with cap guns and spud guns, water pistols and masks, lay a shiny harmonica. It was slightly curved in shape like a smile, and it cost two shillings and elevenpence. On the box it had a picture of a boy with a feather in his hat playing in a woodland, and fluttering all around him were tiny birds drawn to his playing. I loved this object. I dreamt about it. I could hear the sweet music from inside its reeds. I would be that boy, wandering the pathways of Croham Hurst with wild birds all around me singing gratefully to me for sharing my music with them.

Two and eleven. It might as well have been a two pounds eleven. On my sixpence a week it would mean me forgoing Saturday morning pictures for nearly six weeks, and we were in the middle of a wonderful Flash Gordon serial at the moment. Mum had always encouraged us to save our pennies and on checking my errand money I found that I had nine pennies. I was encouraged and let it be known amongst the friends that I was open to offers for work.

Running errands for people on the street usually earned one penny tip, but this source had dried up. Then fortune smiled on me in the form of Mrs. Williams who asked me to be her regular errand boy. From then on until she died I went upstairs to the back of the ground floor where she lay, not quite bedridden.

Each Saturday morning early I collected her shopping list written in her shaky Victorian copperplate. For this job I received the princely sum of one shilling—I was rich beyond compare. Even my mother could not hide the surprise at this huge wage, but the old girl's weekly shopping

was more than two huge bags full and I had to rest on the way back with the handles of the shopping bags cutting into my hands. She might have been frail but there was nothing wrong with her appetite.

What was also unusual was that the coins she paid me with were all old shillings, with the lion on the back and George V on the front. Now I guess she might have been raiding an old money box of her own from some long ago period. Perhaps that was why I got a shilling; maybe she had only saved shillings. I would have been very happy with sixpence and in a way that is what I got.

"Well you better save half of that for the future," Mum advised, and I did. In fact I saved all of it and in less than three weeks I was the proud and tuneful owner of a 'Song Bird' harmonica.

I parted with the money and collected the instrument in a plain brown paper bag, ran up to the top of Scarbrook Road and took out the box, fumbling with the lid and staring with absolute joy at the precisely wrought tiny piece of German engineering. I put it to my lips and blew the first notes. It sounded so sweet to me that I was lost for the next quarter of a mile, only hiding it as I got near to Pump Pail and the rough kids on the Salem Place estate. Then it was up the hill to The Waldrons, tootling and playing all the way. On arrival at the door of the basement I was only slightly disappointed that I was not surrounded by flocks of appreciative birds.

I went to school playing it, and played it at school, and came home from school playing it, and in the evening I played the harmonica. I played all the time, pop tunes, nursery rhymes, movie themes, anything. When Granddad came he taught me *Sally Go Round the Jam Pot* and was quite impressed with my efforts. Just like thousands of other small boys I loved the feeling of being able to play almost without thinking any tune (without sharps and flats) and I even wrote a melody of my own that I can still play. Everyone thought me such a happy child—if I wasn't playing the mouth organ I was whistling and if you pointed a camera at me I would grin for you. I still do.

The truth is that these activities did drive my voices away and filled me with great happiness. The comments that I got from people lifted me, and music gave me a discipline and sense of worth that has never really gone away. I kept the Song Bird in its box until the box fell apart, and from then onwards it was always in my pocket.

One night by the fire I was pressing the shiny top of the harmonica

near my eye and I imagined that I could see forests and rivers in the close reflection. Soon I could see herds of deer and buffaloes and by just twisting the instrument one way or another all sorts of different scenes moved before me. I told Bruce about it and offered him a look but he couldn't see the images that I was able to. When I took it back I was able to see some of what had passed before, but on subsequent days I was unable to call up the picture. I have never forgotten the effect, though.

If music was magical, then magic was just as important. I probably first saw a conjuror at school or nursery and I was hooked immediately. In the wonderment that was Kennard's department store, near the rear entrance on the street level, there was a small counter with a red-faced gent who wore a yellow bow tie and spoke with a northern accent. It was his job to demonstrate the jokes and tricks beloved by small boys everywhere. After Saturday morning pictures I would stand in front of his stall for hours watching him perform with the three egg cups or walnut shells, disappearing sponge balls or card tricks. For the most part I was to remain mystified, delighted and frustrated as I tried unsuccessfully to duplicate his skills. Whenever I asked anyone how they were done I was fobbed off with the phrase 'sleight of hand'.

I wondered what it meant and where you could get a sleight from? The tricks on sale were always about the half crown mark but by saving and running errands I was able to purchase one or two of them. As you might expect, once the secret had been revealed to me I always performed the trick too quickly, but eventually I learned to practise a bit more before performance, and was quite adept in my little deceptions. The thrill of successful completion was always worth the pounding heart and sweaty fingers.

My mum belonged to the public library, and once I had exhausted all the children's books on magic I prevailed upon her to get me some from the main adult section. I would pore over these books for hours and some of them would have pictures of long-dead Edwardian exponents demonstrating the effects.

The explanations would appear under headings such as Effect, Apparatus, and Method. Usually my heart would sink after 'apparatus', where the list of requirements for a particular trick would appear:
1) nitrate of potash;
2) a silver candelabra;

3) a sheet of vellum (calf skin is preferable); and so on...

However, I would still read on to find out how it was done, even if I never had a chance to perform it. This interest led to puppetry—glove puppets in particular—and I acquired a Coco the Clown from Surrey Street, and later even an Archie Andrews ventriloquist doll. Soon I was putting on shows for the other kids in the street, and gradually I collected more puppets and the plays became more elaborate. I was always trying to make things, but my dreams of carpentry have continued to elude me and it would not be right to blame my father's tool kit entirely. Most of my work would have been made from old cardboard boxes, as I would construct machines based on Flash Gordon and old Batman or Rocketman serials from Saturday morning pictures. These designs were made more interesting with morsels of the junk that inevitably fell off lorries delivering scrap to Holloway's yard at the end of the road.

Our financial situation was constantly held up to us and to my certain knowledge Bruce and I never asked for so much as a one penny chew from our mother. We were aware of the heartache such a request would bring. Besides, we did all right—Mum made home-made cake, sometimes with an egg; we had a sweet tin from which were doled out sweets when we'd been even better than usual; and our friends in the street were always getting the odd penny or tuppence to buy sweets with. Both Bruce and I became very good at pleading from our more affluent chums:

"Can I have one?"

"Oh go on, just one..."

"Ahh go on, I'll be your best friend."

"All right then, how about a lick?"

And, more desperately, "Can I have that when you've finished it?"

∾

jock

My mother had managed to get a job at Wilkes the chemist on Parchmore Road on the first of December 1947, my brother Bruce's first birthday. The shop was on the corner of Beulah Road, and faced the police station where the motorcycle section of the division was based. We used to watch the police motorcyclists going about their business, zooming in and out of the place on their maroon-coloured Triumphs.

The chemist's was now owned by a Mr. Waters and on the labels to his medicines he was referred to as the proprietor. He resembled a character out of an Ealing comedy, with prematurely white hair, large-gapped teeth and glasses without rims which slipped down his nose so that he always had an enquiring look whenever you spoke to him. His air was that of an old Church of England parson, complete with a drip on the end of his nose. He was a kindly but frugal man, thinking nothing of transporting cylinders of oxygen on the crossbar of his bike to needy recipients, but at the same time only providing old telephone directories for toilet paper in the outside loo. He had a reputation for believing sob stories, much to the annoyance of Mum who felt that we had genuine need, and he was always loaning people cash on the promise that they turn to Jesus and promise to repay when able. They seldom did either.

There was little or no heating in the shop, and the women were

always complaining of the cold. They might have actually got somewhere if old 'Strongy' had ever backed them up. Mr. Strong was the unofficial dispenser. He made up the medicines, officially under supervision from Mr. Waters, or later on Mr. Jones, who were both qualified dispensers, but usually it was he who did the lion's share.

The chemist's shop in the late forties was a substitute for the doctor's surgery, and in many cases preferred to it. People would come in to discuss very intimate subjects with some of the staff. My mother became an unofficial diagnostician; in particularly difficult cases she would refer to Mr. Strong, who in turn on particularly tough questions might speak to Mr. Waters, but only to confirm his own diagnosis. The shop had its own range of patent medicines and often if they did not have what was needed they might "make you something up."

Strongy was a Liverpudlian, and Bruce and I both thought he spoke funny. He was a short, wiry, stooped man, losing his dark hair. He had one of those unattractive moustaches that looked like the end of a paint-brush; it grew straight out as if daring anyone to kiss him under penalty of being poked by his wiry bristles. Poised like some caged bird, his plum-age a distressed white coat with sleeves too long and his scraggy neck thrust forward out of a collar that was always too big for him, he worked away out of sight but not out of earshot of the customers who queued on the other side of the partition. Weighing minute portions of this and that, a jar here, a bottle there, he moved like some strange alchemist, weaving spells next to the sink with the small brass cold water tap.

"Hello terrors!" he would greet us through clenched teeth as we walked round the back of the shop to where he was working.

"Hello Mr. Strong!" we'd chorus back smiling.

We could tell that he was smiling too under that moustache. Two kids less like terrors would be hard to imagine, as both of us were very shy and strongly disciplined by our mum. There is no doubt we were very well behaved, we dare not be otherwise, but we both understood the nature of our circumstances, and really did try to help as much as we could to make life no harder than it was already. This did not stop us loving to be called 'terrors'—it made us feel rebellious and dangerous. Strongy had that typical Liverpool sense of irony and dry humour that passes as everyday banter up there, but was not always understood by Bruce and myself. Perhaps he thought we ought to be more daring, or maybe he was trying to indicate that he knew how tough Mum was and was trying to show solidarity

with us. We were both very fond of him, and very occasionally he would pay a visit to our dismal flat. His pet names for the two female staff were Blodwyn (Mrs. Owens) and Fan (my mum).

My mother's demeanour was so different whilst at work and it was easy to see why she was so popular with everyone. Confident and breezy and always attractively made-up, she exuded confidence and vitality. I thought she looked so pretty and glamorous and such a pity that it was always zapped out of her by the time she had pedalled the five miles home in all weathers.

As she hung up her white coat and put on the old leather jacket and scarf for the bike ride, she left that other persona behind. By the time she arrived home she had cycled away from her other identity and ridden into that of dutiful Mum with all the cares and responsibilities of raising her two boys.

One evening as she cycled off precariously carrying a rare bag of coal on her back, Mr. Waters called her back, and the rest of the staff thought he might give her a lift home in his motor car. Instead he reorganised the strings and supports she had constructed to carry the coal bag, and gave her some pieces of cardboard to place under the strings so they wouldn't cut into her quite so much. Old Strongy just shook his head incredulously as Mum cycled off into the evening gloom. By the time she got home her hands were nearly dead from where the string had cut into her shoulders, impeding her circulation.

Such pains were soon forgotten in the glow of the supplemented fire. It was always a bit more cheery with a knob or two of coal to supplement the hissing of the damp wood from our Saturday outings at Croham Hurst.

The reps that came to the shop would often treat the staff to free samples of cosmetics, although I heard Mum's reservations over at least one of them who was getting too familiar. The shop gave her a purpose and allowed her to enjoy the banter and gossip that is the oil to ease you through the day. The wages were pitiful but she enjoyed huge respect from the people who used the place and often they would ask to speak to her when they wanted advice or needed an intermediary to the dispenser.

The other lady at the shop was called Jessie Owens. She was a widow and had only just about been forgiven for being Welsh (my father had left us for a Welsh woman). Mum continually found fault with her, but they are still friends at the time of writing and correspond regularly.

Mrs. Owens was an austere-looking woman who had been a nurse. She reminded me a lot of my ward sister at hospital. She was always nicely made up and quite proper. She wore horn-rimmed glasses and had her hair swept back in a bun; her voice was resonant and slightly haughty to my ear, but really it was just the accent and the fact that she sounded different.

Bruce and I had been in nursery care from the first day Mum worked at the chemist. At first she was not able to get us in, as these places were reserved for unmarried mothers. Thanks to our landlady Mrs. Cox, however, she managed to get us both placed. In the early days we were taken in the old twin pram; later when Bruce was bigger Mum would get us dressed and load Bruce on to the little seat on the back of her bike, then with me in tow she would plod up to the nursery before cycling off to work.

Once inside the chemist's she would don her starched white coat, put on make-up and go out to meet the public. This was her stage and she relished the part, reserving complaint for when she got home exhausted. I guess most people knew her circumstances, but this must have added even more to her charisma as she was always so positive whenever we went to the shop, so much so that it was hard for me to recognise her as the same person.

People were supportive in practical ways, passing down old clothes and comics for us boys. Sometimes we would get some old Dinky toys that a kid had got fed up with, and once a builder named Phillips, who was doing up he house where we lived, dropped a load of old toys off for Bruce and me and it was like Christmas coming early.

The reason we went to the shop was to get our hair cut for free, at 'Jock's Gentlemen's Hairdressers'.

"Two halves to the clock, please," was our request and destination on the bus from Croydon. The clock was the Thornton Heath clock tower at the end of Parchmore Road. From there we walked down to the junction of Beulah Road and carefully crossed the busy junction to the chemists.

Once Bruce and I had greeted everyone at the chemist's shop, Mum would usher us out into the barber's next door. Jock would look up expectantly as we came in, and I'm sure his face always dropped a little when he saw us. He would gesture with a sideways nod of his head to a

place where we would sit until the last customer had been attended to.

"All right dear, I'll send them through when they're done," was all that he'd say, the scissors snapping without any break.

Jock was one of the old-fashioned, old school, no-nonsense barbers. His shop was plain, not to say spartan. The interior was painted in green and cream gloss paint, with a row of chairs along one wall and two elaborate barber's chairs facing three huge mirrors.

Adverts for Brylcreem, Seven o'clock and Gillette razor blades hung on the walls, with the sombre face of King Gillette himself looking disdainfully down on us, whilst bottles of green liquids and other unguents stood on the glass shelves in front of the mirrors. In silver vases, waxed spills stood waiting for the odd customer who required a singe, and hanging next to each chair was a huge leather strop. In the centre of the wall hung a price list:

GENTS 2/6
BOYS 1/6
SHAVE 1/6
SINGEING from 9d
SCALP MASSAGE 1/-

I never saw anyone get a scalp massage, and as my only previous awareness of the scalp was through cowboy and Indian films, I wasn't particularly sure that I wanted to. The only thing that appeared to be missing from a previous age was the jar of leeches. Outside twirled the slowly revolving barber's pole of red, white and blue which signified a long forgotten commitment to perform this grisly operation.

Jock's partner in the business was Pat, a northern Irishman who would look up and acknowledge Mum as she provided a little feminine presence in this male enclave. All the men's heads would look up at the same time, and then seeing that the lady had two little lads would return to the *Star, News, Standard, Sporting Life*, or one of the tattered copies of *John Bull* or *Picture Post* that used to absorb me for the hours we would sometimes have to wait before Jock would be ready to see us.

Often by the time we got our hair cut the two barbers would have been on their feet for nine hours or more. At this end of the day our treatment was perfunctory but still kindly, Jock with his smiley mouth

and somewhat gruff exterior, sandy-haired and smelly of breath, whilst Pat with his curly blonde hair parted almost in the middle would ask trivial little questions in his slow baritone whilst he snipped away.

Jock had to succumb to elastic stockings in the end. Pat's leg situation was even worse and he was on the point of having to stop work altogether, when a local engineer came up with a stool that revolved around the barber's chair. It had a wheel which ran on a track, and its uniqueness made the local papers. Pat had his photo taken on it, and for years a fading newspaper picture of it was stuck in the corner of his mirror, but in all the time we went there I never saw him use his mobile stool. This of course meant that he actually walked further than before, because he had to negotiate the stool whenever he moved round to the client's other side.

Whilst waiting to be called, I listened, enthralled by the rhythm of the place as snips and clips interchanged with mechanical shears. The stropping of razors, the scrape of steel on necks, the smell of hair being singed or lather being applied on stubbly chins and the elaborate preparation of hot towels that preceded it. The jovial banter and whispered asides that often resulted in huge guffaws and an imaginary tear being wiped from the corner of Jock's eye at the telling of some risqué story.

"I'll tell you that one later Pat!" he would call to his partner with a big stage wink.

"Oh aye," Pat would respond in his deep sonorous tone. Sometimes the two men would hit synchronicity and two customers take the chairs at the same time and then I would watch to see which would finish first. Usually it would be Jock. Quite often the men waiting would motion to each other, letting someone go in front of them if their preferred cutter was still busy. I usually got Jock whilst Bruce usually got Pat.

The sense that we were in a show was never very far away, because it was only rarely that anyone sitting in the shop joined in with the banter up front: this was Jock and Pat's show, and those allowed to join in had to be in the chair.

To a small boy it was amazing how knowledgeable they both were, able to switch from horse racing to football, politics to humour at the flash of a scissor blade, and all the time Jock's keen sharp brown eyes were on the door as he clocked the entry of each customer. There was the slap of the pomade bottle and the slurp as he rubbed his hands together before massaging it vigorously into the scalp of his customer, then the flick

of the sheet as he dusted the hair from the collar of the man before leaning conspiratorially toward his ear with the enquiry that has become a
cliché:

"Something for the weekend sir?"

I wondered what it could mean, as the electric clock with the Silvikrin
advert and a pretty girl's picture on its face soundlessly ticked away our
waiting.

A local caricature artist was sometimes employed to enhance any special announcement to be made in the shop, and one notice is still very
clear to me: it was a picture of a railway carriage disappearing down the
track in a landscape, and perched on the buffers were Jock and Pat, Jock
on the left one and Pat on the right. Both had on their white coats, with
combs and scissors flying from overall pockets as they clutched their suitcases to themselves.

Above the picture the legend read: 'Jock and Pat are taking their holidays from…' and then the dates that the shop would be closed.

This of course seemed perfectly natural to me as I had been brought
up on Saturday morning pictures and Jock and Pat were obviously no
different to Laurel and Hardy, Martin and Lewis or Abbott and Costello,
and like them they probably slept in a double bed (I knew that Jock was
unmarried) and why wouldn't they go on holidays together? I did have a
problem about their safety travelling by this method, and wondered if we
had been able to afford to pay for our haircuts, they may have had enough
money to buy tickets for seats on the train.

Finally our time would come and sadly the show would end the moment we climbed into the chairs. Jock would work away quickly and
efficiently, with only a cursory question or two as to how things were.
Usually the conversation would be between him and Pat as they summed
up the day or spoke about things that were beyond the ken of two small
boys.

After the electric shears they would progress to the scissors and then
the dreaded hand clippers that seemed to pull as many hairs out of your
neck as they managed to cut. So as not to trouble Jock too much, Bruce
and I often ended up with the longest hair in the school and so as Jock
didn't have to see us too often, we regularly left the barbers with the
shortest cut he could charitably get away with! Then with the slapping
on of some sweet-smelling brilliantine that set hard as soon as it was put

on, and the brush and comb treatment that parted and persuaded boyish locks into thirties footballers' styles (which always made me feel that I looked a bit simple), we were done.

Usually after thanking Jock profusely, as we had been taught by our mum to show gratitude for all kindness, I would try to push the swept-back majority of my parted hair into a quiff before it set like concrete. We would then troop back into the chemist's to be admired and called 'terrors' again by Mr. Strong before walking down to Thornton Heath clock tower to catch the bus back to Croydon High Street. With the walk home through the old town, sometimes Mum would have beaten the bus and arrived before us. The fire would be alight and although the room would not yet be warm there would always be a cosier glow to tea time. Then perhaps a bedtime story, with the tiny particles of hair now lodged in the collars of our pyjamas scratching and rubbing our shaved necks.

Jock continued to cut our hair until a couple of years before I joined the army. Around the time I was thirteen, some of the boys were coming into school with hair that had been 'blow-dried'; I had been looking for an excuse to change hairdressers and this was it. Bruce continued for a while, but soon he too stopped going all the way over to Thornton Heath and the chain was broken. It sounds strange, but such is the vanity of youth, I often wondered if Jock was disappointed that we stopped going to him.

There were many such small considerations shown to Mum, Bruce and me, but this was a practical piece of help and a kind gesture by an honest, hardworking and decent man. Pat was eventually forced into retirement because of his legs, and bachelor Jock finished up a married man after all when he married Mrs. Owens from the chemist's shop next door. They retired to Scotland, where he spent a few happy years before succumbing to a heart attack. The twice widowed Jessie now lives in Wales with her niece.

❧

god

They must have told me about God at nursery school. How else would I have recognised him when he came to visit us in the garden? I learned more at school, and began to enjoy the stories we heard there.

The first story that really impressed me was the parable of the feeding of the five thousand. Obviously Jesus, like me, was very interested in magic and miracles. Turning water into wine was actually a trick that you could buy from a company called Ellisdon's in High Holborn, who advertised their products on the back of comics. Then there was raising the dead and making the blind see, and although his ultimate suffering was deeply disturbing to me, he even managed a miraculous resurrection. It always puzzled me how his disciples had to be convinced that it was him, and as for Mary Magdalen not knowing him in the garden and thinking he might be the gardener, *well!*

In spite of my uncertainty about his finale there was no doubt in my mind that he was a wonderful man, and my outrage at the injustice of his sentence, and subsequent awe at his compassion for the perpetrators stayed with me for many years. These thoughts were further reinforced by Chad Varah's illustrated bible stories on the back of my hand-me-down *Eagle* comics.

Crosses filled me with horror, and images of a broken man hanging on them gave me nightmares, while stories about his exploits filled me

with admiration and pictures of his deeds were an inspiration. We always knew when we were going to have a religious lesson, because the teacher would place an old-fashioned scroll of linen pictures over the blackboard. He would turn it to a particular illustration representing a miracle or parable and tell us all about the woman who searched diligently for a sixpence, or how Jesus walked on water. It was not until later, in Miss Smee's class at Howard School, that some of these miracles were explained.

"There might well have been only five loaves and two fishes to start with," said Miss Smee, "but people might have been made to feel ashamed when they saw the generosity of that small boy and so added their sandwiches and tea over to make up the twelve baskets that were left over.

"Another thing you will find in the bible is that they are very fond of certain numbers like twelve, seven, and forty. It doesn't mean that they were exact figures, it's just like we have twelve months in the year and also twelve pennies in a shilling."

I am sure these pearls were supposed to be wisdom but they were all part of the mystery to me. Jesus had such a kind face and was usually portrayed in a slightly feminine way, apart from his wispy beard, which looked as though he had never shaved. Pictures of him always slightly disturbed me, yet I derived a great deal of comfort in believing he existed—the corollary of which was the enormous void that occurred when I realised that he probably did not. Or if he did, he was probably not the son of God, because God probably did not exist.

My first Sunday School was at the end of our road and was part of the Congregational church in Croydon. Miss Daisy Bales was in charge, with a young man called Mr. Cawthorn and a tiny lady with very bow legs called Miss Argent helping to run things. There was a lot of happy songs including *Jesus Wants Me For a Sunbeam* and my favourite, *You in Your Small Corner and I in Mine*. For some reason my mum decided to be a Sunday School teacher for a short while. She enjoyed good hymn singing and there was plenty of that down at the main church. Her strict discipline and very assertive manner with her girl charges at the Sunday school won admiration from the other teachers and respect from the sometimes naughty girls.

I was often a bit embarrassed by her assertiveness with them, but they seemed to love her and run to her when she came into the yard in which we held our meetings. Miss Argent was scared of my mum at first and

then jealous of her control, especially over the unruly Linnaker family. Mr. Cawthorn, who was prematurely bald and wan, was gentle and not very good at keeping us interested. Miss Bales was tanned and prim with white hair and piercing blue eyes, looking like a seaside landlady, with the addition of that Christian shine that sits smugly on the faces of some true believers.

Those who attended were a mixed bunch, and I suspect now that the children were mostly there so that their mums and dads could have a Sunday afternoon cuddle in private. Given the state of housing at that time, privacy would have been at a premium. One family called Dowser had seven boys and at last Mrs. Dowser had given birth to a little girl. Mr. Dowser seemed to be relieved and everyone thought perhaps they would stop having kids; after all, they weren't Catholics. The seven boys said little about their sister, but eventually it emerged that she was really another brother and their mother was advised to stop dressing the poor little chap in girls' clothes. She refused to do this, however, and for the sake of the family she was indulged until the youngest Dowser began to attend school.

After a slight altercation with Michael Dowser (who was second eldest) in the play area which resulted in him having six stitches in his head, I began not going to Sunday School. Shortly after that, Mum stopped teaching there, although I think she still occasionally went to services in the main church.

I occupied my new-found leisure with roller skating trips and explorations further afield, but one afternoon as I was coming out of school, a man with a small moustache and a microphone, whose name we found out later was Mr. McKay, was standing outside the school gates speaking about a new club that was being set up in a Children's Church.

He promised discussion groups, gym equipment, outings and entertainment. As I stopped to listen and watch, it was apparent that his audience was not the slightest bit interested. I was filled with compassion for the poor bloke. I made a mental note of the address and on the appointed day turned up at the Mint Walk Mission with Bruce and another kid, to find that, apart from an older boy called Philip who came from the Old Town area, we were the only responses he'd had.

He started off by asking us to pray and thanked God for directing our little lost souls to the Mission, while we stared around at our surroundings.

The front edifice was made of corrugated tin sheets in the approximate shape of a church. The centre part was indeed a full size, if small, place of worship, and on each side were smaller wings. One was used as the children's Sunday School on one side, and the remains of what must have been an Edwardian boys' club on the other. We all met in the boys' club part. On the walls were various slogans urging us to be good, not drink and repent. From the rafters hung two or three climbing ropes. There was an old pommel horse, and in one corner stood an intriguing machine that turned out to be a bar billiards table.

Mr. McKay was a working-class Christian man driven by an upper working-class wife who was an enthusiastic evangelical lady. She also supported another fervent evangelist, the Reverend Frank Bustin, and a lovely old lady organist and shining Christian in the form of Mrs. Lily Adlam, who they were all slightly in awe of. A Miss Paul conducted the Sunday morning school. Strangely none of them had children of their own, although Mr. and Mrs. McKay had a temperamental adopted daughter called Brenda.

We were gradually introduced to all these people as they were part of the condition for entry to the boys' club. Mr. McKay promised talks on any subject we wanted "from sport to atomic piles."

"Okay then," said Philip aggressively, thinking that Mr. McKay knew nothing about them, "atomic piles!" Undaunted, however, our leader promised that if we returned next week he would have a talk ready for us. After our first meeting neither of my two conscripts wanted to return, which placed an even bigger burden on me. I could not let the poor bloke down and managed to get someone else to come along to the club the next week, where Mr. McKay warmly greeted the three boys who had shown up. After wandering around the dusty apparatus for a while we were given a glass of orange juice cordial.

"Nice orange juice cordial," I enthused to my unenthusiastic mate. Mr. McKay called us together for his discussion group.

"Now last week, as you may recall," he began, "young Philip here said he wanted to learn about atomic piles."

He pulled out a little red notebook in which he had prepared his talk on the subject, and folded it over to the right page.

He went on, "Now atomic piles are very special piles. We're not talking about the piles what you get up your bottom..."

At this point I lost it completely. Although I tried to follow his

rambling discourse I could not get over the opening line. He had done little pencil sketches to elucidate certain points, and I was touched by his efforts although I retained none of the information.

The following week's group was only attended by two of us, and his talk on racial discrimination opened with the line, "Now a lot of people don't like coloured people who are all God's children although some of them do stink a bit and I should know because I was with some of them in the war..."

I lost it again, and after one more week the boys' club was abandoned.

By this time, partly out of curiosity but mostly out of obligation, I had started to go to Children's Church. The room was a miniature of the main building and the whole thing was run by Miss Paul. She was a small lady, quite young, who wore no make-up and had a rather large chin and tiny gaps between her teeth that gave her a rustic appearance. She always wore a hat in church and lived not far from us, in a small house near St. Andrew's school, with her epileptic brother.

The Sunday morning shows were jolly events, and the characters were from a different culture to anything I had known. Miss Paul bought little prizes out of her own money for children who memorised texts, and for years I had a New Testament that I got from her for learning the names of all of the books of the Old Testament off by heart (for fear that no-one else would bother to have a go).

Miss Paul's simple faith and purity was deeply touching to me, and her distress, when her brother was in the middle of a fit, all the more bewildering a reward from God for her kindness towards us.

Once I pushed through a crowd of people who had gathered down near Reeves Corner to stare at her poor brother lying in a pool of blood, thrashing around on the pavement while she stood there with tears pouring down her face waiting for the ambulance to come. God, I increasingly thought, was moving in very strange ways.

By now I was in the grip of evangelical fever and all I wanted to do was to get people to the Sunday school, not just because of a heightened religious conviction but because these people were so nice I wanted them to feel better. None of my mates had any real desire to attend, but at one point I cajoled at least ten new faces with promises of God knows what to induce them to come down to the Mission.

Somehow I got my best friend Charlie Ranger to go one week, and it

was the week Mr. Hugget was to speak to us. Mr. Hugget's talks were always animated, with illustrations that he pulled out of a battered suitcase and stuck on a felt board. He was also a passable piano accordion player and he belted out his choruses with gusto. We had to join in with just as much gusto, or we would have to do it all again. He was a large man and wore a brown suit with brown glasses to match. He spoke with all his teeth showing and spat a little at the same time; often when he had come to the end of his sermon he would have little flecks of froth at the corners of his mouth. His hair was always cut too short so that it stood up at the crown, giving him a slightly boyish appearance, but I always enjoyed his little moral tales.

Mr. Hugget had set up his felt board and was rummaging around in his battered briefcase for his props. He kept looking up toward Miss Paul and was looking increasingly perplexed. To fill in some time Miss Paul thanked a girl called Moira, who had brought in some Michaelmas daisies to brighten the room, and informed us, "I think it was Shakespeare who said, 'One is nearer to God in a garden than anywhere else on earth.'"

Then Mr. Hugget blurted out, "I've brought the wrong lesson!"

He sat there with his briefcase on his knee and his top teeth resting on his bottom lip in a foolish grin, blinking myopically through his brown glasses at Miss Paul. She was unable to offer any advice, and he suddenly said, "Oh, I'll give them the one I've brought anyway."

There then began a discourse on the Evils of Drink.

This was a talk that he had obviously given many times before and he warmed enormously to his task. He slapped diagrams on the felt board and told us the proportions of water to alcohol in the average pint of beer and that alcohol was basically a poison and what brewers should really say in their adverts was that they sold Best Poison.

At this last statement Charlie, who had been silently chuckling for most of the talk, almost exploded, and an unbelievable amount of snot spurted from his nostrils causing us all to crack up at the back. Although Miss Paul regarded the matter in hand as serious it was not half as serious as the matter that Charlie had in his hand.

By now tears were running down my face, which made Charlie laugh all the more as I frantically searched for my bit of dried bed sheet to offer him. Charlie had no handkerchief, and the more he tried to clean himself the worse it got and the more it produced. Mr. Hugget responded to the merriment that he believed he had caused by becoming even more ani-

mated and began using bigger and more emphatic gestures on his felt board, so much so that his trousers began to work downward and he had to hitch them up before carrying on. This exposed his socks, one of which was shorter than the other, sending Charlie into more paroxysms of laughter until he had to leave the room in order to clean himself up.

"And that's why you should always avoid alcohol!" shrilled Mr. Hugget triumphantly.

He was now bathed in a light sweat, with his trousers hitched a little too high, his glasses awry and steamed up in the cold room, and his hair at the crown standing straight up. At this point Charlie re-entered the room and the sight of Mr. Hugget almost started it all off again, but by now the accordion was being strapped on again and we were getting ready to sing our closing choruses.

In spite of having so many laughs that day I could not persuade Charlie to come again.

By the time I was at grammar school, Sunday had become the busiest day of the week. In the morning I was up and off to the Mission to keep the numbers up, and after half an hour I dashed off on foot to St. Andrew's in Southbridge Road where I climbed into my cassock and surplice to sing in the choir. In the afternoon there was Sunday School back at the Mission, and in the evening there was Evensong back at St. Andrew's. What with all my homework as well, something had to give, and in the end I chose to leave the choir.

There were several reasons for this. Much as I enjoyed all the ceremony of a fairly high church, there was some conflict with my budding socialist beliefs, and even though I was at a grammar school now there was still a bit of snobbery involved, especially about my luminous green teddy boy socks. I was politely asked to stop wearing them, but how else was I to get the lovely Marion to notice me?

Marion was the choirmaster's daughter and she was so pretty it hurt. At practice she would come in wearing her school uniform, and then put on a little make-up before fluffing up her hair in the changing room mirror. I used to watch her with deep appreciation, but she only had eyes for an older boy called Clifford. She was supposed to sing with the boy sopranos but somehow she never stood close to me. I would probably have fainted if she had. I thought she had the sweetest voice.

None of us could read music, although we held the books in front of

us and pretended that we could. The choirmaster was a kindly man, but his support was more visual than anything else. One of the two big songs we worked on was *Oh For the Wings of a Dove*. Our music master at school had played us the version by Ernest Luff and I thought it was marvellous. The trouble was that none of us were good enough to do it, so Marion sang it. I admired her even more. We boys approximated behind her as "the godless came fast" and the congregation seemed to approve at the Christmas concert. There was a sprinkling of other girls but none as pretty as Marion.

One day one of the bigger boys contrived to lock her and Clifford in one of the cupboards, and they stayed in there a long time. When they came out they were a little bit flushed, and I knew by looking at her that she had liked being in there with him. Then her dad found out and went crazy at everybody. I was fed up and knew that she would never be mine even when I got my long trousers, so I left and concentrated on falling in love with girls on the bus to school. I never managed to speak to them either.

It was getting difficult for me to equate my religious beliefs to my growing political sense. Constantly I asked myself, "What if?"

I tried to ponder on eternity and got scared. I thought about death and the sacrifice of soldiers and then the sacrifice of soldiers who did not believe in an afterlife. And then the voices would come back.

Ronald Patterson was a skinny kid who lived up the top of the road. He had a little sister called Susie who sometimes played in our garden, and we thought it possible that under the right circumstances she might show us what she had under her knickers. Ronald, on the other hand, was pretty much despised for being a sneak and a coward who threw stones at other kids and ran away.

He was like a magpie; you felt that if you got near enough to him to put salt on his tail he wouldn't be able to run away, but no-one ever got near to him. Even when he ran the odd errand, if one of us gave chase to get even with him over some ancient feud, he would wait tantalisingly until we were nearly level with him before he'd dart off like the wind.

Ronald Patterson was a tormentor, who would hide behind bushes and fire staples with elastic bands at you so that you could not figure out where they came from, or sneaky water pistol jets, hitting you from directions that you could not work out and even if you did and spotted him you couldn't catch him. From these distances I couldn't even be sure what

he really looked like except he was very skinny with long running legs and a pasty complexion. I always knew it was him, however, because he wore his school raincoat and cap all year round. And we still couldn't catch him.

One afternoon in our back garden Susie obligingly revealed some of the mysteries of her hidden places. I considered it fair trade on the 'I'll show you mine if you'll show me yours' basis but it still wasn't enough, especially as Susie had already some knowledge of boys through her horrible sneaky little brother Ronald. Nevertheless it was exciting and I looked forward eagerly to whatever might happen next.

Unfortunately our activities had been spotted by old Mrs. Williams upstairs, who told my mum, who was furious but only accused me of trying to make Susie go to the lavatory. I felt really chastened and it was quite a long time before I tried to learn more about the mysteries of the female form. Maybe as long as a month. After a lot of nagging and pleading, Lilian who lived across the road obliged me with a quick peep. I was glad about this particular revelation as her dad hated me and Charlie and called us louts, which we weren't. He was always chasing us out of the garden. Once in a blind rage at both of us he called Charlie a slob and Mrs. Ranger (Charlie's mum) went mad and called him all the words she could manage without actually swearing.

"When I think of my husband slobbing *(sic)* his guts out in the desert for the likes of you it makes me feel sick," she told Lilian's dad. She was brilliant, and although her face was red and she had tears coming down her face and he was pale and shaking, we knew she had won and I was very impressed.

I told Charlie that Lilian had shown me her things and we both thought it was great to get one over on her dad. Later on Denise showed me as well. Denise was a bit of a surprise, because when I was made to sit next to her after some minor misdemeanour in class, she offered to show me before I had asked. This was all very exciting and the more so because you knew that the feeling you were having was one that you were not supposed to have.

In history lessons girls sitting together would often titter at Greek statues and this smacked of humiliation to me, as if they were mocking all masculinity. I searched in vain for pictures of female equipment and in the end was forced to add a pencil line here and there to pictures of naked ladies to get my own back and pass the books across the back of the room

to even more titters. Was it all the more exciting because they understood that I had knowledge of such things?

Of course this very natural curiosity and delightful reciprocation was somehow at odds with my religion and produced a great deal of tension as I wrestled with the spiritual over the flesh. In the end Mrs. Patterson heard about the garden adventures and wanted me given a good hiding, but Mum would not hear of it so long after it happened and I resolved to try and curb my curiosity. Ronald had found it a good excuse to fire more stones at me and he was a pretty good shot. I probably thought I deserved to get hit and did little in the way of getting even.

It was early on in my Mint Walk Mission days when the Rev. Bustin came out after Sunday School and asked the children present if anyone wanted to "take Jesus into your heart."

I wondered what it could mean and how many of the kids would stay behind to do it. At the end of the session all the kids got up and went and I realised that no-one was going to take Jesus into their heart.

I felt so sorry for the Rev. Bustin that I went up to him and said that I would do it. I'm sure he was a kindly man and he believed in the word literally. Most recently he had been put in a spot by Philip, the oldest boy at the Sunday school, who like me was beginning to have serious doubts about everything we were being taught. One afternoon Mr. Bustin had come into our lesson and asked if there was anything we wanted to ask him about the bible.

Straightaway Philip said, "I have a question!"

"Go ahead then, Philip," said the reverend.

"Okay. If Adam and Eve had two boys, Cain and Abel, where did their wives come from?"

I was staggered that I had never thought of that one and neither had any of the other kids. How was Mr. Bustin going to get out of this one? I thought he would say that the theory of evolution was the truth, and that Adam and Eve's story had been constructed for the children of Israel to understand, but he took on the question and gave the implausible answer that they would have had many daughters as well, and that times was different then, and that...

"That's incest!" interrupted Philip knowledgeably, and then not waiting for an answer he demanded, "What about amoebas and life beginning in the water and that we are all descended from that?"

We all looked up expectantly.

"That is also in the bible," he said. "Read Genesis chapter 1, verse 20."

We did and it said, *And God said, let the waters bring forth abundantly the moving thing that hath life.*

It also went on about fowl of the air as well, but obviously this ambiguous reference could refer to an amoeba. I was amazed and Philip slightly disgruntled by Rev. Bustin's biblical knowledge, but in the end I favoured Darwin over Moses. The banter between them continued for a bit, and I suppose as far as points scored it was a draw. However I still felt sorry for the Reverend; not only was he beaten by the first question, but Philip did not return to church the following week.

My willingness to 'take Jesus into my heart' would, I hoped, lift his bruised spirits. He did seem pleased as we marched purposefully into his little room at the back of the hall. I do not know what I expected to happen next, but having made the decision I suddenly felt strange as if I wasn't really in control of events. Would there be the sound of rushing wind and fire or would a white dove sail through the window? I hoped not as the window was firmly locked shut. Would he want to see my privates? Again I hoped not, although it was probably all right to show them to a priest.

Once inside the meagrely furnished room we both knelt down and he began praying. I don't remember what he said, but the attention I was getting was wonderful and his strong voice intoned a rambling prayer, the kind that evangelical priests seem to be able to knock out without thinking too much.

After a little while he placed his hands on my head and called out, "If you want joy, real joy, let Jesus come into your heart!"

It was a genuine feeling of elation that I had at that moment, with the Rev. Bustin praying just for me. This was the second time, after my speech to my father, that I had actually made events in my life change by an intentional act. I was pleased with my decision as all my sins were forgiven, and I was sure that included getting girls to take their knickers down and that I would not be drawn away by the delights of the hidden female bits.

I resolved to tell Mum as soon as I got home and felt sure she would be proud of me. I ran home as usual but there was a difference in my step, a lightness and a feeling of relief that I had seldom experienced before. It was a lovely summer evening and the warm air of the day was hinting at

a cool twilight. I crossed Southbridge Road and started up the hill to The Waldrons when halfway up I spotted the unmistakable form, still wearing his cap and raincoat, of the sneak Ronald Patterson.

I couldn't believe my luck. He was ambling up the hill alone, and I was behind him and the last person he expected to see was a deadly enemy like me. Stealthily and lightly I increased my pace, my smelly plimsolls making no sound. I nearly blew it at the last when I crunched a pebble but as he turned around to see what had caused this solitary note, I was on him. I had him by the collar of his mac and before he could pull away from me I had his arm. Now what was I going to do?

"Don't hit me don't hit me!" he begged.

I looked at him. He was older than I assumed, or at least he looked older. I had never been this close to him before.

"You little rat," I said, "you're always throwing stones at me. I'm going to smash your face."

"Don't hit me!" he pleaded again. "I won't do it again I promise."

I still had him by the belt on his raincoat and was floundering about as to what punishment I was going to inflict on him when I remembered that I'd just taken Jesus into my heart. What should I do? I really wanted to give him a slap or at least show the other kids that I had caught the little runt (actually he was nearly as tall as me).

My senses were on overload. I had just had a religious experience and now the thrill of capture. I could, if I had wanted to have the satisfaction, have given him a belt, but what about my heart with Jesus in it? Feeling him begin to tremble and seeing the fear in his eyes, I felt my anger being replaced by pity. In the end I just gave him a push that sent him one step off the pavement and let him go. Like a flash he was off, and as he skidded round the corner into The Waldrons, I wondered if I would get an extra credit from Jesus for my mercy.

What I did get was a rock on the side of the head from Ronald the next time I ran an errand for Mrs. Williams. Still, his sister had shared some mysteries with me. Altogether I supposed that it served me right.

∾

woods

Miss Elwell was a seamstress at the Sleepeezee factory. People said that she was a hard and conscientious worker. She lived upstairs, on the floor above the ground floor, which was a half storey above us in the basement flat. From her tiny single room over the grand, columned front door, she had good views of the road and front garden. In the room was a small cooker, and her bathroom was shared with the Miss Dickinsons who lived across the hall.

She was petite with a sallow complexion and deep brown eyes; she seldom smiled, her gleaming false teeth hiding behind very thin lips. Her hair was dark and parted on the right side, its style unchanged since the thirties; although she never attended a hairdresser it still retained an echo of those days. Her movements were quick and nervous and her voice surprisingly deep for one so slight.

Miss Elwell affected to talk 'posh', often adding aitches where there were none and dropping them where they were supposed to be. She called a certificate 'sustificate', a chimney 'chimley' and Westminster 'Westminister'. She did all the overtime that was offered and her simple dream was a cottage in the country with a rose round the door; for this she scrimped and saved every penny. It was a task that would have daunted most people but Miss Elwell was deeply motivated; she needed to be as

her boss Mr. Price only paid her five pounds a week. She had no friends and never left her room except for the bathroom and work. In September 1947 my father left us for good and Miss Elwell became my mother's friend.

In my memory she was always in our place, but the first time she padded down from upstairs was shortly after my dad left. For reasons that I can only imagine, she admired my mother greatly and was moved to try to comfort her. Perhaps it was Mum's strength not to give in, or her determination to raise these two little ones by herself. Or maybe she was drawn to Mum because of her own inherent distrust of all men (except Mr. Price). There was a rumour that Miss Elwell had been jilted, and her judgment that all men were swine had now been confirmed by my father's desertion.

Both women were working class, but Mum had the broadening experience of 'service' and had learned etiquette and style that raised her practicality above many of the families around us. Perhaps Miss Elwell picked up on this as she showed the younger woman a deference and undeclared admiration that I was always aware of.

1947 was one of the coldest winters on record, and indeed it was a terrible time to be left alone in a cold basement with two kids to keep warm and fed. Like millions of others we had no hot water, and everything we needed, from tea to washing, had to be boiled on the gas stove. There was a fireplace in one room, and we had a paraffin stove that sucked all the oxygen out of the air, burnt curious little fingers, and smelled. It didn't warm the room, but it stopped frost forming on the bedclothes and gave a comforting pattern on the ceiling as the flickering wick threw shadows through the vents at the top.

In those tear-drenched early days of being alone, Miss Elwell's deep tones sought to comfort Mum as she tried to come to terms with what had happened to the three of us. How had she not realised what was going on? Surely Frank would be back, if not for her then for the two little boys that he seemed so proud of.

All the trappings of a young couple were in evidence in our flat: the slow acquisition of a few bits of furniture; photos on the mantelpiece alongside the round mirror on which he had painted butterflies while in hospital. On the hearth stood two boxes that he had covered with plate copper and decorated with a hammered-out picture of two galleons. This had been done with a punch and a small panel-beating hammer from

materials found at work. Mum used to joke that he often found things before they were lost! In front of the fire lay the rug that he had also made as he got well again.

There were pickled onions in the cupboard and meat on Sundays. Though there was nothing that could be said to be new in their possessions, there was the promise of things to come, and because of the garage connections at work, he said it would not be long before they had an old car to get about in.

One day, before the winter had really set in, Miss Elwell suggested a walk in a place she knew beyond South Croydon station. It was called Croham Hurst and was an area of unspoiled hills and woodlands in the middle of the suburbs, with Croydon on one side and Selsdon on the other.

Mum had grown up in the country and walking seemed to help pass the dark hours away, and sometimes she would forget the cold basement that was even colder without him, and so the two friends began the walk to the woods that was to become a Saturday afternoon ritual for the next ten years. Mum loaded Bruce and me into the big twin pram, and with the dog in tow, let 'old Elwell' lead the way.

The route took us up the Waldrons Path and past the nursery school that Bruce and I attended. From there it was down Nottingham Road, across by the Swan and Sugar Loaf, up the slow incline to Croham Road and finally to the woods.

As you entered them on this side there was a drinking fountain, with behind it some toilets, and facing you a steep hill of round pebbles with a footpath leading off to the left. Once climbed, the top revealed a high small plateau of stones and grass, with the ground sloping away to the right. In front was a magnificent view of the surrounding countryside with buildings and homes, and in the distance more trees disappearing into blue grey horizons.

The melancholy of autumn cannot have been the best time to have undertaken that first visit, but perhaps Mum found a reassurance in the almost rural atmosphere, the wet leaves clinging to the wheels of the old pram and her cheeks flushed with the exertion as she pushed us both through the dank sweet beech woods to where the thin sunlight beckoned us to the top.

Here and there she would recognise a late wild flower; she even stopped and picked up a few chestnuts under a tree and with a stick opened them

and popped them in her pocket. Almost without thinking she placed the piece of wood on the pram 'for the fire', and with Miss Elwell pointing the way they should go, memories from happier times replaced the ever-present sadness she was feeling.

She paused to change Bruce's nappy at the entrance as they were leaving. A soft-spoken uniformed park keeper stopped to pass the time of evening, and Mum was relieved that he did not question the small bundle of old wood that she had absentmindedly collected for the fire and placed on the top of the pram.

By the time the little party left, it was almost dusk and with a lightened heart the four set off on the two and a half mile journey home. Mum was hooked.

From then on the trip to the woods was a regular event. It began as a sort of meditational stroll to take her mind off her situation, in the way that people in shock occupy themselves with a trivial task just to keep busy, but it ended up almost the highlight of our week. The discreet collecting of old bits of wood gave way to quite brazen displays, as gradually both Bruce and I were able to walk home and the old pram became loaded up with wood. Sodden as it often was, this would supplement the few bits of coal, and hiss and fizz flickering comfort right through the week until the next outing.

The journey through the houses suddenly gave way to allotments by the railway and lanes that led up past where the new St. Peter's school would be built, and then the last little lane would give way to the entrance and we would scamper off on the familiar paths that became the extensions of our imaginations. Gradually we learned every climbing tree in the wood and where you could run the fastest downhill amongst the pebbles, slipping and sliding with glee and shrieking with delight as the feeling of almost flying possessed us. By the time the trees hove into view Tyler would be practically hauling the lot of us in his anxiety to get into the trees and smells and re-anoint his favourite places.

Mum had begun to take a thermos of tea for herself and a bottle of National Health diluted orange juice for us two. Then there were a few sandwiches added, Marmite for me and jam for Bruce, and we would pause usually by the same tree for our picnic. This in itself was exciting because Mum had always wrapped up the sandwiches in little parcels and the two of us would sit to undo them, a little like Christmas once a

week. When Mum had her tea she would make a bit for Tyler and he would finish off the remains, slurping it noisily out of the lid of the old red flask.

As soon as we had eaten we would be off again on our adventures until it was time to load up the pram with twigs and fallen logs and troop off home tired and happy.

We soon became known to the keepers. They had a small hut which was of immense interest to a little lad like me. Inside was a small table and a couple of chairs, and facilities for making tea. Their uniforms were navy blue and buttoned right up to the top, and they wore caps with shiny peaks. The one who had spoken to Mum on our first visit was called Mr. Bachelor, and his boss was Mr. Sweetman; both were old soldiers from the First World War. Mr. Sweetman had lost an arm in the trenches and wore a false one with a brown leather glove stretched over a wooden hand that, once we realised what it was, Bruce and I found rather scary.

Both men were extremely kind; Mr. Sweetman bore himself more militarily and was less warm to us kids, but Mr. Bachelor was the sort of old boy that was born to be a grandfather. Both men quickly worked out our circumstances. Without fussing over us they always managed to bump into us somewhere on the Saturday and we loved to see them.

As we grew, Bruce and I made new friends and they joined us on our outings to the 'Hurst'. The first to do so was Richard Ranger. The Rangers lived in the next house, which was almost a mirror image of ours, and their rooms corresponded to Miss Elwell's plus a partition which gave them an extra room. Mrs. Ranger was a kind and intelligent woman who soon replaced the ageing Miss Elwell on our walks. She and Mum would talk all the way there and back about everything and nothing, while us boys would get on with the serious business of tree climbing, hide and seek, cowboys and indians or whatever else had fired our imaginations that particular week.

Richard was persuaded to come unwillingly at times, and I distinctly remember my mother telling her friend to "leave the little grizzler" who had decided that he wanted to be carried the last half mile to the woods. Later we were joined by Mickey Sparrow and his brother Paul and various other children from the street, until a veritable little army of waifs made the journey after Saturday morning pictures and Saturday lunchtime.

By now we were all well acquainted with the two park keepers, especially Mr. Bachelor who had metamorphosed into 'Uncle Charlie'. He would often talk with us all and occasionally sit down while we were having our sandwiches. One day he asked Mum if she'd like any apples, and when she said that she would, he told us to go to his home which was close by and ask Nellie his wife to let us collect some windfalls.

On our way home we diverted to the address and knocked on the door, which was opened by a pretty young woman with a lovely smile. This was Ella, Uncle Charlie's younger daughter. She invited us in and introduced us to her mother Nellie and her sister Doff (Dorothy), who was sitting on the back lawn of the lovely big house. Her two children, Robert and Mandy, were running about with their cousins Brian and Maureen (Ella's children).

Beyond the lawn were some vegetable patches and two intriguing sheds, and beyond these were several trees with vivid red apples growing on them and littering the ground. We ran over and eagerly scooped up apples with scant regard as to their worth or quality. Mum patiently told us not to be greedy, and soon we had more than we could eat before they would have rotted. Everyone was so kind and friendly and they asked us to call again. It was the beginning of a family friendship that, in spite of many changes of circumstances, survives to this time of writing.

The apples were taken home and sorted; many of them were wormy and had maggots but there were still enough to provide us with a little treat. The flesh was yellow and sweet and they were awesomely red and autumnal in colour. Before they were all eaten we visited again, and soon we were calling round for Sunday teas.

Nellie was Charlie's second wife but the mother of the two girls. Ella was married to Alf and the young couple shared the house with Nellie and Charlie. Brian and Maureen were striking children; in the summer their skins were dark brown and their hair almost white. Nellie was from Tewkesbury and was slightly deaf, which may have been a good thing in this noisy, happy household.

I had never before been where everyone laughed so much. Even our childish puns were roared at by the grown-ups and it was a marvellous feeling to be able to contribute in this way to the general merriment in the place. Alf was such a happy chap with his sparkling eyes and deep voice, while Charlie had an almost soundless chuckle and his eyes wrinkled and sparkled with mischief. Nellie's laugh began slowly and seemingly

later than the rest but it went on longer than everyone else's to make up for it. Brian laughed as readily as all of them and Maureen, even at the age of three or four had a warm, smoky laugh.

But the laugh beyond all laughs came from Ella. Just to watch her was a pleasure; she was quite stout, though she had slim legs, and when she began, this joy bubbled up from somewhere under her apron to such a huge gurgling, open-mouthed, head-back, thigh-slapping expression of well-being that I waited with eager anticipation for each new beginning, and they were never far apart.

I loved those visits. We thought of the Thorpes—Uncle Alf and Auntie Ella—as real relations, and Brian and Maureen as cousins. Told of the arrival of a new baby for Ella, we waited as part of the family for its safe delivery, and they arrived fairly regularly: first Susan, then Pamela and finally Sandra.

Although they all lived together, the house was divided so that Auntie Nellie and Uncle Charlie had their own front room and Ella and Alf had theirs. This meant that we might be invited by either part of the family and take tea in their respective front rooms. I preferred having tea with the older side of the family simply because Ella used sterilised milk that made the tea taste odd, but the sandwiches were made with real butter and tasted wonderful.

This kind and generous family were not wealthy in any material sense. Alf cycled to work at the water board and Charlie (in semi-retirement) worked 'up the woods'. Their combined wages would have been about enough for one modest small family, and of course compared to us they would have been rich, but Alf hardly had a drink; they spent everything on the children and the family, and saved not a penny. If they didn't have the money, they didn't buy the goods.

Each year Ella and Alf managed a caravan holiday with the kids so Nellie and Charlie could have a peaceful break at home. But they missed them terribly after a couple of days and looked forward to their return. We got cards on our birthdays and little presents at Christmas and were as welcome as any family member to their happy home.

We had always had some fireworks for bonfire night, but no bangers as they frightened the cat and dog. But the first year we went to Ella's and Alf's made up for all the silent ones before. Alf had made a huge pile of timber and sticks in the back garden and laid out rocket launching

positions and boards to fix Catherine wheels to, and there was a Guy Fawkes effigy seated in an armchair waiting to be burnt.

Bruce and I happily donated our five shillingsworth of Roman candles and Vesuviuses, threepenny Catherine wheels and Flowerpots to the fireworks kitty, and joined our 'cousins' for the display. Alf started off the proceedings with some small fireworks (probably ours) and then lit the monster bonfire. As the flames illuminated the garden you could see the whole family bright-eyed in the autumn air and the outline of the runner bean poles in the vegetable garden.

Then the display proper began whizzing and fizzing. The sickly smell of cordite and powder filled the air with a delicious sense of danger. Then a huge explosion as the first of the bangers went off to shrieks of delight and amazement, and wheels whirled and volcanoes erupted and sparklers spat and candles sprayed—and then more bangs and whizzes and spinning wheels and flames and faces warmed by the bonfire as rockets stitched the sky with stars and shared the airspace with rockets launched from all over the country.

Around late September sweet shops began to stock fireworks, and even if you had forgotten the time of year you would soon realise it, as random bangs and explosions occurred around the time schools closed for the day. Little groups of boys spent loose change on penny bangers instead of four-a-penny blackjacks or chewing gum.

Stories abounded of boys who had tied ten and even twenty bangers together to see what would happen, and tales that filled me with horror of pigeons with legs blown off and cats minus tails. It was years before I found out that legless pigeons are usually suffering from a parasitic illness akin to leprosy and that there is a breed of cat called a Manx. There was one up the road that belonged to someone and I always reserved a special pat for the poor thing, believing it to be maimed by fireworks. Bruce and I were not allowed bangers as Mum did not like them. It was just a small detail but I felt and still do that it was one of those little things that make boys raised by mothers alone different to those raised by both parents.

Mum only liked the pretty ones and I suppose I did as well; half the fun of a banger is not knowing that it is about to go off, and once it has there is no more to look forward to. With the non-exploding type you got real value for money, and we would all pass comment on the ones that carried on long after they should have finished, or the ones that seemed

to start again when you thought they had fizzled out. Bruce and I pored over the biscuit tin of fireworks for days before the event reading the instructions and trying to imagine what the effect would be. The price of each device was marked on the side, and I was certainly aware of the cost and that it was all going up in smoke. We also had to light them only one at a time.

Uncle Alf, on the other hand, was into showmanship, and two, three, or even four were the norm. It was extravagant and wonderful, and even at that young age I think we both understood that it was generosity of spirit and pure fun rather than wealth and display that were at the heart of the matter.

Homemade cakes were doled out and the grown-ups had tea with sterilised milk and there was more merriment as Guy Fawkes himself was hoisted up on to the flames and cheers from everyone as he caught fire. I watched in a trance of happiness only allowing the horror of what was happening to intrude on my dreaming as his mask caught alight and his body collapsed into the flames.

Another fizzing rocket left the garden and exploded in a cascade of stars which in turn exploded again into greens and reds falling toward where we stood but vanishing before they touched the ground. All around me was joy and laughter; oohs and aahs emanated from mouths permanently half open, and even Mum was caught up in the display.

Then this hum began again in my head, but this time it did not frighten me. I suppose I was getting used to it by now, and anyway I had company, and it was much more frightening when I was on my own. I looked around to make sure no-one else could hear it, as the fireworks flashed and banged and faces hypnotised by the display and flames beamed from every part of the garden. Coats were handed round as the nip of evening produced the odd shiver amongst the happy group, and then Uncle Alf brought out Mrs. Fawkes and she too was put on to the fire, still sitting in the other armchair that had to be got rid of, to more merriment and sleepy cheers.

When it was over we still had to get the bus home, and Mum said that she thought it was an awful waste of money to spend all that only to watch it go up in smoke, and that made me consider the wastefulness of the event. But the hum in my head had stopped, and both Bruce and I agreed that this was the best fireworks we had ever been to in our lives and once home I fell asleep with stars bursting before my eyes as I

involuntarily replayed the evening. Dreams of people being consumed in flames gave way to children's laughter, apples, and cake. And Nellie, Charlie, Ella and Alf: names to draw up to your chin like blankets and wrap around your worried head until you fell into a blissful sleep.

Our trips to the woods were not stopped even in the middle of winter. On many occasions we ate our sandwiches in the snow! This was when our need for fuel was at its highest, and Uncle Alf had kindly and cleverly made us a proper wood collecting barrow out of the old twin pram. It measured about four feet long by three feet wide and about three to four feet deep. He was a real handyman and this barrow was perfectly put together in one of the two sheds that stood in their back garden. It was painted green and Mum had got an old light green bedspread that she used to cover the top, to hide our spoils from prying eyes on the way home.

At the end of our picnic Mum would call all the kids together to help fill the barrow. We all learned pretty quickly the type of wood that she wanted, and filling the barrow took no time at all. She would break off huge limbs of dead trees by wedging them in between a cleft in a couple of trees and leaning on them till they snapped. I was very proud of her strength and practised doing the same, but I wasn't nearly big or heavy enough.

Mrs. Ranger was now our permanent companion, and although she did not collect wood for herself, she helped with the loading. On the way home, the smallest ones in the party would be hoisted on to the barrow and off we would go. Once a kindly policeman held up the traffic so that we could cross the road. There were eight of us on this trip: Chick Edgerton, Richard Ranger, Mickey and Paul Sparrow, Bridget Brosch and her little brother Lenny, and Bruce and me. As we passed the police-man in the middle of the road, he leant forward to Mum and in a conspiratorial whisper said, "Blimey love, I hope they ain't all yours!"

I distinctly heard him and Mum burst out laughing; it was wonderful to see her happy like this. From then on, when we went on our outings with several kids in tow she would preempt curious glances by stating, "Don't worry, they aren't all mine!" and people would smile or make a little joke.

Chick's real name was Douglas Edgerton, but no-one referred to him as that. I really envied his nickname; it seemed to imply that everybody

liked him, and that he was little, lovable and cute. Actually he was all these things and cheeky too, with dark curly hair. He came to the woods with us on several weekends and endeared himself to my mum on the first occasion by referring to the anemones, one of the first signs of spring, as 'enemies' and telling her that they were his mother's favourite flower.

On the way back from the Hurst we would stop and Mum would buy us a penny lolly. For some reason I always chose the blue one, which was supposed to taste of peppermint but didn't. And very occasionally we might get a Walls ice cream. At this time there was a character called Tommy Walls who was a kind of superboy hero. He was featured in a strip cartoon in the *Eagle* comic and he was used to promote the product. By making the sign of a 'W' with your fingers and thumbs you were supposed to be able to fly. Without telling anybody that I was trying it out I would run around the corner frantically making 'W's and trying to launch myself into the air. Often I thought that I had achieved a hint of levitation, and though I plainly had not quite mastered the technique, I knew that I was close.

I always had a vivid imagination, which was further fuelled by the radio programmes where of course we had to imagine what everyone looked like. Mum read to us no matter how tired she might be, and we loved this moment more than any other. We believed in fairies, pixies, Jesus, elves, Father Christmas, goblins, ghosts, magic and some things called the woodcraft tinys. It was hard to form a distinct picture of these creatures, but I knew for certain of their existence as I often made shelters for them and placed food inside, which was always taken by the morning after they had visited.

I never quite sorted out the relationships in this world of fantasy, and knew that somehow Jesus might be the odd one out—yet there was something that brought them together. For instance, was a goblin bigger than an elf? Did elves marry fairies? Were fairies and angels related? Why were there no pictures of Jesus with pixies and goblins? Was God a bit like Father Christmas? And so on. In my imagination they all had a place, and that place was the woods.

The seasons were more marked in Croham Hurst, and the physical changes in nature were pointed out to us by our mother. She delighted in naming all the flowers as they appeared and she knew all their country names. The first leaves on the hawthorn were called 'bread and cheese' and were to be nibbled and enjoyed as the first fruits of spring. It was

with a mixture of bemusement and pity that our Croydon pals viewed some of this knowledge and behaviour. We ate blackberries in the early autumn, picked the odd mushroom from Duppas Hill, collected conkers from everywhere and saved them till they were as wrinkled as Aunt Naomi. Sweet chestnuts could be found in the Spinney and in the woods, and I even ate beech nuts, though they were fiddly and unrewarding, so most of our friends didn't bother with them.

Coltsfoot, anemones, speedwell, campion, dead nettle, lords and ladies, cuckoo pint, violet and bluebell and dozens of others were all eagerly greeted as they came forth. We learned the names of the poison ones like deadly nightshade and briony (I nearly ate one of these berries once but Mum stopped me and I was quite convinced that she had saved my life). We made tunnels stretching for what seemed miles in the bracken and played games, oblivious of the little scratches to legs and hands that are the inevitable badges of such fun. Once Bruce picked up a piece of wood for the fire that was full of red ants, and Mum had to strip him naked to beat the little biters off him, and he cried as much with embarrassment as pain.

We fell in stinging nettles and found dock leaves to stop the stinging. The occasional wasp sting was borne manfully, eventually. We got clawed by brambles and after the brown scabs had peeled, wore with pride the little white scars that were left for the summer until they faded with our tans in the autumn. We looked for badgers, rabbits and foxes but saw none; made friends, quarrelled and made up again. Sharing this place with new acquaintances was like showing them your favourite toys. It was done with such pride. Along the bridle paths where the branches met overhead, secret tunnels were found. Short cuts were discovered and we would jump out on Mum and Mrs. Ranger after waiting for them to round a bend in the track. They usually obliged with the right expression of surprise and we would scurry off to the next hiding place. We developed muscles like knotted rope, as we dried out the dampness in our bones from the dismal flat, on the hills and amongst the trees and gullies of the Hurst.

Our friendships with the Thorpes and Bachelors flourished and Bruce and I loved going there for tea. Auntie Ella was a wonderful cake maker, and we loved to hear her and her mother Nellie laugh. In fact we both conspired to make them laugh if we could, because that made us laugh as

well. Once, after going to the outside toilet together I said that Bruce did a wee like a watering can; Auntie Nellie nearly had a seizure, and her infectious cackle soon had the whole house rocking with merriment. Mum was fairly strict, so it was a tremendous release to get away with some very slightly risqué things.

Brown as berries we ran through the early summers, Red Indians streaked with blackberry juice, and as the summer moved to autumn running knee-deep in dry leaves as the anticipation to our shared December birthdays prepared us for the excitement of Christmas.

The first Christmas after my father left, there was no money and my mother's family made no attempt to offer any help at all. Her weight dropped dramatically, and the few photos of her taken at the time make her look as if she is suffering from some terrible wasting disease. She has often told me that the Christmas dinner comprised of one lamb chop that she was too sad and distraught to eat. Thankfully this is one memory I do not share. Things improved, and though out of necessity our Christmases were frugal to say the least, we always had a chicken after that, and the holiday was hugely enjoyed just the same.

The Christmas thrill is still there after all this time, and I love the atmosphere of street markets at that time of year. Strings of lights over the stalls as the costers try and offload their wares at knockdown prices so that they can get home and enjoy the fun; people rushing about doing their last minute stuff, kids all shiny-faced and eager.

One year Mum bought a bargain bird, only to find when she got it home that it had not been drawn, but thankfully Mr. Connaughton obliged and the bird had an onion stuck inside its body cavity. In the absence of a fridge it was hung in the 'coal hole' next to the scullery, and by pushing open the coal hole door you could glimpse the chicken's ghostly, white form hanging by a string in the gloom like a lynched corpse, contrasted against the blackness of the interior. It actually frightened me to look at it, so I stopped peering round the door. Nevertheless sometimes just before sleep the image would return long after it had been eaten and enjoyed.

We knew that Christmas was nearly here when, on getting up one day, we would find the front room decorated with paper chains and garlands. Mum always told us that the fairies had done it and we had no reason to disbelieve it as she was certainly too tired to do it after she got in from work. The decorations were always the same year after year; she

had collected them once after a dance. They were carefully put up with drawing pins and after the twelve days had passed carefully packed away again for the next year. By the time they were finally thrown away, they were positively peppered with pinholes at each end of the streamers, and the centrepiece, an old bell in purple and yellow concertina-ed paper, was falling apart.

We always had a tree—or some branches held together to look like a tree—which was decorated with tinsel and coloured balls, two red plastic horses, and a fairy on the top that for many years I was convinced was a real one. We had nuts and raisins, non-alcoholic ginger wine, and raisin wine which we drank out of tiny glasses feeling rather sophisticated as we did.

Mum would listen to the Queen's Christmas message and talk with relief about how much better she was than the old king, who had a stammer and used to make her all hot with embarrassment with the long pauses between words as he fought to utter the next one. We hung pillowcases up and always got presents to open in the freezing morning of Christmas Day. We had to unwrap them carefully so that the paper could be used again; it is a habit I still haven't properly broken.

We had no TV but I think we must have seen so many shows and programmes at neighbours that I certainly don't have any recollections of missing it. We played cards and board games and Mum played too. The fire would be on all day and the flat would feel warm; we could toast bread on a toasting fork made from twisted copper wire whilst Tyler slept and Timmy, the cat who had been brought in to replace Meemo, purred. We all loved Christmas and we were all happy together; it would be difficult to think of a closer time for Bruce, Mum and me because for those couple of days we would all be together with no work to separate us.

Miss Elwell would come down in the evening and sit and talk around our meagre fire as she did on many occasions. One year she helped us blow up balloons to complete the decorations the fairies had put up, and I would play my treasured harmonica for everybody whether they wanted me to or not.

Then one year we were invited to Auntie Ella's for Christmas.

There were no buses on Christmas Day, so we walked there, and with each step our anticipation grew. From the moment they opened the door to greet us, there was jollity until it was time to go home. The house was

festooned with tinsel, paper chains, streamers, cards, and a huge decorated tree with lights of all different colours; there were snowflakes and toys and presents everywhere. The children's faces were flushed with excitement and they seemed to have been looking forward to seeing us as much as we them. There was a roaring fire that was so hot Bruce and I dare not stand too close to it.

Although the children had opened their presents long before, there were a couple of parcels under the tree for Bruce and me, and even a little extra something for Brian and Maureen so that they did not feel left out. Alf and Ella were typical of many working-class families in that they spared no expense at Christmas for their children; and as each new baby arrived, they bought a brand new pram and complete new layette. Bruce and I had never seen anything to compare with the lavishness of their generosity and we were treated so kindly it moves me to think of it still.

When it came to the meal, I was totally unprepared for the sight of the table groaning with all the vegetables, and when they brought in the turkey, I could not believe my eyes. The image of this huge bird had an effect on me akin to watching an expert magician pulling off some amazing trick. I just sat there with my mouth hanging open. There were so many things that I could not eat through fussiness that my plate comprised peas, roast potatoes and gravy, with slices of white and dark meat. It was heavenly, and I resolved if ever we got some money we would have turkey every day.

After we had eaten everything, I had to go to the loo and this meant going through the dining room of Nellie and Charlie, and to my astonishment their table was almost as laden as ours had been, and they had a turkey as well. It was like a scene from a Norman Rockwell painting, and became more so as the afternoon became evening and Auntie Ella started laying the table for tea. There were sandwiches and jellies, mince pies and trifles, and a home-made Christmas cake the size of a car wheel, beautifully decorated by her with twirls and furls of sweet sugar icing over marzipan.

I have never liked marzipan, but Bruce loved it and we traded his icing for my marzipan and all were happy. Then came the Christmas log which was another of Ella's creations. It was a kind of sponge cake covered in chocolate, and perched on a twig on top sat a little robin. After tea, when our fears of being sick had been averted by trying to be still and play some games, we watched the TV which sat in the corner. Then, just

when we thought it could not get better, in came Alf, squeezing past the door wearing the most spectacular piece of equipment I had ever been close to in my life.

Bruce and I watched in amazement as room was made for him to stand where all could see through the haze of cigarette smoke that filled the happy room. Three out of the five adults smoked: Mum smoked her Weights, and Alf and Charlie, who both smoked Ringers tobacco, offered each other their tobacco tins in turn. Then Alf let out the longest sigh on his piano accordion as he charged the bellows, ready to perform.

Alf was not a big man, about five foot six I would guess. He was wiry with swept back straight fair hair, a small nose and twinkling blue eyes already quite lined by smiling. He was a wonderful dad; kind, generous, warm, and one of those blokes who seemed to be able to do anything with wood, from making our barrow to the most complex building of sheds, without the aid of plans or designs—and once erected, everything fitted and was sound.

Charlie and he had cultivated the piece of ground at the back of the garden and it was neatly laid out with winter vegetables in lines. In the summer there would be runner beans and carrots replacing the last of the sprouts that we had eaten a few hours ago. Alf was a real man and here in the ample bosom of his family, admired in every corner, his small but strong frame supporting the instrument that, with the bellows stretched out, must have been the size of a radiogram, he stood poised to play.

As the first notes of *Run Rabbit Run* emanated from the front of the machine, all the children looked at each other and grinned. The reeds rang and we were witness to the loudest music any of us had ever heard. You just had to smile with the magnitude of it all, and soon all of us were singing along. It was wonderful to see Mum joining in and all the adults and children so happy.

Behind the great wheezing monster, Alf's neck strained as if to avoid the constant stream of cigarette smoke that drifted into his screwed up eyes from the roll up that was hanging from the corner of his mouth. Someone brought him an ash tray and he rested the cigarette for a minute whereupon it went out and in between each number he relit it and placed it back in the ash tray. Song followed song and the noise level increased as the kids' voices were raised above the music.

After about an hour, the combined weight of the instrument and the previously consumed Christmas fare took its toll and Alf had to rest. I

wanted to know all about it, and as I sat at his knee he patiently explained what all the buttons did and where the air inlet valve was, and even let me finger the notes and hear the noise it could make. Then there was more tea and biscuits before the mighty accordion was returned to its case for another year and we all had to say goodnight and begin the long winter walk home to the cold of our flat in the basement. We spent several Christmases with these wonderful people and though I remember so much I do not remember a single journey back to our place. The memory too full of wonder, I should think.

One January Miss Elwell died of a massive stroke, upstairs and alone as usual. After the post mortem (she was fifty-five years old) a search was conducted to find if she had any relatives. The spelling of her name was unusual and there were few pretenders to her pitiful estate. By dint of her self-sacrifice and frugality she had managed to save nearly three hundred pounds toward her cottage in the country, and for that money in those days, she probably had enough to have bought one. Instead, after much searching, her savings went to the Crown. Mum remarked on that final ignominy with irony as 'old Elwell' was a republican and would have rather given it away than let "that bunch of parasites" get hold of it.

Miss Elwell was the first person that I would really miss. True, my father's mother had passed on but I did not know her. Miss Elwell's slippered tread down our dark stair was something I would miss, or not understand properly, for a very long time. Why had God allowed this to happen? Had she been guilty of some terrible hidden crime?

The sudden death of anyone who is not at the 'fullness of time' is impossible to explain to children whose logic has not prepared them for the random nature of premature departure. Just when the notion of crime and punishment may have been taken on board, along comes this wild card. The result is anger mixed with a feeling of betrayal and bewilderment. I was deeply troubled by Miss Elwell's death and surprised by my mother's tears. It was not the loss of a companion that saddened her, although I know she missed her; but in our own circumstances of slender hope for an uncertain future, Miss Elwell's failure to see her simple dream come true almost knocked the hope out of everybody.

After the twelfth night, we took down the decorations for another year, some of the balloons by now hanging like wrinkled breasts that we occasionally saw on old African women in nature films. I remembered

that Miss Elwell and I had blown them up together. It fascinated me to think that these receptacles contained her breath and I asked Mum if we should keep one so that she was always with us. Quite rightly Mum told me not to be so macabre, whatever that meant (though I understood what it implied) and we threw them away. But instead of popping the last one, I made a small hole in the top with my teeth and as Miss Elwell's last breath whistled out, I took a deep breath and held it for as long as I could. It awed me to think that she sort of had one last gasp, and that somehow I had communicated with her.

It was the last year that the fairies put up the decorations.

❧

as if in sleep

Trundling through the bridle paths,
Too low for horse and rider now
Even in the warmest summer,
Ruts that never quite dried out

As sunlight trickled through the branches
That grew on both sides of the track
And overhead met in the middle,
Curled, entwined and doubled back,

The children skittered off the pathway
Joined the grown-ups further on
Where the light streamed through the beech leaves
Robin Hood and Little John

The curls of bracken barely showing
Whipped off by swishing hazel shoots
Sharp as blades with patterns carved
By the tribe of Croydon Sioux

On bows and arrows fired and found
Amongst the brambles, sticks for guns
And the dried yolk from the eggshell
That fitted on a small child's thumb

Amongst the willow herb and bracken
Evening insects buzzed and humming
Grip upon the day had slackened
Knowing night was surely coming

A breeze blows up and through the birches
Stirs cathedrals of pines
Wafts through copses still as churches
Above the ferns a child's head high.

Leaf mould underneath the beeches
Sweet decay perfumes the eve
The last sun's ray stretches and reaches
Stragglers who are last to leave

Residents of sandy banks
Badgers, voles and all their kin
Poke out their noses left and right
Venture forth and sniff the wind

Birds are jostling for branches
In oaks and elms and silver birch
Rabbits wash, sat on their haunches,
A fox begins his nightly search

Sunlight fell upon the sandstone
Shadows spread on breakneck hill
(Where someone jumped once for a wager,
The man survived, the horse was killed)

Now the woodcraft tinys come
That live among the roots of trees
Goblins, fairies, elves and pixies
Moved by curiosity

To go out in that other world
Where only children understand
The mysteries of the absurd
Explained away by mortal man

They clamber over garden walls,
Or float like dandelion seed,
Plant toadstool rings upon the lawns
And hide important things you need

And if they're caught when sun has risen
They must stand like statues still
With foolish grins in flowerbed prisons
Waiting patiently until

Shadows blue at evening free them
To the woods from whence they came
Children know this for they see them
In gardens all along the lane.

Back in the woods, lain on the heather
As if in sleep a child lay
No frantic calling would awake him
Creatures sniffed and ran away

And the moon above the pine trees
Let gentle light upon his form
Mr. Latimer would find him
On his rounds tomorrow morn

At once the woods were changed forever
Playtime shrieks not sound the same
Each and every cry examined
Was it for joy or was it pain

For if a child stays as a child
It's often said that he is touched
By fairies who would keep him so.
The love they feel for children's such

That they can't bear to let them grow
And keep one for themselves sometimes
Playing tricks to let us know
That they remember carefree times

They did not tell us where it happened
But soon we knew his age and name
And the man-child that had done it
All the pity and the blame

Was laid at doors in roots of trees
And dandelions cursed again
And garden gnomes were trapped forever
In flowerbed prisons down the lane

~

helmet

The period after my father left home was made all the more difficult for my mother, as there was no apparent family support from her relatives up in the Cotswolds. Mum could always find excuses why Grandma and Granddad never offered any tangible help, but it didn't wash with me. These early years were spent without a real sense of belonging to a larger unit of blood relatives, as neither our father's or our mother's families did very much to reassure us that we were not alone in the world.

Mum always said that the Mays were too ashamed of what had happened, and the Mosses could do nothing as Grandma wouldn't allow it. There was probably some truth in the former, but as for the latter, I can't see myself letting my daughter get on with things on her own the way my grandfather did, whether he was under his wife's thumb or not. I did not resent him, partly because Mum was always singing his praises, and truth to tell he was a dear if dour old man and a true Victorian county man, who had learned etiquette and manners whilst in service as a butler/valet to a gentleman from Holland called van Roulte. Grandma was a working-class Tory; although she too had been in service, her mother had run a small shop in Hammersmith, and she had done the same in Brackley from the front room of their house in Banbury Road.

We had visited my other grandmother, Grandma May, in hospital

where she was confined with debilitating arthritis. It was a sunny day, and she sat upright in bed in an uncluttered ward, with a blue shawl around her shoulders and a white bob cap on her head. I remember sitting on her bed and having to be removed because of the pain my weight caused her arthritic legs.

We brought her a pot of jam with a golliwog on the label. At home I had a golliwog, whose name was George. Later, Mum and I were walking in Park Hill in Croydon when I saw some black men for the first time. They were among the first of the Commonwealth students to arrive in England, and as they drew near I turned to my mother and caused her embarrassment when I told her to "look at the real live Georges."

Grandma May cried when it was time for us to go, and died soon after our visit. Mum says she died of a broken heart because Frank left us.

Granddad May had been an engine driver all his working life, and thought it was just grand when he finally left the steam engines for the comparatively genteel work on the electric trains that ran from West Croydon to Wimbledon. Eventually we were to move to the Miller Road estate that was bordered on one side by that very line, but by that time Granddad was long dead. Mum said he could not live with his sadness, and though he survived his first wife for a long time we did not hear from him much after she passed away. We visited him a few times and I was fascinated by the white ducks he kept in his back yard with only a basin of water to paddle about in.

Once in happier times my father had smuggled me on to the platform of East Croydon station and hoisted me on to the footplate of the *Brighton Belle*, a famous steam engine that Granddad drove to Brighton. Sadly I was too young to remember this, but I do recall my dad taking me to watch the trains there on later occasions, and once seeing an old stuffed German Shepherd dog in a glass case; it looked alive, but I knew it was dead.

My dad had a sister called Ivy, who died giving birth to her daughter Shirley. Grandma May said that God took Ivy because Granddad loved her too much and did not love Frank enough. This story always frightened me. Ivy was certainly very beautiful; we had a picture of her in an old frame on the mantelpiece, but it always faced the wall.

Bruce and I slept in the condemned room next to the living room until it was just too wet to be used for anything but keeping our toys in

(we called it our Playroom after that, though an unhealthier room for play it would be hard to imagine. In it I used to listen to an old radio plugged into the electric light socket. From then on, until we finally left The Waldrons, we slept in Mum's bedroom).

Both of us suffered from bronchitis, and the Valor stove that was to keep the chill off the room also burnt up oxygen as it caused the steam to emanate from the long spouted kettle that was our sleeping companion for several winters.

Comforts were small but much appreciated, and among the biggest of these were the stories that Mum always found time to read to us, no matter what time she got in from work, before we were sent to bed. It was usually Enid Blyton's *Famous Five* or *Secret Seven*. She read so well that we would always plead for just one more chapter, and nearly always got one.

Mum really enjoyed these moments when she too could escape from the drudgery of our existence and be a kid again where there was still hope and optimism. Sometimes she would read Grimm's fairy tales, but their morbidity was sometimes more depressing than our own reality, and several times these were abandoned for lighter stories. I know that this was as much for her sake as it was ours. I was a sad case really, often troubled by nightmares and no doubt traumatised by my parents' split; very insecure and full of self-doubt and frightened by Mum's occasional threats to run away and leave us. This really did scare me. I would sometimes pump away at Bruce until he was aware of the enormity of this proposition, and soon we would both be howling and needing reassurance that her departure was not imminent.

I cannot for the life of me now think that Bruce and I ever did anything so bad as to warrant such a desperate promise, but her life must have seemed like a never ending descending tunnel of darkness at times. Mum was a one-man woman, and when Dad went, he turned the light out. What glimmer of hope Bruce and I produced was not strong enough to light her way forward.

In the winter Bruce and I would inevitably be the last ones indoors, unless Mrs. Sparrow allowed us to stay in and watch television. She put up with loads of kids from the street and we sat politely on the floor with Mickey and Paul and assorted others, loving the Lone Ranger and the Cisco Kid.

It was warmer in the Sparrows' house but I cannot remember where the warmth came from—perhaps it was from all the kids in the one room. Eventually it would be time to leave and we would reluctantly cross the road back to number thirty. Sometimes we would sit under blankets in the big armchairs by the still unlit fireplace listening to the radio. When we were older, I was allowed to lay the fire after first cleaning out the ashes.

The sound of the old split coal shovel on the grate used to make my teeth go on edge, but I could wrap up the cinders as professionally as a worker in a fish and chip shop. When we were very small, well before we could tell the time properly, Mum would stick two pieces of paper on the old American wall clock to tell us when to light the fire that she had laid in the morning before she went off to work. We had the same system for lunch during the school holidays: on the table would be two packets of sandwiches wrapped up in waxed paper, and next to them a bottle of diluted National Health orange juice (we would have had the cod liver oil and malt in the morning).

We would sit there, tummies rumbling, watching the slow movement of the hands before starting our meal: Marmite or cheese for me, and jam or jam for Bruce, although we never ever started before the hands said we could.

Sometimes we would go for picnics and persuade some of the other kids to come with us—after all, our lunches were already packed. Off we'd go, perhaps on our noisy old roller skates, sometimes not very far at all and other times to the far ends of the earth like Beddington Park.

Our imaginations were fuelled by the bedtime stories and fired by what we saw at the Saturday morning pictures. Even the trailer of a forthcoming film would have a profound effect, *The Hunchback of Notre Dame* being one that kept both Bruce and me awake and scared. Sometimes a radio play such as *The Nine Tailors* would haunt me for months. I remember the first episode ending with a body being exhumed and the coroner saying, "My God! Who would want to smash in his face and cut off his hands?"!

Mrs. Connaughton took me to the pictures some Saturday nights. We grew up in the golden age of westerns and great cowboy epics; bows and arrows, cap guns and catapults (hidden) were our stock in trade. Bruce became an expert on the tribes of the American Indians and built Fort

Apache on top of the old Anderson shelter in the yard above Tyler's kennel. Bare-legged and scabby-kneed we roamed the Croydon ranges, ran errands for pennies, and every now and then went totting for paper and rags to sell to Holloway's or Gurney Whites on Southbridge Road. We would have loved a 'telly' and were offered one by a neighbour who was updating, but Mum declined and it was years before we acquired a flickering ghostly black and white set of our own.

Once or twice my maternal grandparents came to visit, and once after my accident I stayed with them at their place in Brackley.

In the black, smelly coal shed of my grandfather's house, reeking of decay, dried onions and impotence, I was reverent. After all this was his storehouse of fuel and he had shovelled it to keep his family warm. He and Grandma also had a cellar, and one day I went down there in the dark with a box of matches and found a sit-up bath and an old bird cage amid the dust. I didn't stay long, perhaps two matches' worth of light, but I saw enough to know that I did not want to know whose bath or whose cage they might have been.

Convalescing at their place, all I knew was that I should be respectful, which I was. I was respectful of my bed that I could not wait to get into even though it was hard with the sheets smelling of Grandma and Granddad's house. The dreams that normally tormented me changed shape in the countryside and I missed the sound of my brother as I awoke in the little room that my mother and her sister Olive shared some thirty years ago. This was the room in which they planned their escape to run off with the gypsies, away from the drudgery of their existence. Stories of how hard they both had to work in order to satisfy their mother filled me with dread, and were often repeated to remind Bruce and I as to how lucky we were. We knew how lucky we were.

Grandma and Granddad did not know how to be with children. The deep tick of the mantelpiece clock measured the silences between them. Grandma expressed surprise at almost everything with her "Well I never" and Granddad expressed virtually nothing. He was the strong, silent type. Well, silent mostly.

One day he carefully built a cement step by the box hedge and I watched in admiration as he scooped shovelfuls of mortar into a carefully shuttered mould. Sadly before it set I managed to accidentally step on it and ruin it. He was very kind and did not shout at me. I'd like to think that I

was forgiven for an careless child's mistake, but even at the time I suspected (in my own childish way) that he was so used to being nagged and dumped on that he would have said "that's all right" if someone had pretended to have accidentally sliced off his penis. That night I lay awake for hours thinking about Granddad.

The whole house smelt of paraffin, which they used to fire their old cooker, and old age. Grandma had even restricted the meagre warmth from the tiny fire in the living room by the application of tea leaves and old wet potato peelings wrapped up in newspaper and placed at the back of the grate ("To keep the fire in," she explained when I asked why, helpfully pointing out that the wet bundle consistently failed to ignite).

There was no TV and the two-valve radio was only used to check the horse racing results. Grandma liked a flutter, rarely more than a bob or two, but often regaled us with the story of how she had gone to the post office to place a bet and spotted a paper aeroplane on the floor. Believing this to be an omen she hastily changed her bet and placed ten bob on a horse called Airborne which came in at fifty to one.

On Sundays Granddad took the *News of the World* for its unbiased political opinion. There were few books, and neither he or Grandma went to the pub which was only next door. I was packed off to bed with my premature nightmares long before I was tired; I missed my home a lot and cried a good deal. Granddad and Grandma didn't know, and I was aware that I couldn't return home as there was no-one to look after me there.

In the evenings Granddad would reread the newspaper and puff on his Woodbines or his 'makings'. Grandma would prod the dishes in an old enamel bowl of tepid water; the very same one that she used for washing her feet. There was no bath and the toilet was outside with no light in it. I tried to go during the hours of daylight, sitting there humming loudly and peering through the cracks in the door for the reassurance that there was still light outside.

There were a few objects in the house to stimulate my imagination. On the mantelpiece in the front room, on either side of the clock, were two shells brought home from the First World War. I hoped they weren't live. One night I thought of them exploding and making Granddad's Woodbine fly out of his mouth with shock and it gave me the giggles for a bit. Then I began to worry that they might explode, then I reasoned that the fire in the grate below was never going to get hot enough to

make them go off, and then I fell into a fitful sleep.

But there was precious little to occupy my time with except my fantasy of being a cub scout. Granddad made me an old push cart and helped me pretend; dressed in my St. Peter's School cap and a blue knitted sweater, I marched up and down the Banbury Road pushing my cart. I had an old gas mask bag over my shoulder, with a piece of newspaper rolled up as a loaf and another rolled up in the shape of an egg inside. Granddad cut out some bits of green paper, and these I stuck in the tops of my socks to resemble the chevrons that the cubs used to wear at that time. I was left completely on my own, and the deserted pigsty at the top of the garden became my hut and the street outside my parade ground.

It was pretty miserable but at least Mum had a bit of a break whilst I was supposed to convalesce. She had brought me to her folks on the train, and although I was still terrified of traffic, the ride on the steam train from Marylebone to Brackley had been wonderful. I was still walking badly and it was decided that I should have a new pair of shoes, which were duly purchased from Mr. Knibbs. I had doubts about these shoes from the off as they had chisel toes (instead of a conventional round toe, these were cut square across the front), but they were new and they were the only pair in my size. I remember wondering at the time how long they'd been waiting to get rid of them on some poor out-of-towner like me. Anyway they were bought for me and everyone remarked on how unusual they were and for such a 'bargain' price. Lying in what had been her room when she was a little girl, all I could think of was a desperate longing to be back with Mum and Bruce in my condemned room where the smell of wet walls was preferable to the smell of Grandma's paraffin cooker and cabbagy kitchen and outside loo with the shiny paper and no lights.

One morning I was outside on parade in full get up when I was approached by two local lads.

"What's on here then?" murmured one of them as he eyed me up and down. I smiled nervously and wondered if they were going to hit me.

"Who are you?" asked his mate, who was looking at my shoes curiously. I thought at the time, because of what everyone else said, that he was probably admiring them and so felt a little bold as I answered.

"I'm a wolf cub."

"Are you now?" said the first one. "Then what's that on your cap? You ain't got no wolf badge." Of course I knew that I hadn't, because I was wearing my green school cap, and in the place where the badge would have been there was my school emblem of the crossed keys of St. Peter. Before I could explain the discrepancy, the second boy offered the explanation that I was a schoolboy at the Cross Keys. It was easier to agree, so I did.

"What's in yer bag then?" continued the first one.

"Just some bread and an egg," I said brightly, not expecting the matter to be pursued.

"Let's 'ave a look then," said the second one, and with that plunged his hand into the bag and pulled out the news paper that had been my egg but that now closely resembled a newspaper. Throwing it down on the pavement he plunged his hand once more into my bag and this time pulled out my loaf of bread that now even closer resembled a newspaper.

"Where's your egg?" demanded the second one.

Seeing the difficulty of explaining the situation I blurted out, "I've eaten it."

The two of them looked at each other suspiciously, then at me.

"You're not from rahnd here are you?" said one.

"No, I'm from Croydon," I replied. I could have said Dar-es-Salaam for all the clarification it made.

"Where's that then?" said the bigger one of the two. He was beginning to get on my nerves, especially as I didn't know how to explain where I had come from.

"You have to go on the train to Marleybone." I pronounced it the way Grandma always did, hoping that they would understand.

"Which way is that?" they wanted to know. I pointed in the direction of the station and then attempted to indicate the direction in which supposed we had come but I became confused and my pointing arm was gesticulating all over the place and I was becoming more helpless and confused. The two boys had plainly never heard of Croydon or Marylebone and cared even less once it was established that I was not a near local. In my experience, near locals are in more danger from their close neighbours than foreigners—unless there are a lot of them.

"Where are you going with that cart then?" they asked me.

"I'm going camping," I answered thinking this would impress them, but even as the words left my lips I knew I'd made a mistake.

"Camping?" they chorused. "Where's your bloomin' tent then?" I must have gestured in desperation to my empty cart because they both started to laugh and ridicule its lack of any content. Then they noticed my shoes.

"What the bloody 'ell are those?" laughed the bigger one.

"I bet he's a dancer!" suggested the other one, giggling.

"Yeah, are you a dancer mate?" echoed his friend. By now I was crimson with embarrassment and close to tears, as I instinctively put my hand up to hide my 'woggle'. Yes, dear old Granddad, in an effort to keep me authentic, had cut off the end of a toilet roll and stained it brown with some boot polish before slipping through the ends of the rolled up scarf that was my pretend neckerchief to complete my ensemble. I needn't have worried because luckily they had discovered the bits of green paper stuck in my socks and were now almost helpless with mirth.

Plainly I was perceived as posing no threat, and after pulling my cap down over my eyes they left me alone. As I dragged my cart and hurt pride back into the garden and furiously wrestled with the toilet roll woggle, I found myself muttering all the things I should have said.

After one or two days in the back garden I ventured back on to the street again but I was not troubled by the local boys, I guess the word was out that there was a simpleton staying at the Mosses' house and they left me in peace.

Grandma and Granddad tried to be nice, but their own kids had been encouraged to leave home by the age of fifteen so the house had been empty of children for a very long time. It was a quiet and comfortless place. I suppose there isn't a lot to say to each other after so long. The clock on the mantelpiece loudly ticked away the minutes that seemed like hours, and the two polished shells guarded its sacred duty to remind me of how long I'd been away from home and how long it would be before I returned.

Above the old sink were a pair of gas masks from the Second World War, still hanging up just in case. The real treasure however hung in the coal hole. There on its own shelf sitting amongst the dust of years was a wondrous item. It was a German officer's helmet from the first world war. Sometimes when I was feeling brave I would take it from the shelf and hold it in my hands and concoct heroic adventures around it. Granddad had a picture of himself taken during the war. He was in full battle dress; my aunt Olive stood by his side and Grandma held my mum

as a tiny baby on her knee. Granddad was in the Middlesex Regiment; his battalion were supplied with bicycles and were nicknamed the Dunlop Brigade.

Putting all these various elements together I attempted to explain Granddad's silences. He had probably wrestled the German general from his horse and thrown him on to the ground. His last bullet spent, he disposed of him with his bare hands and hid the helmet in his 'old kit bag' for a souvenir.

More likely he had exchanged the item with another soldier, perhaps by cleaning his kit for him. I will never know what really happened.

Years later, when they emptied the sparse contents of the house after Grandma died, I slipped into the coal shed and took Granddad's helmet. The house was stripped bare of my grandparents' few remaining belongings, and even the old lino off the floor was ripped up. Upstairs in an old bedside table I found a souvenir of Grandma. It was a nipple protector. I mused as to which of her children had been denied the tender comfort of a soft breast whilst feeding. I think it must have been my own mum. I threw the thing away as we left number 63 for ever. I kept the helmet for years, as it slowly dried out and all but disintegrated, until it was finally lost during a move to our present home.

∾

shave

Mum's sister Olive had left home to work in service at fifteen, and somewhere along the road had met and married Reg who came from Standlake in Oxfordshire. They had two daughters, Christine and Susan, who were one and three years older than me. They were very striking girls, both blonde, but Susan had black eyebrows and beautiful blue eyes and a nervous chuckle, while Christine was very pretty and had a delightful sense of humour. I was especially fond of her.

The first time we stayed with them was when they lived in a council house at Ruscote Avenue in Banbury. I can only remember a little of that visit but my impression must have been good because I know I was very excited when Mum told us we were going to spend a little while with them during our summer holidays. They had moved to a new house in West Street backing on to a recreation ground, beyond which were the goods yards and shunting tracks for the railway.

Bruce and I were given the back bedroom. I think this was the first time we were together without Mum, and everything was different. First of all there was a bathroom, which meant we could have a bath. There were girls' things about the house and Susan had pin-up pictures of Audie Murphy and James Dean on her wall, and there was a piano in the front room where nobody used to go. I spent hours tinkling away there and

Auntie never told me to stop. That room smelt of furniture polish and coal and everything was in its place with polished brass and shiny woodwork. Both girls were having piano lessons from a man who may have been a little effeminate; I heard him described once as looking like 'a water lily floating down West Street'.

The house smelt of bacon and frying pans on some days, and at tea time we had bread and real butter with little Dairylea cheese wedges and vegetables from the garden and allotment; and here was the biggest difference from our own family: this one included a man, and he was our Uncle Reg.

Reg was tall and slim with slightly receding hair and thin lips. His parents had paid for him to have all his teeth out for his twenty-first birthday 'so as to avoid any trouble later on,' and he spoke with what to us at first was an impenetrable Cotswold accent. He also worked nights. Uncle Reg had a shed in his garden where he performed shed rituals— that is to say, no-one knew what he did in there. Most men in those days had sheds where they made things, and to me it was the epitome of maleness with its strange implements on the wall and the smell of oil and wood and sawdust and metal, and lots of old tobacco tins with names like 'Ringers A1' printed on them which were full of screws and nails.

Some men had mild pin-ups on their walls, and Mr. Humphries next door to No. 55 had that famous picture of Marilyn Monroe on his shed wall. For a while sheds were quite exciting, not least for their sometimes erotic content.

Perhaps because he had daughters, Reg wasn't totally at ease with Bruce and me, but he did try. He used to take us to his allotment, and some years ago before he died I jotted down this little memory in rhyme, meaning to send it to him:

My Uncle Reg grew a little fruit and veg
Out on his allotment,
And a carrot wiped clean
On the side of my jeans
Was part of my summer contentment.

...but I never did.

Uncle Reg worked nights at the aluminium factory, and didn't rise until early afternoon, when he would descend to the kitchen and prepare for the day. Bruce and I used to love this time, and would often arrange to be back indoors to observe the ritual.

First there would be the quick patter of carpet slippers coming down the stairs to where I sat waiting expectantly. The door would fly open and there, in trousers and string vest with hair all over the place, he would appear. I did wonder if he arranged his wispy locks to amuse us, but realising that we were not so important to him that he felt it necessary to entertain us from the moment he got up, I guessed that he must sleep with the window open. But there wasn't a gale every night, so it remained a mystery how his hair could be quite so violently disarranged.

His teeth would still be in a cup on the windowsill and his eyes, still slightly swollen with sleep, would blink rapidly as if annoyed with their betrayal of his slumbers. With genuine affection he would notice me in the corner, and as he reached for the kettle would say something which sounded to me like, "Gom mon dew nib Brutus," (he always called my brother Bruce 'Brutus').

"Oh, he's over in the rec on the swings," I would hazard.

"Im gom pooh gert bon frit farl I shouldn't wunner."

"Umm," I might offer.

"In up tom bing bong dayn lotment," said Uncle Reg looking at me directly.

"Oh yes, I'll go and tell Bruce, I'm sure he'd like to go," I answered, recognising the word allotment. It was only slightly better when he put his teeth in, and I'm not sure if he ever had both sets in at the same time anyway. Uncle fascinated me when he ate, because his usually immobile mouth would assume miraculous contortions as he chewed.

As he poured a little water from the kettle into the bowl he would usually say something else as part of the prevarication process before the delicate operation of shaving began.

"Ooh tal Brutus oy god bam blot dig nob nelly ban bog oryte."

"Yes uncle," I would say hoping that this was the correct response.

Once this next operation was finished the teeth would be in and I would be in with a chance. He nearly always repeated anything important anyway. If his lips had moved it would have helped, but I'm sure he could have said "bottle of beer" with no movement. At the time I was trying to master ventriloquism with a miniature version of Archie

Andrews purchased from Surrey Street market toy stall for twenty-three and six—fourteen and sixpence less than the store price. I was very proud of finding this particular bargain as Mum bought it for me for Christmas one year.

After a thorough wash and much slooshing, Uncle Reg would dab his face dry and throw the towel over his shoulders. Then picking up the kettle again, he would pour some water into a special large mug containing his shaving soap. Easing back his shoulders, he would exhale with a sort of a cough and take one or two steps up and down the kitchen.

Reaching for the shaving brush, he dipped it into his washing water, shook off the surplus, and whisked it rhythmically in the mug. To this day I have never seen anyone get a better lather on a brush before a drop was put on his face; the foam would be overflowing like a frothing firkin of best Belgian beer.

Another few steps up and down as he whisked, then whap! as the first brushful hit his face and the massaging into his stubble began. Uncle's stubble was awesome and every night it grew with a determination that gave him a complexion like Bluto in the Popeye cartoons. Today a beard might have been an option but not then; every morning, or in his case afternoon, one's masculinity was reaffirmed by this ritual of mortifying the flesh—quite literally in Uncle Reg's case. When all that was visible were his two eyes and the tip of his nose, framed by the mad hair, he would pick up the razor and stare at it a moment with the hatred of a weightlifter about to try and beat his personal best. With a few more steps up and down the kitchen, a deep breath and a little froth blown from his lips, his eyes would narrow to slits as he looked once more at the libelously named 'safety' razor and then in a quick rehearsed movement lift it up and stroke down from the top of his ear to his chin.

Three things happened simultaneously: there was a sound like ripping calico, or finger nails on a cheese grater, his toothless open mouth acting as a resonator for this dreadful sound; the first drops of blood appeared; and a short gasp of pain emanated from his foaming lips.

He took a few steps, then back at the mirror performed the same stroke on the other side of his face, and the same thing happened again. The teeth-on-edge noise, blood and a muted gasp. A few steps back and forth before he went for the moustache area on his top lip. This was accompanied by little intakes of breath with each short stroke and more

droplets of blood.

Next came both cheeks. He was working quicker now before the blood dripped onto the string vest and it was up with the chin to tauten the skin and the bloody instrument of torture was dug into the whorls and eddies of whiskers that flourished in dense thickets in the lines that connected his chin to his neck.

With each noisy jarring stroke the gasps became louder until they were real cries of pain, the razor now flying along as the task neared completion. Then with a bang he threw down the implement on to the draining board and lifted up both hands full of water and threw it over his face. As he repeated this, the sudsy water turned pink. I could feel my colour draining away as uncle took a few more steps and then picked up the brush and re-lathered his face.

For him the worst was over. The foam on his face became dotted with leaks from all the little nicks in round one, but now he was on the home stretch and sometimes would hum a little something or talk to me through gritted gums and woolly froth.

"Ger schtiff lat Rutus ginks lar gog ler gargoyle," he offered.

"Umm…" I replied noncommittally.

"Well?" he grinned enquiringly at me.

"I didn't quite catch what you said uncle," I explained apologetically.

"Oy said," he began only this time speaking very slowly, "Ger schtiff lat Rutus ginks lar gog ler gargoyle."

Recognising the shorthand for Brutus I offered to go and get him and this seemed to satisfy him, though he did mutter mysteriously under his breath and foam, "I bet 'e will."

Once more the shave began, only this time it was much quieter, the length of the bristles now shortened and like piano strings the longer they are against the sound board the deeper the note. The sound now resonating from uncle's mouth was like someone sandpapering a tobacco tin.

Finally the shave was complete, and if the blade had been new it would now be useless, but I never saw uncle change a blade so I can barely imagine his pain. As he stood there, blood dripping and foam everywhere on his visage, he looked as if he'd done six rounds with Rocky Marciano.

Uncle was resigned to his daily torture and undaunted he threw the weapon down on the draining board like a weightlifter throws down the

bar when he fails to make a lift, and rinsed his face once more in the water that by now resembled what you'd find in a beaten boxer's bucket. Then, taking a piece of Bronco from the toilet, he would tear off little bits and dab them on his tongue before sticking them on all his little wounds to stem the flow.

What a man! How I admired him! I wondered how long it would be before I would be shaving; not too long, I hoped, or else I might have to get a tattoo.

These days with Olive, Reg and my cousins were probably some of the happiest of our young lives. There was an order to each day and Bruce and I, long able to organise ourselves, were about our business and only came in at teatime. Auntie was kindness itself and though she sometimes got cross, there were none of the rages we had got used to with our mother.

Once I heard Olive tell Mum not to be so hard on Bruce and me, telling her we were "really good kids", and once I heard her threaten Christine and Susan with the words, "If you don't behave I'll send you off to your Auntie Win [our mum]".

That soon shut them up. I actually found this reassuring as I know we both tried to be good, but with all she had to cope with, Mum was sometimes hard to please.

We attended their local Saturday morning pictures and wandered through their market that had gypsies selling herbal cures, and we ate fried potato scallops on the way home, past the smelly brewery and the big rec where the magnificent steam locomotives thundered through on their way to London.

There was a brook there and we went fishing for tiddlers and sticklebacks and redthroats, and once we put a dragonfly baby in with our catch and it slaughtered several of the fish before we could remove it. It dug these horn-like things into their throats and it upset us all greatly. We wandered the fields and played games, fished in the rivers, climbed hills, ate watery homemade ice lollies that a lady made in her fridge and charged one penny for, had tea with the family and finally fell asleep to the sound of trains shunting trucks and carriages way across the rec, their puffing shuddering steam and smoke occasionally blowing smoke rings into the red green blue gold summer night sky and guiltily I wished we could stay here forever.

Uncle and Auntie were very kind and used to help an old couple called

Woodward on an unpaid basis, Reg doing the garden and Olive doing the housework. Quite why they felt obligated to do this I don't know, but people generally seemed to help each other more then, and favours done were usually returned.

Reg was also a voluntary bell ringer, and one day took Bruce and me to see them practise. Just past Banbury Cross, a little way back from the road, stands the beautiful St. Mary's church. Its circular shape and mellow sandstone made it something of a landmark.

When we went in to climb to the belfry the church was surrounded by very ancient tombstones but later, to my horror, they were mostly dug up and turned into paving around the periphery of the church where the soft stone soon relinquished their memorials to passing feet. As a child I found myself doubly worried by what became of the remains beneath the stones and the final anonymity for them once their names had vanished. This rekindled memories of *The Nine Tailors* for me. As we entered the tiny bell space the noise was unbelievable, and partly because of that and partly from the sight that greeted us, both Bruce and I looked at each other and grinned.

There must have been eight bell ringers there; most were men but there was at least one lady, and they shouted their greetings to Reg and acknowledged us with smiles. Reg took his place among them and added his bell to their cacophony. I could perceive an order to the peal but the rhythm was very irregular. All the pullers were red-faced and sweating with the exertion, and many of the men were in some state of disarray: stretching up to pull the ropes resulted in trousers and shirts parting company, and what seemed like acres of underpants had become exposed.

Bell ringing is a two-handed job, so there was no possibility of adjusting one's dress until the session ended. The bell ropes had sheepskin grips of red and white and it was confusing to note that the 'clang' did not synchronise with the pull but at a little time after; this is because the bell is attached to a beam which is rocked by the rope, and as the bell tilts so the clapper hits the side.

Watching them all working together, it was as if there was a time delay and the soundtrack was a couple of frames behind the action. All this only added to the confusion of the senses, and a comic ingredient was added to the scene when Uncle Reg's trousers slipped from his skinny waist, staying precariously balanced on his hips as he puffed and sweated with the rest of them.

Bruce and I gazed in wonder as the weight of the bells practically lifted the men off the ground. We were allowed to hold on to a rope and were actually elevated a few feet, a marvellous experience. It was probably the loudest thing we had ever heard up until then, but more was to come as one of the blokes left his post and, taking Bruce by the hand, led us up a narrow wooden staircase to the place where the bells were fixed.

As we climbed through the little trapdoor the noise was literally deafening. The swaying of the huge bells and the terrifying din awoke the memory of the *Hunchback of Nôtre Dame* trailer. We were almost hypnotised by the rocking motion of the bells themselves; I began to feel dizzy and very frightened, and Bruce even more so, as I used to tease him about the Hunchback. At home I'd made a haunted house out of our damp old 'playroom', where I'd fixed up some cocoa tins which I'd told him were the bells of Nôtre Dame, and he'd been so scared that he wouldn't go in until I'd removed them, but now I was as glad as he was to get down from there.

Banbury's other claim to fame, after the famous nursery rhyme, is that it boasts the biggest cattle market in the country. We went several times, but that used to make me sad as I soon released that, in spite of Auntie telling us otherwise, some of the animals were not going to new homes but were destined for mint sauce and mustard. Nevertheless it was exciting watching these huge beasts slipping and slithering down the ramps of lorries and to hear the squealing of pigs, the crying of calves and the mournful moaning of cows recently separated from their offspring.

The air was full of Woodbine and pipe smoke, and it stank of shit as terrified animals evacuated their bowels in the strange environment. Gumboots squelched through the unspeakable mire and red-faced men spoke and joked in loud hearty Cotswold accents whilst auctioneers gabbled in high speed code that both mystified and amazed us. I was staggered by the size of the balls on a bull, and when I heard the price of a calf, I seriously wondered if we could accommodate it in the back garden at home.

I had been unlucky with pets at that time, as a rescued kitten that I'd attempted to rear had all but died on me. I'd only fed it on Puffed Wheat (I had presumed that because our own master mouser Timmy liked this breakfast cereal that a kitten would love it). His cries had revealed his whereabouts in the old bedroom, his life was saved and a new home found for him.

Not so my pet jay, a full-plumaged fledgling who had miraculously avoided the attentions of our cat and survived for three days perched on a waste pipe in the area around our basement. On the third morning I had gone out to feed him with some bread (which they don't eat) and as I got right up to him he just made a strange cry, lifted his lovely wings and placing them over his head in a final display, dropped dead in front of me. I was inconsolable and cried on and off for several days. It would have been bad enough finding him dead but for him to wait for me before dying was cruel. I blamed myself, though I could not have provided the meat that he required for his survival as we only had meat once a week ourselves and we gratefully ate all of it between us. All things considered, perhaps a calf was not a good idea.

Beyond the cattle market was Uncle's allotment, and in neat rows his crops were displayed: runner beans, lettuce, carrots, parsley, onions and even flowers all shared the bit of ground. Reg would take his single-bladed old knife and cleanly cut a lettuce to take home or scrape a carrot for us both. Never before or since did a carrot taste so good. As the summer wore on we began to understand his speech more, and he was never less than enthusiastic when he spoke to us boys. He also grew some vegetables in his back garden, from which a gate led out to the rec, a huge piece of open ground. It was largely unsuitable for football (which didn't interest us anyway) as the ground had been pushed up in undulating waves to assist drainage, but it was always well used by local kids.

One evening Uncle asked if I could ride a bike. I told him that Mum wouldn't let us have one because we lived in town, and he said that I was old enough to learn anyway. So after tea one warm evening he wheeled his old 'sit-up-and-beg' out of the shed through the back gate and into the park, where I clambered aboard. Supporting me upright by holding the saddle, he ran along till I had enough speed to balance and then let go in the time-honoured way.

I was amazed at uncle's stamina, as I was now pedalling at a fair lick. What a man he was! I shouted that he should let me try on my own. Not getting any response, I glanced back to see him back at his garden gate and realised I had been on my own and self-propelled for a while. I immediately fell off. Unhurt, I got back on and Uncle pushed me and away I went. Then he taught me how to get on and off, and soon I was riding all by myself all over the rec. What a feeling of freedom and speed! The

whole thing was exhilarating. I had to be called in to go to bed or I would have cycled till dawn. Sweaty and tired I fell asleep with a grin as wide as a cycle chain.

Bruce learned at the same time, and though we didn't get our own bikes for a number of years, we now had the skills to begin our rehearsals for leaving home.

I never saw any open display of affection for each other from either Olive or Reg. I suppose they just rubbed along like some old-fashioned couples did before separation and divorce became so commonplace, and Auntie never seemed to bother about trying to make herself glamorous. Her hair was sort of parted and rolled up at the back, and she wore a crossover apron all day. She looked a lot like Mum, but she laughed more readily and was always kindly without being over-fussy. She wore the same sort of underwear that old ladies did, sensible stuff made out of cloth, whilst Mum wore embarrassingly scanty (for the time) nylon bits of frippery. The lascivious Mr. Humphries next door always had a comment to make, and I think Mum sort of enjoyed the mildly risqué remarks.

"I can always tell when yer sister's 'ere because of the washing on the line," he would chuckle.

I quite enjoyed the thought that he found Mum sort of sexy. She did try to impress in certain ways as if to test her attractiveness, and she always wore make-up and dressed up smart for work, as far as her wardrobe of hand-me-downs would let her.

∽

fairies

The most famous resident of The Waldrons was a pre-Raphaelite style painter called Cicely Mary Barker. This sweet lady was tall, but almost bent double with a terrible stoop. She was rather splay-footed with large feet, and always seemed to be smiling, her large teeth protruding slightly. She wore a huge-brimmed straw hat and strode on her errands with purpose and gentility. Perhaps because of her stoop she did not seem to recognise individual children, though she knew many of us; she never spoke to us, but you sensed that she liked the fact that we were there playing in the street. Maybe it was that permanent smile.

Miss Barker is known all over the world for her illustrated books for both children and adults; her 'Flower Fairy' stories and poems are the best known. Our neighbour Mrs. Leisk's two attractive daughters, Anita and Valerie, posed for two fairies each, and Anita remembers having to stand holding a broom pole to represent a flower stalk. She was the Tottergrass fairy and her sister the Pansy fairy.

Contrary to rumour, Miss Barker did not make the costumes that the children wore. Her models wore their own clothes, and the gossamer threads and petals were added from her imagination afterwards.

She had also illustrated a children's bible that had been written by her sister Dorothy. The two sisters looked after their very elderly mother

who wore frightening surgical boots, one of which had an extended built-up sole made of cork. The three of them lived in genteel order right at the top of the street and directly opposite the Halfway House with all its concomitant pandemonium.

She had a studio in her back garden, and one day she approached Mum and asked if I would be allowed to pose for her. The Flower Fairy books had by then been completed; instead, the character I was modelling was a little boy in a country smock and hobnailed boots, in a story about a swan. Bruce also modelled for her, and we became a composite figure. She usually stood to draw and she had half glasses that her stooped frame peered over. I preferred it when I was facing away from her, as when I had to look straight at her I sometimes wanted to laugh. Her gaze was very different to the way one would look at someone if they were having a normal conversation, and with her protruding teeth she did look a bit odd. For a long time I didn't see the paintings, only the drawings. One was a profile, and for the first time I saw the shape of myself sideways on—or was it Bruce?

On the wall of her studio she had fading newspaper cuttings with pictures of Brumas, the polar bear cub at London Zoo, and although they were beginning to go yellow she kept them there to keep her young models' attention.

Perhaps because she guessed that I would be interested, she let me look at her sketch books, and I marvelled at her ability to reproduce faithfully likenesses of everyday objects.

Once when needing to draw a pair of boy's leather boots, she had journeyed all the way to Cumberland, believing that boys there still wore them for everyday use, only to find when she returned that a lad across the road whose name was Roger Conio wore them all the time. She was able to chuckle at this, which I thought quite remarkable. I realised she must be rich to be able to travel so far just to draw boots, and my suspicions were proved correct when, after the posing was finished, she gave me four shillings and sixpence and allowed me to keep the jeans that I had worn for the drawings.

Eventually I did see a painting from these sessions when she exhibited a portrait of me in an show that was held at Allders department store, and I was very excited about seeing it. I was wearing the hat and smock that I wore for the sitting, and with great pride and a loud voice I announced to all nearby that it was me in the picture. A lady leaned

toward me to verify my assertion and smiled.

I believe it was Miss Barker who was instrumental in getting me into the choir at St. Andrew's, because she was upset when I left. I love her pictures of the flower fairies because of their originality but mostly because she draws out the beauty of the street urchins who posed for her, some of whom I can still recognise from kids in our road.

For many years I thought that Valerie Leisk was the model for the Snowdrop fairy, and even though she didn't pose for this particular one, it is one of the sweetest paintings. Even at the time it reminded me of Hans Christian Anderson's *Little Match Girl* and I used to wonder if her bare feet might be cold in the snow.

I've mentioned before that my mother read to us every night; I remember that halfway through reading one of Anderson's stories she suddenly put down the book and said that she could no longer continue reading them because they were so unremittingly miserable and were enough to give anyone the willies. I was surprised but glad and we moved on to Enid Blyton or something a bit more cheery. She always said that it was to protect us from having nightmares, but I had them anyway. I suspect it was to stop her having them herself.

Mum needed escape from the drudgery of her life, and in a way I think reading these and other 'Sunny Stories' reminded her of protected but happy times in her youth when she worked as an assistant to the old Nanny that raised the young Marquis of Hertford. There must have been books available suitable for the young aristocrat, and Bruce and I in our poverty-stricken surroundings inherited the love of those safe and sensible, and often very funny, reading lists.

Perhaps this influence made us a little bit softer but the fact that our country-raised mother taught us by repetition all the names of the wild flowers we came across as we played up in Croham Hurst, Bruce and I picked little bunches of flowers for her and did not in the least consider it unmanly. This was a definite perk of being brought up by just a mother, although I think that shedding this softness made the pain of entering the real world with its macho values that bit more difficult.

Eventually both Miss Barker's old mother and her sister Dorothy died. The old house must have been too big for her, and the last time I saw her—though she didn't see me—she was wearing a huge pink straw hat and striding splay-footed down Violet Lane. I think she bought a little

house there and retired. It really could not have been more appropriate.

Earning money as a model for Miss Barker was not going to provide a regular income—we always needed a few pennies more. Mum gave us pocket money that started off at sixpence a week, but as that was consumed by Saturday morning pictures it was soon raised to ninepence, giving us a surplus of threepence. These were the pennies that should have been used to buy luxuries, but from the beginning we were encouraged to save them. This meant that we always had enough to buy her a Mother's Day box of chocolates or a hyacinth for her birthday, and we were very happy to do it. She was always very appreciative of her little presents and handmade cards, even when Bruce made one with a bomber plane delivering her birthday wishes.

Mum also paid for the sweets in the sweet tin, plus the occasional Mars bar that was carefully cut into as many as eight sections and shared out through the week. She also paid for our weekly comic, *The Topper*, and later *The Beezer* as well. On trips to the woods we would get the odd ice cream, and with neighbours always asking us to run errands for a penny or tuppence reward, we were more or less on parity with the rest of the kids on the street. But we could always have done with more.

One day I suggested that we have a go at raising some extra money by totting. Mum was not at all keen on the idea, but relented when she realised we would only be collecting paper salvage. With Bruce in tow to give me confidence we began knocking on the doors of the friends in the street. We progressed to those we did not know, and soon we had enough paper to go to Holloway's yard.

Holloway's was a scrap metal business. They also dealt with rags, newspaper and woollens. It meant that there was a constant throb of noisy activity at the end of the street. A non-stop parade of horses and carts, open lorries and even blokes with hand carts made their way to deliver the scrap that afforded many of them a living.

As we nervously made our way inside, the rough-looking blokes who worked there gave us odd looks, but seeing us with our bags of paper, one of them told us to go up to the paper scale and wait. Across the yard was a man working at a machine that chopped up pieces of metal as if it was plasticine. We both stared transfixed at its awesome power until the operator gave us a big wink and we grinned back.

Next to his machine was an open arched doorway, and through it a tunnel that led to a room in a cellar under the road. There was movement down there and as I focused through the bright sunlight of the afternoon I could see a woman with a curious hooked knife tearing rags in the gloom with a single light bulb above her head. She pulled the shapes of old garments, sleeves flapping, from a huge pile on the floor then hooked them up and slashed at them with this wicked looking knife. As they flailed about they looked like people hanging there, and I looked away. A cigarette dangled between her lips and I thought it must be the saddest loneliest job in the world.

As we stared, a man came up and tipped our pathetic bundle on to the scales and weighed it without a word. He wrote something on a piece of paper, handed it to me and told me to go up to the office and get it cashed.

With one last glance at the woman in the rag cellar I scuttled off up the wooden steps and gave the lady in the office the slip of paper, in return for which I received one shilling and eightpence. I hurried back to Bruce and we scurried out of the yard. It was so much money we decided to save it and put it in our money boxes that Uncle Reg had made out of cocoa tins.

That evening Bruce and I sat putting our ten pennies each into the slot in the top and listened to the satisfying clank as the hit the bottom, then we took the lid off and did it all again. The next day I changed my pennies into halfpennies so that I could count twenty coins in and out of the money box.

After a few days we tried again but not nearly so much luck, and some of the people said that we were a nuisance. We left the paper at home and resolved to try further afield. We were only moderately successful, lacking the bravado of some lads. We did, however, collect some rags and separated the woollens because you got more for them, and were even offered an Anderson shelter which we weren't able to dismantle. A pity, because we would have made a fortune out of that.

Eventually the blokes down at the yard got fed up with us too and started to take the mickey.

"What have you got in there, son," one of them asked, "loose cigarettes?" All his mates laughed, and although I'm sure she wouldn't have been able to hear, the woman in the rag cellar looked like she was laughing as well. We both went red, and after I got our money we did not go

back totting for several years until after we had moved.

Some time later I had a dream about a mad woman in a cellar who hooked bodies of children up on a hook and slashed at them with her wicked crooked knife and I knew that we'd had a narrow escape.

In November 1952 something unthinkable happened. A policeman, Sydney Miles, was shot and killed, allegedly by two youths attempting to rob a sweet wholesalers not far from where we lived. We did not take a daily newspaper but we knew everything about what was going on because people talked about it endlessly.

We all knew that Christopher Craig had shot the policeman and some knew that Derek Bentley was epileptic and mentally about eight years old; at some point he had visited the chemist where my mother worked and had to hand over a note for the things that the family needed. Craig's elder brother Nivan had also been in the shop and been pointed out to my mother by the dispenser Mr. Strong as being "a bad lot."

Everyone was appalled at the death of a policeman, but the trial was over so quickly that I think everyone was in a state of shock.

No-one really thought Derek Bentley would be executed. Mrs. Connaughton brought down the paper with the terrible news of the 28th of January. There was that same smudged and grainy photo of the young Bentley, cigarette dangling from his mouth in an arrogant laddish pose which suggested toughness and mischief at the same time.

Now the paper told me that Bentley was dead. In response to all my bewilderment and the awful silence that followed the news all my voices were murmuring at the same time, and I begged for an answer with every look that I could give my family and the few grown-ups that we came into contact with.

My mother could only wearily manage, "Well at least now it's over." How wrong she was.

Mr. Diamond moved next door in the basement flat. He was a nice man, who unfortunately had lost his wife recently with polio and had three little ones to raise: Nicholas and Geoffrey, who were respectively two and four years younger than me, and a brand new baby called Linda. He also had his mother and father-in-law to help look after the children, who seemed incredibly sad.

I took it upon myself to welcome the boys to the street. I had just

learned a new swear word, which I was sure was not as meaningfully bad as bleedin' or bloody, and decided to use it at every opportunity. Because the boys took a little while to settle in to their new home and life without mother, it was a few days before I actually had a chance to speak with the two of them. One morning on the way to school I spotted them hand in hand on their way to my school, and ran to catch them up. They both had on their new school caps and looked very apprehensive as I shouted hello.

"Are you going to fucking Howard's school?" I asked cheerfully, enjoying my new word. Recoiling slightly with the shock of being so familiarly addressed they nodded.

"That's the same fucking school that I fucking go to!" I confessed. "Is this your little brother?"

"Yes," said Nicholas, looking even more nervous and probably wondering if this foul-mouthed maniac might eat his small sibling. Geoffrey smiled a toothy smile.

"I've got a little fucking brother as well!" I announced as we drew near to the school gate. Further attempts to converse were put aside as we went into our respective classes, but I felt I had gone some way to assure them that there was a friend nearby.

On the way home from school that evening as I was balancing on top of a fucking garden wall, Christopher Bond questioned me on my new all-purpose adjective and to the wisdom of using it at every opportunity.

"Oh, it doesn't mean any fucking thing," I said, adding, "it's only like saying flipping which is probably a worse swear word."

"I don't think so," said Chris, "anyway I wouldn't say it to my mum."

"Oh, my mum wouldn't mind," I said, secretly wondering if I should dare and deciding not to.

Unfortunately the word slipped out later that evening in a moment of exasperation when some cardboard contraption I was making failed to work.

"I can't find the fucking scissors!" I exploded.

There was a sudden hush like the world coming to its end.

I realised at that exact moment that Chrissie Bond had been right, as my mother looked up from the fireplace and asked slowly, "What did you say, Ralph?"

"I can't find the scissors," I replied, as the colour drained from my face.

"You said something else as well," she said. "Another word."

"Oh that, it's a new word we say at school when we can't find things like where's the *flucking* scissors," I said, heavily emphasising the L which is usually left unpronounced in normal speech.

Of course it was no good and Mum saw right through my pathetic excuse.

"If I ever hear you use that word again, Ralph, I'll wash your mouth out with carbolic soap. No-one ever uses that word in front of me. Your father did once and I told him the same. Don't you ever use it again, do you hear me?"

"Yes Mum," I agreed, and I thought to myself, that was flucking close.

As Christmas grew near it occurred to me that with my new found skills on the mouth organ there might be a chance of earning a few pennies by carol singing. I spoke to Bruce and said that if we got Mickey Sparrow along and a couple of other kids, I could play the mouth organ and they could sing and we were sure to make some money because most carol singers didn't have anyone to play for them. Bruce could see that we might be in with a chance, so we had a rehearsal. It was only then that a slight doubt entered my mind.

If you have music in you then you are blessed, and if you can make music as well you are doubly blessed. If you like music but cannot make it, at least you have partial blessing, but if music means nothing to you at all then pity is all that should be accorded you. Unfortunately my two accomplices fell into these last two categories. Bruce liked music but could not really find the notes, and seldom got off in the right key even with me trying to indicate higher or lower with my eyebrows as I blew as hard as I could to try and give him an anchor to the tune. Mickey hated to sing anyway, and when we finally got him to oblige he sang everything on one note not daring to move from the safety of the one he had found. This was especially difficult for me, as I started to think that they were doing it on purpose.

"NO!" I would shout, breaking off to join them in a bit of singing.

Bruce would wrestle his way up to the right key, but as soon as I left to return to the harmonica he would flounder and Mickey would drone on with his one note dirge. Neither of them wanted to go out and try it, but after investing all this time I was not going to give in.

I realised even before we embarked on our mission that my eyebrow signals would be redundant in the dark, and I had to come up with an

alternative. Bruce suggested using hand signals, but I was not so good at these for some reason and occasionally moved my hand up for a down note which, when corrected in mid-note, tended to reduce Bruce's effort to a yodel. Mickey didn't even try to follow and continued to drone away, but at least he had most of the words.

Then I had a minor brainwave. For our birthdays both Bruce and I had received a small torch. This had been a great choice as it was supposed to give us the confidence to negotiate the dark passage to the bathroom past the stairs. It did not manage this entirely but it did help in using the bedside chamber pot. I had missed it several times and fairly recently had managed to pee in my shoe that I had pulled out by mistake. Bruce and I entertained each other with light shows and I found another way of fear transference when I discovered that if I slowly moved my open hand over the beam reflected on the ceiling I could say that the monster was going to get him as my hand assumed gigantic proportions before smothering the torch lens and reducing the room to death and blackness. Eventually this game palled and I stuck various shapes on the front of the lens to scare him or entertain us both but nothing worked quite as well as the 'haunted hand'.

By now Mickey was adamant that he did not want to go carol singing even with the untold riches we had told him would soon be his. I pondered on those whose parents gave them the odd penny and thought that he was a bit spoiled. Certainly his younger brother was. If Paul was to so much as whimper, his mum or Midge (his unmarried aunt who lived with them) would give him some money and we would all troop after him down to Warren's sweet shop for a lick of his sherbet fountain or whatever he bought.

Mickey was finally persuaded to come when I made Bruce give him his torch. I explained I would need mine so as they would be able to see my eyebrow conducting and clues as to time. We had rehearsed several carols including *Once in Royal David's City* and *While Shepherds Watched their Flocks by Night*. We considered who might be the most sympathetic to our music of the people in the street, and eventually decided that our landlady Mrs. Cox was probably going to be our best bet.

After one more rehearsal of our dismal chorale, and with a somewhat heavy heart, we trudged across the road to number seven and climbed the steps to her front door. We started off with *Once in Royal David's City* and I thought it sounded dreadful, so I stopped it after the first verse and

we went into *While Shepherds Watched* which sounded even worse.

There was nothing for it but to knock on the door after several what seemed like minutes of banging, ringing and waiting the door was finally opened by old Mr. Cox who was, you may remember, virtually stone deaf.

"Yes!" he bellowed, looking down at the hapless three.

Bruce stuck out his hat as he'd been instructed to do, and the old man looked at it for a second or two before he said, "It's not mine."

"No, we know that," I shouted, "we're carol singing and we want some money." Then I remembered. "Please."

"I can't hear what you're saying," said the old man, "I'll get Mrs. Cox to see you." Off he went down the hall to where the old couple sat in their kitchen, which was as far from the front door as you could get in their apartment. No wonder the old man couldn't hear us.

"Hello Ralph and Bruce," said the old lady, "and isn't that Mickey with you?" She peered at the three of us in a curious but kindly manner. "What can I do for you?"

"We're carol singers, Mrs. Cox, and we've just sung a load of carols and we were hoping for some pennies."

"Are you?" she beamed, "well I didn't hear anything as we were in the back end so you better sing me some now that I am nearer to you."

The ensemble looked crestfallen but we had gone this far and so I boldly struck up again with *Shepherds*. After some frantic eyebrow movement my choristers reluctantly joined in halfway through the second line. With an audience, my wayward harmonisers went a bit quiet on me, and I thought we sounded somehow vaguely Scottish as my reedy mouth organ squawked out the tune whilst these two droned on below.

We had not even begun verse two when she walked off to get her handbag, and coming back, took out her purse and gave us two pennies. That seemed to be the going rate as the night progressed. One lady complimented me on my playing but said nothing to the drones, who by now were fairly philosophical about the enterprise. One man came out and started laughing right in our faces and gave us two more pennies to sing one verse again while he dragged his wife out to hear us. She laughed at us as well. Several times Bruce got the giggles, which made Mickey laugh, and our shape was clearly beginning to suffer, as well as a kind of exhaustion setting in.

Looking back I think our presentation would have been more suited to Hallowe'en than Christmas, my torch shining from below my chin

giving my already contorted face an eerie strangeness. My eyebrow sig-
nalling had given me a headache, and my body was aching from willing
on my unenthusiastic and mournful sounding vocalists with every spasm
and shoulder flick I could muster. Halfway down Violet Lane we had all
had enough, and Mickey wanted his split there and then so that he could
go to the shop. I think we finished up with a shilling or so each.

Summer games took place in the Spinney. As you looked at it from
our gate there was a postbox that I fell off from time to time, and just
beyond it a huge ibrox or evergreen oak. I also fell off this once and tore
a lot of skin from my backside, which would have been more bearable if
Mum had not insisted, to my utter embarrassment, on showing Mrs.
Connaughton.

This was our adventure playground; there were trees and bushes and a
store for the road sweepers to keep their dust cart in, and in the autumn
there were chestnuts and conkers. Around the perimeter the road became our running track and the bushes provided cover for games of a
more enquiring kind. Once in the middle of my becoming a boy detec-
tive I discovered a whole pile of what I took to be blood-soaked bandages.
I was totally convinced there had been a murder or at least a stabbing
(Mrs. Connaughton had told us about a knife fight down at the pub in
Salem Place the previous Saturday). For the life of me I could not understand the reluctance of any of the adults to take my find seriously, but
eventually someone must have done. I was told not to go near them and
that they would be dealt with, which they were. It was years later before
I realised they were used sanitary towels.

As the nights drew in I was forced to keep the games going longer
and longer; if our friends got bored they would just peel off and go and
watch telly so I had to be good. The alternative was to sit indoors waiting
for the hands on the old American clock to reach the two bits of paper
that had been stuck on the seven and twelve to indicate seven o' clock.
This was the time that Mum left work, and usually it meant that the fire
had to be alight and going well by the time she came in exhausted through
the door.

Sometimes Bruce and I would sit under a blanket together until the
time was right, then I would do the honours and light the old newspaper
and damp wood in the grate and hope for the best. Mum was good at
laying fires and to this day so am I. It was rare that we needed more than

one match to get it going. Our cat Timmy was a better frogger and toader than he was mouser, and ceaselessly dragged in the bodies of dead amphibians for my mother's approval. But we loved him anyway and I was convinced that he was the prettiest cat in the world. He would sit one side of the fire and Tyler the other.

One night as Mum prepared some tea for us all I was dreamily gazing into the flames while Tyler was sitting with his back to the fireplace. Suddenly, without any warning or provocation, he lunged forward and bit my face.

It was an extraordinary thing to have done. His teeth closed around the inside of my left lip and his top teeth under my left eye. As soon as the bite was made he let go and I recoiled backwards in a state of shock with blood spurting everywhere. I must have screamed, and my poor old tired mother came rushing in and in utter disbelief surveyed the scene in front of her. Bruce explained what had happened and Mum tried her best to stop the bleeding before we all trudged up to Croydon General Hospital. Luckily the evening casualty room was quite slow that night, but the smell of ether and disinfectant got to me, and I began to tremble as the dreadful memories of my stay there came back.

The wound to my upper lip took three large stitches—but should have had more—and the top injury just one. The thing I remember most was the feeling of having manly bristles on my upper lip in the form of the thin wire stitches that were inserted and the fact that the young nurse who administered the tetanus injection broke off the needle in my leg and they had to use pliers to pull it out. My biggest fear however was for Tyler. Mum, naturally, was furious but I knew how she loved her dog and I had to think of an excuse for his behaviour.

In the end the story I made up went along the lines of, "I was stroking Timmy as he sat by the fire and the buckle of my sandal accidentally pressed on Tyler's foot which caused him to jump at me in pain and jealousy."

It was a bit thin, and I suspect that she knew it all along, but it gave her the excuse not to have him put down.

On my return it was as if nothing had happened between us two. Tyler greeted everyone with his normal wood-splitting tail wagging and must have been surprised at the coolness of the welcome he got in return. I enjoyed my hero status a little as well, especially as it could have been viewed as if I had been in a manly scrap of some sort. I think I even put

on a little swagger as I walked.

On the weekend as usual we went up to the woods and as usual ran about playing games and climbing our favourite trees. It was a normal sort of outing except towards the end of the afternoon I began to feel very strange. By the time we were ready to leave and begin our homeward journey I had begun to look ill enough for my mother and Mrs. Ranger to be concerned. I was very dizzy and hot and my colour was deserting me.

Soon I was unable to walk and they lifted me up on to the wood barrow and hurried to the nearest phone box. By now I had gone a sort of grey colour and had all but fainted. How Mrs. Ranger got the wood barrow home with her push chair I don't know; I had passed out by the time we got back. The ambulance arrived and took me off; as it neared the hospital I had begun to come up in a rash, which then started to turn into small blisters. My mother was almost beside herself by the time the doctor had seen me and declared that I must have had an overdose of the tetanus injection.

This diagnosis was confirmed by our own wonderful Dr. Martin, whose sonorous Welsh tones gave us all such confidence to get well: "You see, my dear, it appears that they gave him rather too much of the serum for anti-tetanus and now the poor boy has the illness proper."

I can't say that he ever soothed me with that clear penetrating enunciation of his, but he did inspire confidence. He always wore a suit and half-rimmed reading glasses in gold frames. He had grey hair and very dark eyes with eyebrows that seemed permanently furrowed with care. I imagine he used the same voice to tell you that you were dying as he would to tell you that you were going to survive. His delivery lacked any trace of sentimentality and he would deal out admonishment in the same tone as praise. Everyone loved and feared him in equal measure.

The only time there might have been a hint of embarrassment shown on his part was when Mrs. Sparrow was safely delivered of her third child. Dr. Martin helped bring him into the world and Mrs. Sparrow insisted that the little boy be named after him. On hearing that the good doctor's first name was Lambert, she compromised and named the child Paul Lambert Sparrow.

I eventually regained consciousness in the small ward that I had been placed in three years previously to avoid the tormentors of the children's ward. For the next few days I was woken every few hours to receive doses

of antibiotics. It was touch and go for a while, but I was soon home again, although much weakened by the experience. I began to feel quite guilty about these mishaps and paradoxically realised how lucky I had been.

Not very long afterwards I arrived late home from school to find quite a little crowd gathered at the top of the basement steps. Poor old Tyler had gone crazy and had attacked everyone who had gone close to him. My mother and the vet were there already and she was the only one that could get anywhere near him.

The diagnosis was an inoperable brain tumour and Tyler was put to sleep. It was tough on all of us, and a replacement dog that the vet provided us with was too boisterous for Bruce and I to handle and we had to give him up too. Still we had Timmy the cat, and soon I had pet mice and even a guinea pig.

Several of my school friends had joined the cub scouts. I had longed to be a cub since before my accident. I suppose it should have been a warning to me of all disciplined activity, but I continued to confuse obligation and duty with being good or correct. The mysteries of 'sixers' and indecipherable songs like *Ging Gang Goolie* left me bewildered and embarrassed, and the sausage-cooking outing was a washout, during which I lost my penknife and my pocket money.

The games, devised I guess to foster a team spirit, were lost on me, as I had no desire to win apart from running races, which are not team sports. The only thing I really remember was the cub play, where I was given a walk-on part on the small stage at the scout hall. It was a play about a man who hears the football results on the radio, realises that he has won the pools, and then one of the kids finds the coupon in his pocket and they are not instantly wealthy after all.

The audience found this very funny but I thought it sad, especially if my mum had done it and we'd had a chance to escape from poverty and then I'd found the coupon in my pocket. It did not bear thinking about and I wondered which might be the best form of suicide and how I could explain or ever come to terms with my slackness.

At one point Brian Atkins, who was at my school, got up and sang a song in a beautiful boy soprano voice, and all the mums cooed and aahed at him. He was a slim blond boy with an angelic face, and I was jealous of both his voice and the effect it had on his audience. That night I practised singing like Brian Atkins and learned *Golden Slumbers* which I sang

to Bruce on many goodnights.

After a while I thought I was probably good enough to join a choir. The best church choir was thought to be at the Croydon Parish Church and Miss Barker was kind enough to ask if I could join. She told us with some small embarrassment that they only took Grammar School boys and I was still at primary school. I thought this unbelievable. Did Jesus really worry what school you went to I order that you might sing his praises? I doubted it. Other forces were at work here, so I applied at Miss Barker's favourite church where she had designed one of the stained glass windows and was accepted.

By now I was involved with three churches: the Mint Walk Mission, the Congregational Church and the Anglican church at St. Andrew's, as well as the cubs. Of course one of them had to go, and just before Mum had scraped up the few coins for my second-hand cub uniform, I got into a small scrap with a boy outside the cub hut. I took a swing at him with the wolf's head on the pole that we had to march with, he ducked, and with my usual co-ordination I managed to hit the gate pillar, causing the wolf's head to burst just above its right eye. A pile of stuffing fell out on to the road and I thought it best to go home and construct an excuse as to why the cubs and I were not really suited.

For some time I had been having doubts about my future with this organisation, because I had been taken at my word when refusing payment for my errand running, saying that it was "my good deed for the day"; and now I was being run ragged with the neighbours always asking for me to go to the shops so that they could avail themselves of my free service.

Needless to say Mum was disappointed, but we sold the cap for two shillings and I wore the jersey without the badges for a long while.

Eventually, some months after my tetanus scare, I was well enough to have my tonsils out. For a hospital veteran like me it was a doddle. Nine days inside and ice cream to eat with jelly—no problem! This operation was done at Mayday Hospital, where my brother was born. It made a nice change to be in a new hospital, and I was also one of the oldest on the ward at nine years old.

When the Sparrow family acquired a TV, a dozen or more kids would troop or sneak into their tiny front room to watch the Lone Ranger and Tonto or the Cisco Kid. It was great to sit amongst them and stare at the

black and white screen, but part of me missed the outdoor games that we seemed to play more before the TV arrived.

We never ran out of things to do in our street. Bows and arrows, soapbox carts, roller skating and for a short time roller skate soap boxes, where we took the wheels off a pair of skates and fixed them crudely on to wooden axles so that the trolley was only about an inch off the ground. Not only did this add greatly to the sense of speed but it made a fearsome noise as well. You could get two trolleys out of one pair of skates.

Probably one of the best presents Bruce and I ever got was a pair of rubber-wheeled roller skates. I travelled miles on my skates and led a troop of kids with me into uncharted territory, often miles from where we lived, and somehow got us all back home again. Of course skates were not as good as they are today, but that feeling of speed and silence, where we felt we were able to speed the world up to the tempo we wanted it to go, was marvellous. Often at the end one of these epic trips, long after I had taken the skates off, I could still feel the motion of moving. Just like when you come off a ship and you can still feel the motion of the vessel. The one small hitch with rubber wheels was when a tiny piece of grit or small stone got under your wheel it stopped it dead. This did not necessarily tip you up, but worse, it spoilt your rhythm.

Wheels gave us freedom and I longed for a bike, but Mum made it quite plain that after my accident I would not get a bike until I was at least twelve years old. The waiting was torture.

Much later there was a push scooter craze and again I was off for miles and miles of pavement travel. My fear of traffic all but a memory, my legs grew hard and strong, and if I wasn't on wheels then I was running.

And if I wasn't running I was blowing. My enthusiasm for the harmonica had stayed with me, and eventually led me to persuade my mother to fork out the sum of twenty-nine and eleven for a hefty looking instrument, the Super Chromatic.

Around the age of eleven my friend Charlie Ranger got a ukulele, which cost thirty-seven and six.

By this time (it was now the middle fifties), Elvis had arrived on the scene, and the guitar, like Elvis himself, became king. It is hard to overstate the impact Elvis had as far as the guitar goes. Prior to this, the instrument of the working class would have been either the piano accordion (for portability) or the piano, for the pub sing song. The guitar was

a rare bird, and its place in the orchestra or bands of the day not properly understood beyond a few jazz aficionados. The main reason being I suppose that you could hardly ever see or hear it. You couldn't hear Elvis's either, but you could certainly see it, and it was sexy.

I was intrigued, and after some persuasion managed to get Charlie to swap his uke for my harmonica. This did lead to a slight altercation between our mums over the discrepancy between the two prices, but it was resolved and I kept the mysterious stringed implement.

After we moved, I learned to play it with the help of the George Formby Ukulele Method. Although it was all but a guitar in miniature, I can't say it was in any way sexy.

According to the George Formby book, all you had to do was to tune the strings to the tune of *The Campbells Are Coming,* then put one finger on the third fret of the first string and by strumming in a downward movement you obtained the chord of 'G'. It worked! Next came a two-finger chord of 'C' and then a hard three-finger chord of something strangely labelled 'D7'.

Put them together with the words under the picture of the chords, and out came *Way Down Upon The Swanee River.* It was fantastic. I was away almost immediately. Thankfully I could hear when the chord was right or wrong, and within a few days could just about accompany all the new skiffle hits on it.

Skiffle had arrived about this time with the marvellous Lonnie Donegan version of *Rock Island Line.* It is hard to think of a better beginning to this movement. I loved this track and played it over and over again with that slow build-up of speed until my green felt ukulele pick was a blur in my hand. I was soon playing Buddy Holly tunes as well on this plinky little instrument.

∿

warts

Howard Junior School was an ordinary Victorian building in Dering Place, Croydon. I was transferred there, with other children from the immediate area, when St. Peter's School closed.

It had separate entrances for boys and girls and one for 'mixed infants'. I started there at the age of about six and a half, in Miss James's class, and from there went to Miss Burt, who had eyes of different colours and who wore her hair in a bun. She walked with great strides and her face went a little red whenever she spoke to one of the two male teachers in the school.

Miss Burt introduced us to the stories of Brer Rabbit, which I loved. I was by now reading very fluently, and my writing was good if not particularly neat. My spelling was reasonable and I looked forward to the next year when we would be given pens and inkwells to use.

Around this time, in the early 1950s, appeared the great London smogs. We were all used to fog, and as kids we loved to run and disappear from each other in the playground, only to reunite with our friends from a different direction. Fog enhanced some of our games and enabled you to be part of magic. I loved the eeriness of the shapes of trees in the Spinney or the muffled outlines of the few cars in the street and the way

colour was almost reduced to black and white. Usually the sun burned the fog away by morning playtime.

Smog, however, was different.

Smog settled on Croydon like a wet blanket of smoky smothering cloud. At first it was funny because two or three paces away from you, your friends disappeared entirely, but at its worst you really couldn't 'see your hand in front of your face' if your arm was outstretched.

Traffic all but stopped and only valiant bus drivers crawled along familiar roads using their sixth sense and memory to guide them to the next paraffin flare. Inching your way to school, holding on to garden walls and straining your ears for oncoming vehicles, tested your hearing and faith to the utmost. Over everything hung an eerie muffled silence.

Then people started to die. The old were particularly at risk. Bruce, Mum and I, all of whom had suffered with bronchitis, began coughing. Mum tied scarves around our faces, and by the time we got to school there were black sooty stains where our mouths and noses had drawn in the filthy air.

When the newsreels of the time were shown in cinemas, they produced a few laughs as you could not really see what had been filmed, and people once again seemed to draw reserves of fortitude from their remaining vestiges of wartime spirit.

My best friend at this time was Chick Edgerton, who was distantly related to the Leisks, our neighbours across the road. Chick was considerably shorter than me, but he was a very fast runner. He also did well at simple hand-to-eye co-ordination, which I was hopeless at, but we became pals anyway.

One day during the lunch break we were running around the junior boys' playground, fairly bored, when Chick thought it would be a good idea to do something naughty. We decided to write down all the rude words that we could think of on a piece of paper and show it to one of the little girls in the playground next door. We got quite excited by the prospect, and using a stub of pencil and a scrap of paper we scrawled down words like: winkle, bum, titty, pee, fart.

With each new word we had a giggle, and when we ran out of naughty body parts to list we went on to swear words like: dam (sic), sod, bugger, fuck.

We knew these were bad but had not the faintest idea what they meant.

Our laughter now attracted the attention of a red-haired boy called Terry, who was a real handful and a little slower at reading than Chick and I.

He wandered over to us by the playground wall and wanted to see what we were doing. Because we were both slightly nervous of him we handed him the paper. This was a big mistake. Terry looked at the wobbly writing and made no sense of it whatsoever. The fact that we were laughing at our rudeness was lost on him, but he rightly presumed that we were up to something. Unfortunately, because he couldn't read, he mistakenly thought we were laughing at him and his eyes narrowed as he considered what to do. Suddenly he took off across the playground.

Chick took off after him like a rocket. Terry knew he could not out-run Chick, and now thinking this was a great joke he ran straight up to the dinner lady, Mrs. Holder. After tormenting little Chick by holding the piece of paper above his head, he was just about to run off when Mrs. Holder snatched it out of his hand, unfolded it and silently read my childish hand.

She looked at Terry and asked, "Did you write this?"

"No miss," he said, "it belongs to Chick and Ralph."

She looked up and motioned to me to leave the refuge of the wall I was trying to climb into. Once I was by her side she read the list again as if to reassure herself that such awfulness warranted the decision she was about to make.

"Go and stand in the hall by the cloakroom," she ordered.

Hardly believing the sound my heart was making, we both went and stood where she said, minutely examining the green gloss paint. We stood fairly close together, but such was the discipline in the school we hardly dared try to talk to each other. Outside, the distant but still exuberant sounds of the playground seemed a long way away.

I don't know if Mrs. Holder planned for us to see the headmaster, but on his way back from lunch he had to walk past us on his way up to his study.

George Wilson was a smallish, slightly pompous man with slicked-back brown hair and a pencil moustache. He always wore a suit, and liked to think that he possessed a sense of humour. We had a boys' football team, but neither of our male teachers were very sporty and Mr. Wilson's most oft repeated euphemism for losing hopelessly at our matches was, "We didn't quite manage to win but it was a very good game!"

As he walked past us I noticed to my horror that he held our pathetic

scrap of paper in his hand.

"Come with me, you two!" was all he said.

We dutifully followed him up the three flights of stairs to his room. He told to us to wait outside his study, where we stared at a picture of boats by Van Gogh.

After several more minutes we were summoned in to the small room. Mr. Wilson turned to face us and asked which of us had written these words on the paper. My heart was making so much noise that I hardly could hear myself answer.

"I did."

"What did you do?" he asked Chick.

"I helped him," said my friend. Chick looked so relaxed, I felt I would be all right once the shame of being caught had gone. Without another word our headmaster went to a cupboard by the wall and took out a long thin cane. It had a small piece of string tied round the top and I noticed that it was split quite a long way down its length.

"Hold out your right hand," he ordered Chick, who did so without hesitation. Then, spinning quickly on his toes and giving a little jump, Mr. Wilson brought down the cane on Chick's hand with a swish and a slap that I can still hear. I instinctively looked at Chick's face: not a sign of pain, thank goodness. Then, as I kept looking, I saw all the colour drain from his face, as with no change of expression huge tears welled up and overflowed his eyelids, splattering on to the floor. His hand had clamped up but I saw no more as I was ordered to hold out my own hand.

Mr. Wilson seemed pleased with his effect and with a flourish of a man who takes a pride in such things repeated the little twirl leap and contact with my hand. I had never experienced such a shock before. The cane not only stung my hand like an army of wasps but it gripped it momentarily between the split and must have pulled at the centre of the stripe it left on my palm. My hand clenched and I wanted to put it under my arm but was forbidden to do so.

Our headmaster then put the cane back into the cupboard and told us, "Let that be a lesson to you both. Now go back to your classes."

Tears were silently pouring down our cheeks but I could make no sound except a kind of muted sob. The pain was unbelievable and was getting worse. I could barely open my hand to look at the damage. I felt sick and violated. Somehow I got through the afternoon, and from across the classroom I could see Chick trying to prise open his own hand to

look at what had happened. On the way home I stared at my hand. Across the palm was a thin pinched red line and each side of it was a white one. By now the weal had swollen up, and opening and closing the hand was painful.

By the time Mum came home from work the redness around my eyes had disappeared and I managed to keep the whole event secret from her. The pain lasted until well into the evening and I was sure that my mother would see the mark. Even at bedtime my hand still throbbed, and in the morning there was a slight blue tinge as the bruise began to appear.

The next day, apart from comparing the marks to our hands, Chick and I did not speak to each other. It was as if we might inadvertently pass more trouble to one another. Most of our friends knew what had happened and sort of sniffed around us the way animals do, keeping a distance from one of their number who might be mortally wounded. Terry was really upset by the incident, but could not articulate his contrition for our punishment. It was nearly a week before we were both free from pain and could use our hand for writing properly again.

Teachers usually dealt summarily with classroom offences but this was one of the few times I remember the head caning such a young pair of children.

It was not until much later that I found out that many of the teachers were members of some brethren sect. I have no idea if that was what gave them the right to be quite so brutal with some of us. There didn't seem to be an undue emphasis on religious education at the school, but there was a very strict regime and a high degree of expectation backed up with very firm handling. I was certainly anxious never to be caned again, especially on my hands. The preferred way of quick summary punishment was to have your sock rolled down and be hit on the calf muscle two or three times with a ruler.

Miss Smee had no need to threaten any of us with violence, as her reputation was awe-inspiring. I dreaded going into her class, but as an A-stream child I was expected to pass the 'eleven-plus' exam for grammar school selection, and Miss Smee had certain methods that had proven very effective.

She was one of the old school, who believed that children should not speak unless they were spoken to. It took her ages to learn our names and she never discussed anything with us. She played the piano with great

ferocity, seated on several thick books to raise her up to the required height.

She was very keen on singing, and to help us open our throats, she forced a ruler between clenched teeth and rattled it up and down until our mouths were open wide enough to let out our praises. Those of us who were unable to hold a tune or who refused to try were called 'growlers' and no more was asked of them. The selection process was to walk down the line whilst we were singing and to send any out-of-tune offenders to one side.

Our classroom was an old laundry, and there was an inscription to that effect over the door. The desks were on two levels and Miss Smee conducted her lessons from street level. She had two mobile blackboards, one on each side of her desk, and behind the one on her left was a sink with hot and cold taps. Miss Smee used to smoke Churchman's cigarettes, which were quite strong; she would have frequent coughing fits which were quite productive and by nipping behind the blackboard she could expectorate into the sink. Some of the more sensitive pupils were nearly sick when she did this, but I was inured to it by my mum's ferocious cough from her roll-ups.

Miss Smee made us collect waste paper and milk bottle tops. I got over the paper obsession, but milk bottle tops stayed as part of our family duties for years, and it was only when I found out that it took three railway trucks filled to the brim to pay for one guide dog that I stopped collecting and made donations instead. It was wonderfully liberating to stop hoarding silver paper.

Miss Smee constantly preached the virtues of National Savings, and excelled at teaching us mental arithmetic by saving the lesson until last in the day or last before lunchtime. No-one was allowed to leave until so many correct answers had been achieved. The calculations had to be done at speed, as she rattled off the numbers like someone reading the weather forecast: 6 plus 9 minus 3 times 2 plus 6 divided by 3... and so on.

Her voice was gruff and masculine, with a broad local accent that mellowed on school open day to that of a sweet old lady. I was hardly able to believe my ears as the old tartar sweetened the parents and even managed a smile, revealing teeth the colour of mahogany.

No-one was allowed to interrupt her lessons, and hands raised for requests when no question had been asked were largely ignored. This had dreadful consequences for me.

One morning after break I suddenly needed to pee. I tried not to think about it but the more I tried, the more I was sure that I could feel my bladder filling up. There was ages to go before lunch break and finally I was forced to raise my hand to be excused. Miss Smee was in full flow on some subject, and though she must have seen my hand, now waving with anxiety, she steadfastly took no notice. Now my knees were unhelpfully knocking together rhythmically as I tried not to concentrate on my growing discomfort. Soon my other hand was forced under the armpit of the raised one in order to give it more height and I was leaning slightly to one side. Next I was bouncing to the rhythm of my knocking knees, and my face was getting red, but still there was no acknowledgement.

Finally I could stand it no longer and got up and ran down to her desk.

"Please Miss," I began, "may I be ex…"

I got no further because she rounded on me.

"How dare you interrupt my lesson. Get behind the blackboard!" she ordered, and miserably I crept behind it, wondering what would happen next. For a moment. standing was a little easier, but within a few seconds I was back hopping from one foot to another. I had on a pair of brown corduroy short trousers that my mum had made for me from an old skirt from the lady upstairs. It had a pocket in it and I thought that if I were able to reach in maybe I could hold my willie and stop myself peeing.

Unfortunately the pocket was rather too short to reach the vital part and as I struggled in my desperate dance to find myself, my concentration was unable to focus on both needs and I peed myself. At first it was such a relief and the sound of the pee so alien to classroom noises that no-one noticed it. I stood there watching it happen and wondered if it would ever stop. Within a few seconds I realised that it never would, and after several gallons had splattered over the stone floor, and with a cry of woe and humiliation, I ran for the swing door and pushed it the wrong way before bursting out into the playground and running to the boys lavatory. Whereupon I stopped peeing. I stood in front of the urinal and pulled up the side of my trousers and of course there was nothing left to do. I felt so miserable I wanted to cry. Suddenly the thought of going back to class was too much, and with my damp brown corduroys flapping round my skinny legs I hoofed it off home.

Mum was very sympathetic and the next day went in to see Miss

Smee, who professed to understand, and when at last I could be per-suaded to swallow my humiliation and return to school I was amazed that no-one ever made any comment about my accident.

I was not the only one to pee in Miss Smee's class. Shortly afterwards Susan Hayward did a silent pee whilst sitting at her desk and then my friend Vernon Burford obliged, and by so doing cemented a friendship which survives to this day!

Meanwhile, in Mr. Ogle's class Trevor Gunther pooped his pants. Once I had heard about poor Trevor, a mere piddle on the floor was nothing and I started to get my confidence back.

My humiliation had been exacerbated by a growing awareness of girls, and not just wanting to look at the hidden parts; I genuinely wanted them to like me because I was certainly attracted to several of them in my class.

We had to do country dancing on Friday afternoons and this was both a joy and a curse. A joy because it meant I might have the opportu-nity to dance with Sandra Williams. When I returned to school after peeing on the floor I was placed next to Sandra and instead of being embarrassed at having a piddler sitting with her she told me she was glad that I had been put there because she liked me. This was a tremendous boost to my ego, and I immediately decided I liked her as much as Irene Wood, a very pretty blonde-haired girl who lived not far from us, near the wooden houses on Southbridge Road.

Things should have been looking up. Girls liked me and although it would have been sissy to have admitted it, I liked girls. Of course all the boys hated country dancing, and I agreed with them that it was stupid, and we had to dance with girls that we did not like, and sometimes these girls smiled at us in a way that made us suspicious. Sometimes their hands were sweaty and sometimes they held too tight, but every now and then, one of the pretty ones would have soft sweet hands and I would get a warm feeling when I touched them. Which is where the curse came in. It should have been wonderful, but for one small problem, which eventu-ally became several small problems.

Warts.

Just as I was able to enjoy the tactile sensation of fleeting touches with the prettiest girls in the class, a series of warts arrived on my hands, caus-ing me deep embarrassment. Naturally I thought that everyone could see

them, but what was worse, the girls might be able to feel them.

The first wart appeared near the first joint of my right thumb, and then one came on the back of the same hand. Another appeared on my left hand, and then one in the palm of my right. As if this wasn't bad enough, people insisted on telling me the folk law of warts.

"Have you been playing with eggshells?" was a frequent question, first asked by my mother but repeated by several others. There were also the country variations to deal with.

Uncle Alf suggested, "Rub them with a bit of raw meat and bury the piece as far away from the house in steps as you have warts on your hands. Do this during a full moon and when the meat has rotted the warts will have rotted too."

This sounded promising as it hinted of magic and spells. The trouble was that in our family we hardly ever had any cooked meat, and rubbing it with a sausage or a piece of spam did not promise the same mystical effect. Somehow Mum got me a piece, but even as I was rubbing it on I started to have doubts. In the end I expect a fox dug it up and ate it, as the warts stubbornly remained.

Uncle Charlie told me to rub them with elderberry leaves. This left green stains on my fingers and hands.

Someone else told me to cut notches in an elderflower stalk (one for each wart) and bury it, then when it had rotted like the meat, my warts would be gone.

Granddad suggested that I had probably been playing with toads.

Grandma agreed and said there was only one thing to do and that was to rub them with elderberry juice. This I did as it was plentiful and cheap: there were bushes in berry all around us. It stained my fingers and hands purple, but apart from showing everyone where the warts were sited, failed to have any effect.

Back in Croydon, Miss Elwell from upstairs helpfully suggested strangling them. By this time I felt this would be a suitable punishment for all the misery they had caused me. The problem with this method was getting the cotton round the thing in the first place. After considerable patience on the part of my mother, we succeeded and eventually the wart on my thumb dropped off only to be almost instantly replaced by another.

I think people started to make up cures for me to try. When someone suggested putting the same number of cherry pits in my shoes as

corresponded with the number of warts I had, making me barely able to hobble to the front door, I finally gave up and we went for the more conventional method of burning them off with acid. This was painful but it almost succeeded.

Unfortunately, before they were ready I would pick them and they would bleed, and apparently (another bit of wart folklore) wherever a trail of blood from a wart stops, another wart will appear. So I finished up with twelve of the horrid little bastards over my fingers and hands.

My warts had got the better of me and Mum had to arrange surgical treatment to have them removed.

Weeks of treatment at King's College Hospital in Dulwich came next where my warts were electrocuted, burnt, needled and painted. Blisters were lanced and infections treated. Old warts died; new ones arrived. It was misery because nothing worked and even the surgery only seemed to make them pop up somewhere else on my hands.

Even thus afflicted I still sort of looked forward to Friday afternoons and dancing about with the pretty girls in the class. I felt I had come up with a suitable way of disguising my afflictions by offering my preferred dancing partners, instead of an open hand, a rather unfriendly fist for them to hold. This can't have impressed the objects of my desire, but I guess girls are used to boys being scared to show their deeper feelings, and no-one ever asked me about my style as we hopped about the floor to the music from an electric gramophone. I would jealously watch where my favourite girls were in the room, and in the meantime give my open hand to Nancy Wayklin or Maureen Prendergast.

In the end, in a fit of anger and panic, I scrubbed the warts away with a piece of pumice stone, which made the bathroom look like an axe murder had taken place, and they never came back.

Our last class at Howard School was run by Mr. Harvey. He was very tall with a large head and dark hair. The school had a very high pass rate for the eleven-plus and he must have been under a lot of pressure to get results. This is no mitigation, however, for his appalling behaviour toward some of the children in his care.

Although there was another male teacher, Mr. Ogle, at the school, Mr. Harvey was the first male adult since my father that I had ever been in regular daily contact with. His reputation preceded him, but for our first few days he was so gentle and softly spoken that many of us began to

think that maybe all the reports had been exaggerated. Miss Smee's approach had probably toughened us up, and although I never saw any real affection given to the children by any of the staff, up until we were nine or ten there had been an attempt to haul all the kids along together. Now we were blitzed with work, and those that fell behind were almost written off by Harvey as he strove to get eleven-plus results.

Before our actual exams there was some light relief in the form of a school pantomime. Mr. Harvey scripted a version of *Babes In The Wood*. It was very funny and parodied many of the school characters, especially Miss Smee, who Mr. Harvey was in awe of. In the panto she was clearly recognisable as Miss P. Nut. She even had a servant carrying books about on a cushion mimicking her piano playing position.

Mr. Harvey cast the play and all his favourites got major parts. When it came to the two robbers, he chose Ronald Strudwick for one of them...

"...and the second robber will be Ralph May."

I couldn't believe that I had been picked to play a part. What was more, the role was a comic one, so it meant that Mr. Harvey thought I was funny. I liked that perception even if I felt sad a lot of the time and heard strange voices. I began to think I was a devil-may-care character and for a while I started skipping to show that I was light of heart.

The play began with Ronald and I walking backwards toward each other and bumping into each other, which gave us our first laugh and made me feel wonderful.

I also got to play the mouth organ. In those pre-rock'n'roll days the hit parade comprised some dreadful material and at the top of the charts that year had been a song called *Where Will The Baby's Dimple Be?* I was supposed to play it on stage and one of the teachers had written out all the words on the blackboard. It was great when we played for the school children as everybody joined in, but in the second performance when the parents came to watch, most of them just sat there. They applauded me when it was over but didn't join in at all.

This was my first public performance and I can still see one mother's face staring at me while I played. She had a puzzled look and I was not sure how to interpret it. Perhaps I was well received in part because my right hand was swathed in a huge crepe bandage to protect it from my recent wart surgery. Perhaps they felt sorry for me.

The panto was a big success, but our moment was soon over and the oppression really began. I don't remember any more stories being read to

us, and all our lessons were about sharpening up our IQ. We had endless tests of the type we would face for our examinations and all levity seemed to leave the class.

I cannot imagine what horrendous things the class could have done to send our teacher into almost uncontrollable rages, but somehow we managed it. I can still see the look of terror on Victor Sageman's face when he was being shouted at from close quarters; in a temper Mr. Harvey's complexion went purple and his insane bellowing must have been heard all over the school through the partitions that separated the classrooms. His reputation was well known by all the kids who slowly worked their way toward their final year at junior school.

He often used a slipper on the boys. One of his favourite tricks was to line up more than one offender and punish the first one but not the other; but because the boys were bent over they had no means of knowing whether they were to receive the punishment or not. His greatest venom was reserved for two kids in the class, Stephen Gardener and Dawn Bates. In the end Stephen developed a stammer because he could not pronounce his "th" sounds, and after a particular session of torment, ran away from class and never returned.

Stephen was a war baby and never had a dad. He had been to my house on several occasions and although I saw him quite a few times over the years, he appeared not to recognise me. This was strange as we had only sat two rows apart in school. He was a gentle lad but a bit over-weight; he got a job working down Surrey Street market and eventually had his own stall. I always recall him telling me about some sour-faced individual: "He's so horrible even his friends don't like him!"

At least Stephen survived with his dignity. Poor Dawn suffered the whole year she was in the class.

Dawn was a skinny girl with mousy hair tied into two pigtails. She lacked grace and charm and was a rather plain kid. She always seemed to work hard and had travelled through the school with me, although I didn't even notice her until our last year. For some reason Mr. Harvey hated her, and because she was a girl he could only hit her around the head, which he did frequently. Why cases of child abuse are seldom re-ported by children may be partly explained by the whole class's reaction to these mental rages which Harvey seemed to go through. After throw-ing Dawn about the room, and on one occasion banging her head on the radiators, we just sat in stunned silence. For a long time afterwards the

atmosphere was one of terror with hardly a flicker of movement among us.

Whatever Harvey threw at the poor girl she weathered and tried to get back to the safety of her desk as if it would protect her. Once she repeatedly scrambled back on to her seat only to be thrown out of it on to the floor again, and back she crawled while Harvey grabbed at her hair and hurled abuse at her at the same time.

I cannot think what caused these rages and why she was treated this way, but it was horrible to watch. It was made even worse by the way he returned to normal after such episodes. He would begin talking in a voice of oily calm and even joke with one of the brighter children, usually one of the boys. This would produce a forced laugh from the recipient of his attention, and as Mr. Harvey's complexion returned to normal so did the atmosphere in the class. I could not take my eyes off the man during these bouts, and it was not until another form master in class 3D at secondary school struck Chris Masters full in the face with his fist and made his nose bleed that I have been so scared of an adult.

Harvey went on to become a headmaster at another local school.

∾

PART THREE

BENNY & CO.

picnic

After years on the housing list our number finally came up, and Mum, my brother Bruce and I were moved from our semi-condemned basement flat in The Waldrons to Miller Road, a council estate off the Mitcham Road in Croydon. It heralded a major change in our lives.

Number 17a was known as the show flat; it was the first one to have hot water and an indoor bathroom separate from the lavatory. At last I was able to have my first bath in my own home. It was luxury. My mum had often had baths at Mrs. Leisk's across the road, but Bruce and I had always had to make do with the tin bath and a couple of kettles of water.

The estate teemed with life and vigour of a very different sort to that which we had become used to. My mum had accepted the flat after biking over to see it, and as the three of us stood in the little sitting room overlooking the chimneys of the Croydon 'A' power station and in the shadow of the gasholder (we called it the 'gasometer') that dominated the estate, she burst into tears.

"Never mind Mum, it'll be all right," I said.

"You don't understand, boys," she sniffed, "I'm not sad, I'm so happy."

From that moment on I knew we were all going to be OK, but I also knew it would still be tough; even as we had come in to check the place over I had heard the language the boys were using on the street, and it

wasn't the same as the way they spoke where we came from.

On the day we moved in I heard a boy playing the mouth organ, and behind the enormous overgrown hedge that ran down the lane between the houses I sat on my doorstep and played a song I knew. Within a few seconds a voice enquired through the hedge who it was playing, and that's how I met Tony Potter, his brother Jamie and their friend Benny. The Potters lived over the road and Benny lived at 11a which was the mirror image of our flat at the other end of the block.

Benny had a moderately bad stammer, which meant he had to kick start most of his sentences with "and", but this had still proved difficult so he had found it better to add a "g" to the vowel, hence nearly everything he said started with "gan-gan". Benny was an ideas man, and without ever assuming the mantle of leadership, his influence on our activities was immense. He also had an uncanny knack of coming up with nicknames that stuck.

At The Waldrons I was one of the older boys, but here we were all about the same age; Tony was a year older than me and Jamie and Benny were a year or two younger. We were all 'bulge' babies, fathered by servicemen back from the war, and there were loads of us. We had street cricket and elaborate games of Release-O and Tin Tan Tommy Knob; we played Knock Down Ginger and had raids on the council dump that was just down the road in Factory Lane, where we nicked bits to make bicycles.

The older boys were all 'Teds' and a couple of the really ancient ones, like Paul Potter and Harry Barnet, were in the Merchant Navy. Some of them went to boys' clubs where they did weights or boxing, and it was all very laddish. So different from the insularity of The Waldrons, a world of its own where the very poor still rubbed shoulders with some of the comparatively well off; here everyone was poor and working class, and I felt it prudent to knock about with some of the younger boys whilst I found my way.

Beyond the Purley Way and the power station lay the factories that employed many of the people from the estate, and just beyond the factories stood the sewage farm. In another direction there was the skinning factory at the edge of the estate, and not far from that the corporation dump and the knacker's yard, and we often joked about always knowing which way the wind was blowing.

Before hanging out any washing Mum had to wipe the soot off the plastic clothes line, and if that did not mark the sheets there was always the chance of an aerial bombardment from Mr. Kelly's pigeons, which exercised around the smutty air of the estate. Sometimes fumes would waft across the estate and make us feel dizzy and nauseous, but most of the time we took no notice.

In front of the sewage farm was a patch of waste ground, completely overgrown with scrubby trees and elderberry bushes, and in front of this was a huge crater from a wartime bomb aimed at one of the factories, which some of the older boys used to trial their illegal motorbikes.

Over to the left of the main plant there was a small detached three-bedroomed house and a little garden with a few apple trees in an otherwise overgrown wasteland. This was always referred to as 'Farmer Brown's orchard'. I never queried it at the time, but looking back it was almost certainly a name that Benny thought up: we were at the sewage farm, therefore the man who lived there all the time must be a farmer, and all farmers are called Brown. It's obvious really.

This whole area Benny had christened the 'playing fields' because they were fields where we played, but they were always referred to as the Playnies. The boys used to go there on a regular basis for a number of different activities: mucking about, meaning just going across to see what would happen; racing our home-made bikes around the crater; or occasionally making raids on Farmer Brown's orchard.

Early on in our friendship Benny asked us if we'd ever seen any 'johnnies'. I said that I probably had but I couldn't remember exactly, so Benny offered to take us. Once across the Purley Way we walked down the railway tracks that served the factories, across the 'white road' and straight on, with the playnies on the left and the processed waste fields on the right, where tomato plants grew in abundance in the summer (even after all the treatment of the sewage the tomato seeds stay potent and ready to germinate).

Just before the sewage farm proper was a railing across the road and an inspection platform. From here it was possible to watch the raw sewage flow into the plant. After staring in wonder at the size of some of the stools that flowed past I was ready to leave, but Benny insisted we must wait as we hadn't seen any johnnies yet. I wondered what he meant. We didn't have long to wait, for very soon a used condom floated past, closely

followed by another and another.

"Cor look at that one!" yelled Benny, "and that one, fuckin' 'ell 'e must 'ave 'ad one like a rollin' pin!" Then he burst into his whistling laugh.

"There goes another one, coo look at that. What would you do if you 'ad one like that?" At last I realised what we were looking at. It was a truly humbling experience for a twelve-year-old. These things were enormous, and it forced me to ponder all sorts of things that I was only just ready to grasp. The younger Benny had even more to perplex him—or rather, less.

The Potters who lived opposite were a very unusual crowd. Mrs. Potter was of Anglo-Indian descent and liberally used Indian words in her speech. Mr. Potter was largely out of work with his chest, which he made sure would stay that way by smoking Capstan full strength cigarettes. I remember sitting in their spartan front room one afternoon with the sun streaming in through the windows, watching him exhale as much smoke as the steam coming out of the cooling tower chimneys, and wondering how he managed it. His hair was a grizzled grey colour. I never saw him with his teeth in and I never saw him smile.

It was rumoured that they were a rum lot and that Mrs. Potter had been involved in some street trade during the war, but it only added more spice to my imagination. Paul, the eldest boy, as I mentioned before, was away in the 'merchant'; Albert was semi-delinquent, dangerous and frightening; Tony was handsome and honourable; and Jamie was a moaner and hadn't been circumcised properly. Benny said that when he had a piss, the end of his willie blew up like a balloon. There was one girl in the family, Donna, who was very pretty and sexy and didn't live at home; Benny said she was 'on the game.'

The Potters also had a dog, imaginatively named Spot. He was a cross between a wolf and a collie, so Jamie said.

"He must be a wallie then!" said Benny, which almost caused a fight. Spot was largely concerned with homosexual activities with other dogs, but if none were available he would spend most of his day rubbing the mange patch on his back under the bars at the end of the alley. The bars were placed at each junction throughout the estate to stop the kids running out into the roads.

Sometimes the boys would go 'shtrewing' and this was where Spot came into his own; he was reckoned to be the best shtrewer in the neighbourhood. The first time we went across to the playnies to go shtrewing I was puzzled, but later horrified at the sport which awaited me. Once on

the playnies we combed the waste ground for old bits of corrugated metal and formed a circle around its perimeter. Spot would be alert and waiting for his moment.

One of the boys would call "Ready!", the sheet would be flipped over and if there was any 'shtrews' underneath, Spot would have them.

I had enormous problems with this. Although my brother and I had been brought up in poverty in most accepted definitions of the word, our mother had always made sure that our imaginations were richly stimulated by reading. She had read to us from a very early age and no matter how tired she was she always found time for a couple of chapters of something before bed.

I'm sure Mum was motivated to read to us not only for educative reasons, but to escape the drudgery of our grey existence and to perpetuate a feeling of childhood optimism; and through the stories I had always vaguely thought of small creatures as living in little warrens and houses in tree trunks, with a set of values and morals not unlike those instilled in us at Sunday School. For me to see tiny shrews and field mice ripped apart by mangy old Spot was more than I was ready for.

We were also keenly aware that we were under scrutiny from the lads, especially Benny. I had quickly decided not to copy their accents, but this was easier said than done. The boys on the estate used wonderful language. They littered their speech liberally with swear words, especially "bleedin'" which my mother hated the most; but more interesting to me was their use of Romany words among the slang terms. Thus a dog was a juk (rhymes with hook), rain became parni in the sky, and a stranger was always a mush (like bush).

They also used a good deal of cockney slang which was all new to me, and I began to feel that we were quite genteel by comparison. I can remember listening in awe as the boys recounted the episode where Freddy Barnet and Robby Elmwood attempted to climb the gasometer at the end of Miller Road. The boys had to climb very narrow, almost vertical ladders up about four stages.

"'alf way up Freddy's bottle went," said Benny, "an' 'e 'ad to come dahn."

Why he had to take a bottle with him I couldn't understand, or what difference it would have made if he lost it, but so impressed was I with the bravado that I pressed him to explain.

"What, he took a water bottle with him or something?"

"No, 'e shit 'isself," Benny explained.

Gradually the mysteries of rhyming slang were revealed to me. Bottle and glass equals arse, so saying your bottle went meant your arse went. Having plenty of bottle meant not shittin' oneself—in other words, courage.

I don't know whether Freddy actually defecated with fright or was just too scared to continue. I made up my mind anyway that one day I would climb it—and I did, and ran across the wobbly dome on the top. It was a great buzz, and my bottle held.

Our gang was made up like this: Benny, Jimmy and Ronnie Barnet, my brother Bruce, Tony and Jamie Potter, Jimmy Wren (cousin to Benny) and sometimes little Bobby Best, who was the youngest. Of course there were girls in the street but the boys had long grown out of their company. Well, the youngest ones had, and the older boys would have liked to play different sorts of games but were not quite sure of the rules. It was a strange feeling, noticing that you were suddenly growing interested in a girl who, only a term or two before, made you so irritated that you could hardly bring yourself to speak to her.

The girls down our street were the Longhurst girls, whose parents did not allow them to play with any of us, Amy Blair, Maureen Forester, Pat Elsie, Jeannie Wren, Charlotte Price who was very strange, and little Lucy Best who was as pretty as her brother was plain.

Maureen was fifteen and just about to start work in one of the factories beyond the Purley Way. She arrived at the bars one day to mind one of her little brothers, when the idea of the picnic on the playnies came up.

"Everyone's got to bring an egg," said Benny. Bruce and I were crestfallen. "Or a potato," he added, quickly perceiving that we might have a problem with the egg. Benny was like that; seemingly of average intelligence, he was capable of great and quick understanding, and his sharp observation gave him a pragmatism that would make sure that he would get his way.

Benny was chubby with cherubic features, blond curly hair, a little hooked nose and lips that were never closed. This sometimes gave him a vacant look, but he never missed a trick and his eyes were always darting about, taking it all in. His mother was a large-hipped woman, slightly reserved and prone to gossip, while his dad walked like a sailor and kept pigeons. He had a centre parting and was kindly, and Benny had a brother

called Robert who was deaf and dumb.

"We could 'ave a fire over there, no-one would mind," said Benny, "an' we could cook things, it'd be a right laugh."

We all thought that it would be a laugh but nothing was finalised until Maureen suddenly said, "I'll be your cook."

That was it, suddenly we were motivated and the news spread rapidly. Soon a little gang had arrived and everyone was talking about what they were going to bring and what a great laugh it would be and that we ought to leave Spot at home because he didn't like fires, and so on.

The next day saw us all arriving in dribs and drabs until we were assembled loosely under the 'white trees'. The whole area was like another planet; the trees actually had white leaves and it was only much later that I realised this was because of the thousands of starlings that gathered there to feed on God knows what at the sewage works, along with the seagulls so far inland.

There was just a light breeze which occasionally rustled the trees, and a hot sun sat high in a blue sky as we scurried about collecting bits of wood. Benny and I had found an old dustbin with the bottom rotted out of it, and we judged that it would make a great burner. We stood it on four bricks, and paper and twigs were placed in the bottom. Maureen laid out her kitchenware: a large saucepan, some butter or marge which was already beginning to melt in its paper, and an old black frying pan.

"Right, let's have all the food," she ordered.

All the food? What food, I wondered, as I laid my potato on the ground next to the melting butter that had now got some twiggy bits of grass mixed into it. Bruce laid his potato next to mine.

"That's a big one," I found myself saying, "I hope Mum won't remember it and notice it's gone." Bruce looked worried for a moment.

Next came Ronnie who had both an egg and a potato, which he laid next to Bruce's. A little too close; Bruce was forced to move his a little further away so they didn't get mixed up. Bobby Best had an egg and a potato, and so did Jimmy Barnet; Jamie Potter had only managed a potato and half a loaf of stale white bread. All of this was laid out on the ground and we all stood back to admire our banquet in waiting. By now a little more twigs and grass had made their way into the butter as Maureen gently lay down her own egg and potato.

All this time Benny had been watching everyone's contribution without uttering a word. When he was sure that there was nothing left to be

laid alongside the rest, he slowly put his hand in his pocket, and with a little flourish pulled out a potato that was about half a pound on its own. Then from his windcheater top pocket he carefully removed an egg and placed it next to the others, and finally, with a dramatic "dah dah", he spun around to face us all, reached into his other pocket and pulled out a sausage!

"You flash sod," muttered Ronnie as Benny waved his prize in front of us all held between his finger and thumb.

"I bet you nicked that," said Jamie.

"No I never," said Benny.

"Yes you bleedin' did!" said Jamie this time even louder.

"You ain't 'alf a lie," spluttered Benny again (he never called anyone a liar, always a 'lie').

I was dreadfully jealous as we only had a sausage if there was an 'r' in the month, and then only one each, but I said nothing. Maybe he might give me a bite of it later, I thought, and immediately realised how stupid this idea was.

Benny was taking huge delight in our envy and was now holding the sausage in front of his flies and waggling it rudely at Maureen. I looked anxiously at her to see what her reaction might be; she told him not to be a dirty little devil but she was laughing at the same time. I began to think how pretty she was.

"It looks like yours, Jamie," said Benny.

"Piss off!" said Jamie, more angry than embarrassed.

"At least this one don't blow up at the end when I 'ave a piss," taunted Benny.

I noticed Maureen looking puzzled by this remark, and felt very uneasy, but only for a moment as Jamie suddenly leapt at Benny, hitting him in the belly with his head. Although Benny was a solid sort of boy, the sheer surprise of the attack set him off balance and he was forced to take one step backwards to remain upright.

In doing so, he trod on Bobby Best's egg. Benny looked dismayed as nearly everyone else started to laugh at his predicament, which only increased as little Bobby flew at Benny and tried to grab him round the throat. Based on their size there should have been no contest, but we all knew about Bobby's legendary temper. He was capable of fearsome rages and was totally fearless with regard to his own safety, and amazingly hardly ever came to grief in spite of having a go at boys a lot bigger and older

than himself.

After a little struggle we managed to prise them apart, and Maureen said that Bobby could have her egg. I began to think how *kind* and pretty she was.

After the dust had settled and Benny had satisfied himself that the egg could not be salvaged in any way, it was decided to light the fire. Everyone wanted to do this, so in the end Maureen said that as Bobby had lost his egg, he should be the one to strike the match. There was no argument with this, and with one match the old dustbin's contents were ablaze.

Unfortunately so were the lower branches of the tree under which we had built our kitchen. None of us had thought about the siting of our fire, and with the summer sunshine and hot weather, everything was as dry as tinder.

"Ssssssssssssssssssssssssshit!" stammered Benny and backed away from the inferno that was now crackling and roaring inside the old bin, treading as he did so on Jamie's bag of stale bread.

Before another fight could blow up, Jimmy Barnet came from nowhere and kicked the dustbin on to its side so that the remaining contents spilled on to the ground, then grabbing hold of an elderberry bush yanked off a branch and began beating the flames out on the tree above our heads. We all followed suit and eventually managed to put out the blaze.

When everything was once again under some sort of control we all looked at each other and began laughing.

"Di'n it bleedin' go!" marvelled Benny.

After the excitement we resited our stove in a little clearing, gathered up the trampled bread and potatoes, poured the now quite melted butter into the black frying pan and began again to collect wood and scraps for the fire.

Ronnie and Jamie meanwhile had started a game of knife throwing. The idea was that you aimed the weapon as near to your opponent's foot as you could, and where the knife landed you took up that position, your legs gradually getting further apart until one of you fell over or received a stab wound to the leg or foot. It seldom came to this though, and the game was usually abandoned after a few rounds.

"You'll 'ave to lend me the knife," announced Maureen. "I forgot to bring one for the potatoes."

The boys handed it over and sidled off into the bushes. I watched Maureen set about peeling the potatoes, which proved difficult because, although the knife had a sharp point, the cutting edge was very blunt. Maureen was reduced to laying the spud on the ground and sawing at it, which made for a lot of waste. The resulting square peeled items were further sliced into chips, and each one was then wiped on her dress and stored in the frying pan with the melted butter and twigs.

Suddenly there was a sharp cry as Maureen's grip slipped and she sliced into her finger. It bled profusely and I felt quite sick and thought I was going to pass out. Luckily Benny, who had been arranging his sausage and two of the eggs somewhat genitally, had a handkerchief. I say 'luckily' reservedly, because Benny was one of those kids who always seemed to have a runny nose. His mum insisted that Benny carry a handkerchief with him at all times, and it was a well-used item that was reluctantly accepted by Maureen.

I couldn't bear to watch as she wrapped the rag around her finger, so I busied myself with lighting and tending to the fire. Once again the flames crackled and roared and soon they were leaping above the top of the bin. The heat was ferocious and Maureen was beaten back from her stove until the flames died down. I watched fascinated as Maureen valiantly moved toward the heat, holding the saucepan in one hand and shielding her face with the other. Someone had turned up an old aluminium milk crate and slung it on top of the bin as a kind of grill, and Maureen carefully placed her frying pan on top, moving back with her eyes streaming.

Amongst the sticks and general rubbish collected for the fire was an old tyre, which was now burning merrily with thick black smoke and giving off a terrible smell. Undaunted but beginning to perspire with the heat and pain in her finger, Maureen changed position with the wind, and I could see her face now lined with tracks of her smoke-driven tears.

Intermittently she darted toward the swirling pan to prod a chip with the knife that had wounded her. The hankie bandage was by now drenched in butterfat, and trailed into the pan as blood from the cut dripped in amongst the cooking potatoes. Maureen began to look as if she had been in a fight; her hair was drenched, her face was smeared with soot and blood, the bandage flapped loosely on her damaged finger and a steady stream of tears ran down her cheeks. I thought she looked beautiful and

was almost overcome with compassion, but I also felt sick.

The boys were slowly drifting back from what they'd been doing in the bushes, and Benny and little Bobby returned from throwing stones at the johnnies. Ronnie and brother Bruce had returned from Farmer Brown's orchard with some tiny little scrubby green apples, which everyone started throwing at each other.

The sight of poor battered Maureen only stopped them for a while as everyone engaged in a funny little ritual dance around the fire in order to avoid the black burning rubber smoke that seemed to follow us wherever we went.

"When we eatin'?" someone demanded.

"When we 'avin' our eggs?" asked the egg owners.

"When they're bleedin' well cooked," came Maureen's harassed reply.

"I'm starvin'," muttered Benny. "Can I 'ave mine now?"

"Look," said Maureen, "they ain't even cooked yet."

"I don't mind, I'll 'ave em raw," said Benny hungrily.

"Yeah, let's 'ave em now!" we all chorused.

At this point Maureen was happy to concede defeat, and one by one we queued up to take a chip or two each. Pierced with the wounding knife, basted in gravy made from her own blood and butter, we attempted to eat our scalding rock-hard potatoes. There was many a burnt lip and scalded tongue, to say nothing of terrible swearing from young mouths of tender skin who had dropped the food on to the jungle floor and tried to wipe off the grit only to find that the spud was inedible.

By now all our eyes were streaming as we sat Indian-style with black lines down our cheeks, spitting out bits of twig and grit round the fire.

Benny handed Maureen his egg, which she broke expertly on the side of the pan and tossed into the now burning fat. Benny grinned round expectantly at the rest of us when Jamie sullenly pointed out that he hadn't got a plate to eat it off. A moment of anxiety crossed Benny's face, then he jumped up and quickly disappeared into the bushes, arriving back a few seconds later with a bit of an old cardboard box about the size of a saucer. He offered it up to Maureen, who somehow managed to slide the egg on to it, leaving most of the gravy in the pan. For a moment Benny looked triumphant, but while he was gloating he took his eye off the 'plate' and his slippery feast slithered off and on to the dirt floor. Everyone guffawed and hooted, and for a moment I thought Benny was about to burst into tears.

Then defiantly he muttered, "I'm still goin' to eat it!" To our assembled amazement he picked up the egg by its white and, after dropping it once more and then picking off the worst of the dirt, popped the whole lot into his open mouth like a mother bird feeding her young.

Suddenly the other egg owners were not interested in having their eggs after all. Although nothing was said, we were all pretty impressed by Benny's defiance. Maureen had certainly had enough of her role as little mother and was sitting down inspecting the soiled nature of her light sweater, picking little bits of twig from it and lightly flicking at the butter-splattered stains that had landed on her breasts. I wished she would have let me help her.

Ronnie and Jamie had wandered off again to light up a fag and little Bobby Best had disappeared somewhere with his egg. Benny and brother Bruce were lobbing bits of wood into the fire. I was chatting with Jimmy while secretly admiring Maureen and wondering what we would do next, when an egg came hurtling through the trees and hit Jimmy smack in the forehead.

There was a moment of stunned disbelief as we all realised the enormity of the situation. Jimmy Barnet was easily the best fighter pound for pound on the estate; he boxed for the boys' club and fought at just about any other opportunity as well. If the egg had hit anyone else there would have been enormous hilarity but now there was silence.

It was a silence that stilled the birds in the bushes; a silence that quelled the chattering flames; a silence that stopped the sewage flowing in the farm. The sun momentarily hesitated in its passage across the summer sky. We thought about the great Kenny Manley fight on the Canterbury Road rec, and the time he almost killed Rory McLean in the snooker room at the Rectory Manor Boys Club by locking his arms round the legs of the table so that he could exert more pressure round the boy's neck he held between his thighs. Two grown-ups had had to hit Jimmy with billiard cues to make him release the kid, and that was all because Jimmy thought Jamie had called him a guttersnipe. It's very doubtful that anyone in our neighbourhood would have used such an old-fashioned word, but it was well known that if you wanted to put Jimmy into an uncontrollable rage all you had to do was to address him thus.

I have often wondered what Jimmy imagined a 'snipe' was. Could it have been an evil rat character that lived in the gutter and survived off the spittle and waste that found its way there before being flushed down

the drains, or was it some huge indefinable monster of his imagination? Certainly I would never know as I was far too scared to even mention the word within several miles of his hearing.

Perhaps he saw it the way I saw the 'ape of the lights'. My old Grandma was a Victorian of high moral principles and iron discipline, whom her daughter (my mum) hated, it seemed to me and Bruce. She was a Hammersmith native born and bred, and her speech was littered with superstitions and colourful sayings like, "He's as soft as an a'porth o' lights!"

'Lights' were the lung offal that was often boiled up and fed to the domestic pets of the house, and whoever it was she was referring to was obviously as soft as one halfpenny worth, but to me for years it was King Kong draped in fairy lights. It didn't seem silly to me at the time. I will always wonder what Jimmy saw.

Suddenly an anguished cry burst from the bushes.

"Sorry Jimmy, it was me, I was aiming at Ralph, I never meant to hit you, honest Jimmy, you got to believe me!"

Recognising the voice as that of little Bobby, Jimmy slowly stood up and without wiping away the egg walked over to where Maureen was sitting and picked up one of the remaining eggs.

"Come here, Bobby," he said, his voice showing a menacing calmness which struck terror into all our hearts.

"Don't 'urt 'im Jimmy, please," said Maureen quietly.

I tried to speak but only a croak came out, so I shut up and watched as if in a trance as the only moving thing on earth advanced slowly toward where the cowering Bobby was quietly snivelling. Jimmy bent down and, placing his hand in the bush that held the offender, slowly lifted him into view by his ear.

A new episode of Edgar Lustgarten's *Tales of Scotland Yard* was already taking shape in my mind: I could hear his sombre tones and clear diction announcing the horrible Murder On The Playnies and how after a gruelling cross-examination in the witness box I had finally admitted that it was my fault, and that if the egg had hit its intended target little Bobby would still be with us. I began to shake but was unable to move; like everything around us we were frozen in time.

Jimmy, still with the evidence of the direct hit on his forehead, brought the distressed figure of Bobby to the remains of the fire. Looking up to confirm that we all had his attention, he pulled Bobby's trousers out at the back and placed the egg in his underpants and under his bottom,

then tweaking the ear slightly in an upward direction he leaned forward and said in a voice of utter calm, "Sit on it."

Immediately the earth started moving again as little Bobby looked up at Jimmy and realised he was going to live after all. One by one all of us began to laugh as little Bobby, only too glad to play his part in the situation, slowly and theatrically sat down on the ground. None of us heard it break, but we all saw the expression on his face as the goo spread between his legs.

As the sense of relief spread through our little group, a bit of knockabout bravado ensued, and just as Jimmy had refused to wipe off the egg from his forehead until he'd had his retribution, so Bobby bore his punishment manfully and left the shells inside his trousers. Benny suddenly remembered his sausage and after cutting off a stick and sharpening it to a point, picked up the twiggy pink member and after a lewd waggle at Maureen, pierced it with his stick and started to cook it over the dustbin. Most of the tyre had been consumed, but there was still a smell of burning rubber permeating the air along with that of the pork sausage. The others drifted away out of nose-shot of the cooking and I watched Benny twirling his treat over the flames that were still occasionally firing up as drops of fat hit the embers below.

"You fancy 'er don't ya?" he asked me. "I seen ya lookin' at 'er tits. I bet she's got nice tits, but you're wastin' yer time boy, she fancies that kid Pepper, the one that goes out with Gillian Pallister, she's got the best tits on the estate."

"How do you know?" I demanded, embarrassed and blushing so deeply my face nearly bled.

"'ow do I know what?" asked Benny innocently. "That you fancy Maureen or that Gillian Pallister's got the best tits on the estate?"

"About Gillian," I mumbled.

"My mate's 'ad 'em out, one in each 'and, they're like that!" Benny described the size and weight with his free hand.

This was too much for me. I was getting aroused by all this talk and the heat, and I was just about to turn and join the others when I noticed that Benny's stick was burning and his sausage was on fire. I don't know whether he was following my gaze but he looked back at his stick just as the flaming morsel fell off the prong and into the fire. I quickly turned away so that he wouldn't be sure if I saw the tragedy and went to join the

others. They were playing a game that was getting a little bit too rowdy for Maureen's liking, and I could see that I was not the only one to find her nearness stimulating. In those days most boys wore Y-fronts and some lads nothing at all underneath and a few of us were already teenagers and arousal was easy to spot. Suddenly we were joined by Benny.

"How was your sausage, you greedy fat bastard?" shouted Jamie.

Only I knew that the hurt look in Benny's eyes had nothing to do with the insult, but was entirely due to the loss of the item in the flames of the dustbin.

"Don't you worry about my sausage, mush, what about your balloon dick sausage," spluttered Benny.

"Yeah, show 'er your knob," suggested little Bobby to Jamie, and everyone sniggered. Maureen had a mixture of feigned shock and curiosity, and we all looked at her expectantly to see how she would react.

"I've seen a dick before," said Maureen.

"Yeah, but not like Jamie's," Ronnie and Bobby chorused together, and everyone sniggered again.

"Look you lot, I've 'ad enough of all this talk," said Maureen, "I'm goin' 'ome," and with that she turned back toward the dustbin and her few utensils.

The afternoon was coming to an end and a balmy breeze was rustling the leaves of the elderberry bushes. The acrid smell of burnt rubber had been replaced by a real wood smoke scent in the air, shadows were lengthening and all of us were in various states of dishevelledness, Maureen amongst the worst of us. A handful of swallows were swooping above the sewage works and the tired and smoky band of kids from Miller Road were reluctant to call it a day.

"I got an idea," said Benny, and he whispered his plan to us all.

Maureen was inspecting the cut on her hand as we approached, the old dustbin lay on its side and our pitiful little kitchen was dismantled and ready to be carted off home. I had my instructions and when all the boys were in position I nonchalantly asked Maureen if we should put the fire out.

"Oh yeah," she said, "I almost forgot about that." Then I banged the frying pan with a stick really loud which was the signal to begin and with a jump Maureen swung around to find a circle of boys all peeing on the fire, then on my next bang on the pan, they divided the circle and folded back to reveal Jamie in full flow and ballooning willie in hand.

It was pretty impressive. In the company of the rest of the boys the last remnants of Jamie's inhibitions were shed and he peed with great force and brio, and the fire hissed in response. Maureen on the other hand turned tail and ran out of the trees and bushes into the open, hair flying and shoes slipping, soon to be followed by our gang.

I paused to pick up the bits and pieces and her jacket before chasing after them all. Just before the bomb crater she was brought down by Ronnie, and the others all fell on top of her. Amongst a great flailing of arms and legs could be heard a lot of laughing and giggling, but by the time I'd got there most of the lads were back on their feet. Maureen was crying with what looked like tears of laughter and relief that nothing had really got out of hand, and we all set off again toward the railway line and the bridge over the Purley Way.

We must have been quite a sight as we traipsed up the lane to our street, covered as we were with bits of straw and grass, streaked with dust and soot, smelling of smoke and rubber, with bloodshot eyes and bramble scratches, fingers stained with berry juice and stomachs rumbling.

As we got nearer home I found myself walking with Benny and little Bobby.

"I nearly got an 'andful di'n I," said Benny, "but that Jimmy Barnet could see what I was after an 'e pulled me off of 'er."

Little Bobby was quiet for a while, then he said in a voice that trembled a little, "I felt 'er tits."

We both looked at him for a second or two, then he giggled and shook with mischief. Bobby was the youngest of the lot of us and it was he who had the prize we all wanted. It was years before I was ever to feel such jealousy again.

Never did such a lot of us ever go to the playnies again, and Maureen soon started going out with a boy from the next street. We were never really friends in the same way, but she always spoke to me when we met. I loved the sound of her morning chatter with friends at the bars at the end of the lane, and their laughter coming home from the factories near the old playnies. But she never knew how I'd once felt.

Jimmy went on to become a fine amateur boxer, little Bobby vanished from my ken and we heard that Ronnie had died prematurely with the same heart complaint that killed his sister Pam. Tony Potter joined the

Royal Navy at the same time that I joined the boys' army. Jamie surfaced again at his sister's place, coincidentally above my mother's new flat in Thornton Heath, where the noise and 'entertaining' nearly drove Mum crazy and we had to get her moved to save her sanity.

Benny lost his deaf brother after a fit when the boy turned twenty-one. Benny himself married a girl at the top of the road, and as far as I know still lives there.

∾

hedge

It was accepted that after the war a lot of kids were brought up by grandmothers, aunts, and in some cases even by neighbours. The idea of extended families is not really new and you don't have to go very far back in most families to find a child that came into the world before its parents were married.

On the Miller Road estate there were several children who were brought up by their grannies. One of these was Charlotte Price. She was an odd child and spent most of her time on her own. Her old grandfather was a complete eccentric, but he had died just before we moved to the estate. Stories abounded about him and his wife. In spite of our common financial state, they seemed a different class from the rest of us, and were reportedly old-style revolutionary socialists. Some of the older residents in the road confirmed that the old man used to wait till the sun went down in the summer and stand naked at their bedroom window playing the violin. I couldn't decide what was the funniest aspect of this activity: the nakedness, the timing, the violin or just the display. The old ladies talked about it and laughed behind their hands at the memory. He was known as Pop Price.

His wife, Charlotte's grandmother, was odd as well. She wore an assortment of brightly coloured clothes and hats and was the most bowlegged person I had seen since Miss Argent at my first Sunday school.

All the elderly women on the estate were given the honorary status of Granny, and within three houses lived Granny Wren, Granny Cockell and Granny Price.

The former two ladies had total respect from all the kids, and the pair of them used to take turns keeping an eye on all the games that took place on the road. A couple of words from either in the way of remonstration would be obeyed with little dissent. Both of them used to lean on their garden gates, and Benny said that their arms had gone bad from all the leaning they had done.

Granny Cockell was very elderly with only two teeth on the bottom left of her mouth. Her voice was stern but not loud, and she sometimes had to issue her rebukes more than once.

Granny Wren had more teeth, was somewhat younger and walked with a brisk shuffle to the shops and back. She was very Romany-looking and had a voice as gruff as an old soldier, but her eyes always had a twinkle and she laughed off comments on her deep tan as having picked up its Mediterranean colour from "walking up and down the Mitcham Road."

Granny Price, on the other hand, was a genteel old girl; she had very little authority over us kids and none at all with Charlotte. Her amazing rolling gait made her unmistakable from hundreds of yards away. Although quite elderly she carried her bags of shopping in both hands and swayed like an Indian bullock up Factory Lane with her load. Charlotte never went shopping and threw massive tantrums against her granny whenever she was asked to do the smallest thing. The only time she was respectful was when her mother paid the odd visit to the estate by taxi.

"She's on the game," said Benny. He said that about so many people that the statement was beginning to lose credibility, but there was no doubt that Charlotte's mother was like nothing we ever saw on the estate. The taxi would pull up and in a swirl of fur coat she would alight and pay the driver through the window using currency of such high denomination that none of us recognised it. Her hair and make-up were always immaculate, and she swept into the end of terrace flat like an actress. She had a fabulous figure and invariably wore sweaters that showed it off as her elegant fur coat opened and flapped in the breeze. Like Charlotte she had intense eyes under the make-up and the glasses she sometimes wore. Charlotte's eyes just looked small, and she wore her glasses all the time to help correct a slight squint.

These visits never seemed to last very long, and soon the cab would

return and she would be whisked off ("back on the game," said Benny), leaving a slightly pink-eyed squinty girl standing forlornly at the gate watching her mother drive out of sight.

At twelve, Charlotte was much taller than the other girls, and while many of them were now adding little fashion accessories to their dress, she was still being dressed as a child with her bright red hair tied in a ponytail, or sometimes in plaits which suited her less. Other girls were starting to get noticed by the boys on the street, but not Charlotte, who still wore ankle socks, little cotton dresses tied with a bow at the back, and a ribbon in her hair.

All the houses and flats on the estate had privet hedges in front of them, and because our house bordered the alley, we had the longest hedge to cut. We also had the bluntest shears with which to do it.

When we first moved in, it took Bruce, Mum and I three days to work our way down the outside and a week to trim the inside, after which we just about kept it in check. Most of the hedges of the houses on our side of the road were nicely trimmed. One or two on the other side were positively ornamental.

The Prices' hedge, however, was dreadful. It had grown up and out and drooped over the pavement and into the garden in a tangle of dense branches, and as spring gave way to early summer it was plain that something had to be done. It was difficult to drop hints, and even when old Granny Price was forced to walk in the road to get past the hedge, she seemed not to notice. Finally one warm evening Granny Wren stopped her in the street as she was returning from the shops.

"Your bleedin' 'edge needs cuttin'," she suggested. Granny Price put down her bags for a moment and squinted up at her hedge.

"My goodness, yes it does!" she said, as if noticing it for the first time ever. "I'll have to see if I can find the shears and sort it out."

Granny Wren gave a gruff chuckle at the acknowledgement and resumed leaning on the gatepost. Granny Price picked up her bags and slowly waddled through her gate.

The cutting of hedges seems to work like the domino effect. Someone does theirs, and another follows suit, and in most cases a lazy neighbour is eventually shamed into cutting his hedge by the neatness of those either side of him. In the case of the Prices this was slow to happen,

and it was not until we had broken up for the Whitsun holiday and all our hedges were trimmed that old Granny Price was seen by us kids valiantly hacking a hole through her gateway.

It was a warm afternoon and the old lady had adopted a short-sleeved sweater and floral apron to embark on this task. As I watched I realised her shears were even worse than ours. The scissors seemed to merely grip the fronds of privet and I watched transfixed as huge flaps of fat beneath her upper arms wobbled and shuddered when she tried to rip the branches from the main body of the hedge. Our game of street cricket came to a pause as one by one we stopped to watch her efforts.

"We ought to offer to help," I said.

The rest of my mates looked at me incredulously and then Benny shouted, "You should let Charlotte do that, Granny Price!"

When the old lady finally realised that she was being addressed, she conceded that Benny was right and slowly turned and spoke to Charlotte who was playing quietly in another part of the garden. There then followed a one-sided shouting session as Charlotte loudly protested that she should not do the work. This petulant voice was something we had got used to, and it was a fact that Charlotte's protests were always louder when she knew that some of us kids were listening.

Suddenly there was a noise none of us had ever heard before from over the jungle of privet as the old lady finally snapped and a clear voice rang out, "You take these shears young lady and begin cutting that hedge NOW!" This was followed by a slapping noise and a shriek.

Us lads all looked at each other and grinned. *She had it coming* was the silent agreement among us all, and soon through the hedge came muffled stuttering sobs, of hurt pride more than pain, accompanied by rhythmic clipping noises.

Our game of cricket wandered aimlessly on, and gradually through the hedge Charlotte's sobs turned to little tuneless humming noises as the cutting settled into a neat regular pattern. The sun grew warmer and us lads slipped off our shirts, to expose singlets and skinny chests with arms in various shades of brown.

As our game dwindled toward its close, Charlotte's red hair began to show above her hedge, and as she worked her way backwards and forwards along the front facing the road, more and more of her face appeared, now slightly flushed, and then the tops of her bare shoulders. Then from behind the foliage she began cutting from the bottom of the inside to the top in

great strong chops of the shears, all the while singing her tuneless little song.

From time to time I glanced at her progress, and as she cleared away the leafy outgrowth from the inside border it was possible to make out her movements through the lace curtain of the depleted front foliage. She bent to pull some leaves from the ground and I suddenly noticed that she had taken her top and skirt off and was cutting away stripped to the waist, wearing only her school knickers.

Several other lads had noticed at the same time because the bowler had paused to look, effectively stopping the game. There was nothing unusual in children running about in their knickers and nothing else during the warm weather, but what had made this different was that Charlotte was suddenly no longer a little kid. The sight that we could so tantalisingly glimpse was of a beautiful coltish young girl, her flaming red hair tossing from side to side with her movements and her young breasts bouncing in time with each swish of the blades. To the sound of a cricket bat hitting the pavement the entire team crossed the road as one to the Prices' hedge.

"'ow's it goin' Charlotte?" asked Benny as nonchalantly as he could. Charlotte looked up surprised by the proximity of the voice.

"Who's that?" she squinted over the newly-cut top. Ordinarily Charlotte looked better with her glasses on, but now the fact that she wasn't wearing any added to her 'natural' look. The streaks of dust in the beads of perspiration and her quizzical peering, to say nothing of the lines down her cheeks from the smack that had so chastened her, made me feel a little protective toward her.

"'ow's it going?" asked Benny again.

Now Charlotte recognised the voice, and could make out the forms of the half dozen or so boys that were pressed up against the hedge trying to look over the top. Charlotte delighted in the attention; I was simply overwhelmed and feeling a little light-headed. Suddenly one of our number appeared with a pair of shears and began cutting the front of the hedge enthusiastically, and from where I and one or two others were standing more of Charlotte's gorgeous form began to emerge. In the next few minutes hedging shears were appearing from sheds all up and down the road as eager lads jostled to work next to the redheaded girl.

Some of the boys engaged in brief competitions with her to get her breasts to move more by snapping the shears shut more fiercely. One of them suggested she use his shears as they had just been sharpened, and she eagerly accepted. Soon there was a boy on each side and another

three in front of her, all snapping and cutting away as Charlotte giggled and thrilled to all the attention she was getting. I hung back but could not take my eyes off her.

It was only a car horn that alerted any grown-up to this fun. As usual the boys had set up a wicket in the middle of the road and put various markers to denote lines and boundaries, and the car refused to drive through them. No-one was prepared to give up his position near to Charlotte to move them either.

It was Granny Wren who shouted to us, "Move that bleedin' wicket out of the way!" and noticed the crowd of boys all working in the hedge.

"What's going on here?" she wanted to know, her suspicions aroused by this unusual enthusiasm for work. By this time Granny Price had come down but saw nothing unusual in the boys' interest. In fact she went so far as to thank us all.

"I think it's very nice that Charlotte has so many nice friends willing to help her," she said.

Granny Wren left the authority of her gate and in slippered feet came to inspect the scene. She was quick to realise the attraction, and shaking her head slightly in disbelief at the naiveté of the old lady, pushed past us lads and told us to clear off whilst she spoke to the older Price. In rebellious, sulky little groups, the boys stood in the road and watched as Granny Price told Charlotte to go upstairs and change. Without a murmur the young girl turned and went to the front step, but just before she went inside, she paused and gave us all a wave. Perspiration had rivered lines down her face in the dust from the privet hedge and traced patterns across her breasts, and as she waved they gave one last jiggle and she was gone.

When she came back outside, she was washed and wearing her little girl's dress with the bow at the back. Although we all knew what lay underneath, she was once again on her own when it came to friends. But for a brief moment she was the undisputed star of the road. None of us ever forgot that preview of what to expect when we had girlfriends of our own, and Granny Price got respect and her hedge cut.

❧

straws

Like kids everywhere, I longed to work at the fair, and we only lived a mile or two away from Mitcham Common where the Easter and Whitsun Fairs were held. At the age of about twelve I acquired my first black shirt with a button-down collar; I had a shilling tin of lavender brilliantine, home tapered trousers, and my tie knotted the wrong way round so that the thin end faced the world, and in my mind I was a Teddy boy.

I thought Teds were the best thing. Of course, I had no money to dress like they did and I had no beard to grow sideburns either, but I could make up a pastiche of what they wore and practise the way they walked. Teds always worked the fair; they had tattoos and took incredible risks standing on the whirling machines, leaning against gravity and nicking a bit of small change from the excited punters. They looked so cool as they made the girls scream with excitement, pushing the Waltzers round so that the rib-crushing centrifugal forces made them shriek as the air was forced out of their lungs. Dresses went awry and we caught tantalising glimpses of what we were not really supposed to see as the music roared out of the fairground speakers: *I Found My Thrill On Blueberry Hill...*

The posters announcing the fair would appear a few days before the advance party arrived with some of the heavy machinery and one or two trailers. It didn't matter that you knew they were coming, you still got the same rush of excitement at the thought of all that colour and noise. The

caravans ringed their position like wagons in a western film as they built up the site from within the protection of their walls. At night lights were seen in these trailers and eventually television aerials were in evidence alongside the elderly but immaculate Scammells and Albions that hauled the fairground rides to each new destination. The Common was our domain all year but when the show people arrived it was definitely theirs.

None of my mates dared break through the cordon of trailers and trucks, and in any case each one seemed to contain a dog with a bark loud enough to knock down the walls of Jericho. One night, however, I did creep inside the cordon on my own whilst my mates stood at a discreet distance. It was a strange sight that opened up in front of me: all the stalls were covered up and only the lights from inside the caravans illuminated the scene. Then some monster dog began a frenzied barking, and I was only just back to my friends before a couple of men appeared with the beast at the rim of the vehicles and let us know if they ever caught us again they would set the dogs on us.

Stories of the fabulous amounts of money to made at the fair abounded, and I decided that it was time I swallowed my shyness and tried to get a job on one of the glamorous rides. I would be able to buy a pair of black jeans which I would have tapered like Rory McLean, only not so tight, and stand leaning backward on the Waltzer making the girls scream. They would admire my skills of balance and manliness and also my honesty. I would not fiddle the change that the boys handle with distracted indifference (I was always convinced they would forget mine, but I always got it). If there were no jobs on the Waltzer, there was always the Whip or the dodgems.

The job I got was on the Pick-a-Straw stall. By the time I applied, everything exciting had been taken by much older lads. I'd gone up to the Duck Shoot stall and asked the bloke in charge and a young lad if there were any vacancies on the rides. I must have sounded posh to them and the lad nearly had a fit of laughing, but he told me to go and see his auntie on her stall. She asked me if I could give change and was I honest, and said she wouldn't tolerate any nickin' or fiddlin' and took me on to start that same afternoon at one o'clock.

There followed one of the most miserable weeks of work I have had before or since. Although disappointed by my failure to secure a glamorous job, I was still quite pleased to have got something. I began to wonder how much money she would give me, as this had not been discussed. I

was sure I would have enough to get a Teddy boy suit, but more than that I had no idea.

The job was simple enough. All I had to do was to walk round and round the stall carrying a large mug stuffed full of drinking straws and shouting, "Pick a straw!" for which the punters paid sixpence. Hanging on the uprights that supported the roof were prodders made from bits of coat hangers; the participants would insert these into their chosen straw and poke out a piece of paper with a name of an old movie star printed on it.

If their name corresponded to a name on the stall, then that would secure the item represented by that film star. So if you pulled out Dale Evans you would get a pencil sharpener, and for Bing Crosby you got a 48-piece tea service. It took me two or three days to realise that there were probably no Bing Crosby names in the straws. At first I was more excited than the punters as they poked out their tickets, craning my neck to see if they had won it. It soon became obvious that the whole thing was a con and that there were far more Tab Hunters (no prize) than there were Dale Evanses.

I felt so bad in the end that I began telling little kids not to spend their last sixpence there, as I couldn't bear to see them go away with nothing. Once I gave away a chipped and battered plaster elf to a little girl who had lost to Tab Hunter, and the old girl even questioned me about how I had got rid of it. I blustered some excuse which she grudgingly accepted. In spite of this apparent disloyalty, the old girl was pleased with me and after the fourth day could even remember my name, though she still called me 'boy'. I can only think that in spite of me actively discouraging speculation at the stall, her profits were up, simply because I didn't steal from her.

Her oafish nephew got me to part with my collection of second-hand comics, which he promised to return. I soon realised that he couldn't read and that he liked to look at the pictures, but it kept him off my back and once or twice he let me have a free go on the .22 rifle range, which I was surprisingly good at (I was useless at most hand-to-eye sports).

I only stayed the week, and by the Saturday I couldn't wait to get away, but I couldn't leave until I'd been paid. The music had been irresistible, but the weather had been miserable and rainy, the girls and boys that nightly thronged the rides had not even noticed me, and as we wrapped up the stall for the last night and I prepared to receive my wages, the old girl addressed me.

"Well boy, you've been a good kid and I've talked to me old man and we'll take you on with us if you like. I know your old mum is 'avin' a struggle with two boys at 'ome and I should know 'cos I've raised four meself. Now you tell 'er that we'll look after you and you'll get your proper schoolin' and proper food an' you'll travel everywhere we go. We're off to Southampton after this and you can leave with us tomorrer if you want it, now what do you think?"

As she made her little speech she counted out in half crowns the sum of twelve shillings and sixpence and pressed the large coins into my hand. The mixture of emotions at this time was extreme. This woman was more or less offering to adopt me and take care of me, and I could become a traveller and be free as the other lads who worked the rides and drove the wagons and trucks. I could wear my hair long and greasy and live on hot dogs and candy floss, I could meet hundreds of girls and become experienced and get tattooed and have an earring put in. I could leave the council flat and be free.

Not on twelve and sixpence a week I couldn't. I counted the coins in my pocket again. I couldn't believe it—twelve and six! A whole week standing under a soggy canvas poking out a mug of 'lucky' straws at people and not cheating the old girl and this was my reward. I stood outside her trailer and mumbled about not being able to leave as I had to attend school and look after my little brother. She once again told me that I would get all the schoolin' I needed with them. I thought of her strange offer of motherhood, then of the callous exploitation of my honesty and stupidity, and a tear trickled down my cheek. She didn't notice.

I managed a goodbye and thank you, and without looking back at me she said, "We leave tomorrow at eight, if you want to come and yer mum says okay, be 'ere an' we'll take you with us." Behind her at the caravan table the old man was looking at the paper, and he slowly shook his head from side to side and blew out a cloud of Old Holborn smoke.

"Bye boy," he said. I walked away from the fairground angry and confused, and when I got home I lied to all my mates about the money I got paid and then realised that her oafish nephew hadn't even returned my precious comics.

∾

d-day

"Have you ever 'opped the wag?" asked Benny nonchalantly one evening. We were all leaning on the bars that were situated outside our tiny flat. They were there to stop kids running straight out into the road from the alley that ran down the side of the houses and the kids sort of met there and hung around while they waited for inspiration to hit them as to how to spend their time.

"'ave you ever 'opped the wag?" I turned the expression over in my mind. This was a new one on me and Benny was always doing this. He seemed to have a vocabulary that was all his own. All the other kids knew his words but seldom used them. It took me weeks to work out what a 'juk' (the Romany word for a dog) was. 'oppin' the wag? Could it be rhyming slang, I wondered, all the kids used this cockney derivative. Wag, bag, fag, shag? All these thoughts raced quickly through my mind. I drew a blank but already Benny was starting again.

"'ave you ever 'opped the wag?"

It was probably some sexual thing, I decided, so it was probably best to deny it. I answered as lazily as I could, "No," then added, "not really."

There was a pause and Benny said, "Either you 'ave or you ain't."

So I said, "No, definitely not."

He kicked a small stone into the gutter and said, "Well you ought to,

it ain't 'alf a laugh."

There was a short hesitation as I pondered what it could mean when he offered, "We could both do it, it's more a laugh if we both do it."

Oh Christ, I thought, it *is* a sex thing and Benny wants us to do it together. I was constantly amazed at Benny's precociousness, as he was only eleven but seemed to know so much. After a while I asked when he was thinking of doing it. This seemed to be the safest way of continuing the enquiry without committing to the act.

"I was finkin' Wednesday," said Benny, and for the first time he looked round at me and I saw not a hint of embarrassment at his proposal. It was still term time, and as we went to different schools I asked what time he wanted to do this thing.

"All day of course!" was all he said. All day? What on earth could it be about? I kicked a small stone into the gutter and turned round and looked down the lane.

"Well, I couldn't do it Benny, you know I have to go to school."

"Exactly," said Benny, "I know, that's why I said it. It's Derby day." He pronounced Derby like the Americans do. I was more perplexed than ever, this wag 'opping was somehow connected with horses and I was becoming even more wary.

Then Benny asked, "'ave you ever been to the Derby?"

I turned round to face the road. "No, I haven't been interested in it."

"It's only up Epsom. We could go and 'ave a laugh," he said without stammering.

"Look Ben, I have to go to school, I already told you."

"Yeah, you could 'op the wag, an' we could go." Oh Christ, we were back to 'oppin! Then it dawned on me that he meant me to play truant.

"You mean to bunk off school, don't you?" I said with relief.

"Yeah," said Benny, turning round to face down the lane, "Let's both 'op the wag."

And 'op the wag we did. In the end it was Benny, Ronnie, Bruce and me that 'opped the wag that June morning and met down at the tiny station at Waddon Marsh. This was the first stop on the loop line to Wimbledon, and the regular train service added character to our estate. Years before, my paternal grandfather had considered his train driving career hit the heights when he was promoted to the electric service and he could wear a collar and tie to work, returning home almost as clean as when he started. The train was only ever two coaches long, and after rush

hour it was often completely empty. We climbed in and immediately Benny started to behave badly. He threw his legs up on the seat opposite and pulled out a packet of Weights.

"'oo wants a fag?"

"Stop showin' off," ordered Ronnie.

"I ain't showin' off," said Benny, "if you want a fag you can 'ave one that's all I'm sayin'."

He only had a pack of five, so we all took one, leaving him with one for later. I was the only one who could inhale the smoke, and soon our little coach was full of cloudy fumes.

"You can't even take it down," teased Ronnie, as Bruce and he puffed away with much flicking of ash.

"Yes I fuckin' can," said Benny.

"Let's see you then you lyin' git," said Ronnie. Benny attempted a tiny inhalation but predictably ended up in a coughing fit, which caused Ronnie and the rest of us much amusement.

As the train pulled away from the next stop, Beddington Lane, Benny said, "We got to change at the next station, Mitcham Junction." Just before the train drew in Benny threatened to pull the communication cord, but we stopped him and I breathed that he better behave or we'd leave him on his own. For the next part of the trip he sulked a bit, but he was no trouble.

It was a beautiful morning as we left the station and asked a man the way to the racecourse. At first he must have thought we were taking the mickey, and then seeing that we were genuine he stated deliberately that to follow the crowd might be a good idea. I was embarrassed that I hadn't thought of that, it was so logical.

We dropped in behind a group. I was surprised at the numbers of folk that were moving toward the downs. We all looked at each other and grinned the way kids do when there is excitement in the air. I rattled the loose change in my pocket and wondered how far I would get on three shillings and sixpence; I bet myself that Benny would have at least ten bob and I was right.

Benny had his first toffee apple at eleven o'clock and his first candy floss shortly afterwards. Now he's down to nine shillings, I calculated, as I resolved not to start spending until we had achieved parity. That meant he had to spend another five and six. It was going to be a long afternoon.

We entered the downs at the top, where hundreds of cars were parked, and the level of conversation rose around us as people glimpsed the course and the sweep of the scenery that warm sunny morning. Over in the distance could be seen the tops of tents and a few fairground rides; in fact it looked bigger than our own Mitcham Fair, one of the high points of our social calendar.

"Come on," shouted Benny, "look at all the bleedin' tents over there." We quickened our pace slightly, but there was so much to look at I wanted to take it all in. Soon our pace had slowed again. All around the top, people were gathered in groups as tipsters shouted that they had the sure winner of this or that race. I wondered why, if they knew they would be willing to pass on such valuable information for a paltry half crown. Not that a half crown was all that paltry, especially if you only had a few bob to your name like me.

As we edged along, gawping at everything we came across, a huge crowd was listening to Prince Honolulu. Not that they had much option but to listen, his voice was so loud.

Every time he hollered, "I gotta horse, I gotta horse!" the crowd smiled and acknowledged his famous cry. I remember him as being very big, with a huge voice and a head dress of exotic feathers. In his hand he held a brown paper envelope in which he swore that he had the name of the Derby winner. There was a steady stream of takers for this prize, and as I watched it dawned on me that he only had to list all the horses, and as long as that number of people bought his tips, one of them would be a very satisfied customer. In fact he was part and parcel of the entertainment as we moved along through the happy crowd.

Soon Benny had his first hot dog, and Bruce and I pretended not to notice as the first little jabs of hunger reminded us that it was mid-day. Couples and groups sat all around us on the grass, with everything from a sandwich to small hampers of food and bottles of warm beer; and way over by the track, the crowds were being drawn to the rails like iron filings to a magnet.

Benny ate another toffee apple and washed it down with a bottle of R. White's cream soda, which he offered round and we all gulped down a few sickly mouthfuls. As the horses pulled in the punters, so the music of the fair drew us to the rides above the course. It was a proper fair, with side shows as well as rides, and us kids were in our element.

Benny and Bruce invested in a ride on the 'chairoplanes', and while

that ride was going on, I planned to visit a tent that promised the longest rat in the world. I was just about to pay my tanner when I heard some kid say to his mate that he could see where they had sewn two rats together, and what was the point of seeing a rat floating in a lot of yellow liquid? The picture on the outside showed a terrier cowering in terror before a snarling rat of gigantic proportions, not some mouldering specimen in a bell jar.

I was relieved at saving my sixpence, as I had once before succumbed to curiosity at Bognor and parted with hard earned pennies to see the two-headed calf. The pictures on the display outside showed rosy-cheeked children stroking the heads of a beautiful young creature, but on entry to the booth, all that was on display was a jar about the size of a pickle jar at the fish and chip shop, in which floated the tiny embryo of an aborted two-headed something or other. It was about the size of a puppy and had been disembowelled and sewn up with some white thread. It was as much as I could do to force any food down me for several days.

Benny and Bruce had been on their ride and were both eating candy floss.

"That was terrific weren't it, you feel like yer flyin'," enthused Benny, looking over at Bruce for confirmation. It might have felt good, but I thought Benny was looking a little dodgy myself.

Then there was a hammer and bell machine, and skinny blokes with brown arms and ghostly white bodies in string vests made the bell ring, whilst bigger blokes failed for some reason. I watched the abstracted way the barker broke the fall of the striker with a stick, just before it returned to rest. He took the sixpenny toll with the same hand as he used to hand the punter the hammer, and didn't even look at the geezer as he continued his urging to "Try your strength!" or "Ring the bell, impress the gels!"

I looked around, but there were no unattended girls for me to impress, and the hammer looked too heavy for me to lift, let alone hurl over my shoulder and on to the spigot of the machine.

I almost blushed at the thought of the humiliation if I failed to get the clapper to move, and my fears were vindicated when Ronnie, after some prompting from Ben, decided to have a go. He had to hold the hammer so near the head in order to lift the thing that it had no travel to gain momentum, and the hammer merely fell on to the spigot sending the clapper all of twelve inches up the fifteen feet of the graduated board.

"Weaklin'!" crowed Benny, gleefully reading the classification of

effort from the board.

"Fuck off," countered Ronnie, his face more red with effort than embarrassment. Benny was giggling and sweating at the same time; Ronnie made a lunge at him and Bruce and I pulled them apart before anything happened. It went a bit quiet for a moment as we sauntered round the various stalls. A little way off from the rest was a bloke dressed for some reason as a cowboy and speaking in a cod American accent.

"Guess your age! Guess your age! Only one shilling!" All he had by way of props was a box that his punters stood on, and then he walked round them assessing their age. As a backdrop to his box, the rules of his gig were set out: *If I cannot guess your age within two years you can have your money back.*

"D'you fancy a go, Benny?" I asked.

"Not if he takes two years to guess it, we're only 'oppin' the wag for a day," observed Benny cleverly, though it took me a minute to work out what he meant. I wished I was as fast as Benny.

"I don't do kids," muttered the cowboy from the corner of his mouth, his accent suddenly more English. The others began to drift away, and I watched as a few punters duly parted with their shillings to be told what they already knew. He appeared to get all the ages right, and it crossed my mind that if he guessed a woman to be younger than she was, she might be so grateful that she would pretend he got it right. The longer I watched, the more impressive it became; he was getting all the ages right, and in the short time that I watched he must have earned about ten or eleven shillings. I was very impressed.

He must have seen how intrigued I was. During a lull in his labours, he turned to where I was standing and from the corner of his mouth whispered cryptically, "You have to look around the eyes. It's the eyes that tell the story," and then he was back to work.

I grinned and went red. He walked round the back of the customer and gave me a large wink, as I was now privy to the secret. Again he was on the money, and another shilling went into his pocket. I wandered away, wondering if he had a son to pass on these skills to. Perhaps he had been waiting for the right kid to come along to pass on these age-old secrets, and he had chosen me. I was flattered and couldn't wait to try it out on someone.

Suddenly I realised I had lost the others. I gazed at the throngs of people milling about and a panic hit me. Onions and cigarette smoke

and sticky smells were on the breeze, and Little Richard records crackled above the general noise. Other voices closer to my head were all talking at the same time and I felt a little dizzy.

"Come over 'ere Ralph," spluttered Benny, snapping me out of my distancing feelings, "there's some tarts in a tent over 'ere wiv no cloves on." He raised his eyebrows and pursed his lips and blew a gasp of air through the small gap between them.

"They're stark fuckin' naked!" He burst out in a huge guffaw.

"What are you talking about?" I said, still coming to from my away moment. I was really pleased to see him and as usual his enthusiasm was very contagious. Bruce looked a bit embarrassed but I still looked to him for confirmation of Benny's assertion.

"What Ben's saying is that there's a striptease tent over there," and he gestured with his hand. Without saying anything, we all wandered off in that direction.

Outside the small marquee was a little man with a huge voice drumming up an already interested group of punters, while we lurked at the back. His spiel indicated that these three lovely girls would reveal all their charms in discreet artistic poses for the price of two shillings.

I felt my own hand check the few coins in my pocket and looked at the others.

Benny said, "Two bob to look at them old birds, you must be jokin'. One of 'em looks as old as my mother." This was probably true, but another one was so pretty, with dark hair and a sweet smile, that I had nearly fallen in love with her before the barker finished his pitch. Soon the men in the crowd started to pay their two bobs and I stood watching them file into the tent.

Ronnie turned to Bruce and Benny and said, "They won't let us in anyway, we're too young. Let's go on the dodgems." I told them to go and I would wait for them here. The three of them took off in the direction of the cars while I stood outside the tent, listening to the lascivious murmurings and chuckles emanating from within.

Other noises mingled with the crowd, and voices again muttered just out of earshot inside my head. The thought of the men leering at the pretty girl disturbed me, but the thought that I could see her naked exerted a greater pressure on my adolescent body. After what seemed like an age, the flap opened on the tent and the men emerged, blinking slightly

in the sunshine and grinning to each other.

The barker came out and once more began drumming up the crowd with his well worn patter. He was assisted once more by the one who was as old as Benny's mum, who also took the money on the door, and she was joined at the entrance by another slightly younger girl with a fairly large nose. Finally my pretty one came out, to a few wolf whistles, and that was it. I plunged my hand into my pocket and grabbed the two bob bit, and as soon as some of the men had paid their entrance I joined in the queue, and the lady who was as old as Benny's mum took my money without looking at me.

Inside the tent the heat was overpowering. All the men lit up at the same time and began jostling for position. I worked my way to a corner, and by standing on tip toe and craning my neck I could see the stage quite well. The barker climbed on to the tiny stage and stood in front of the curtain, which looked like a stained bed sheet with a small triangular tear, revealing a small amount of movement behind it. The lady who looked as old as Benny's mum scurried back out of the tent, allowing a flash of sunlight on to the tawdry scene within. Another flash of sunlight indicated that she had arrived at the backstage area and the barker began a short spiel.

"What you are about to witness is an artistic display of some of the world's finest paintings depicted in living tableaux form by the lovely ladies you saw outside. Because the great artists of the past found nakedness to be quite acceptable, some of the poses you will witness will contain nudity. We 'ope that this will not cause offence and must point out that to conform to the guidelines of the 'ome Seckertary there will be no movement allowed during the performance. I thangyew."

From somewhere behind the scenes an elderly gramophone struck up and the man announced, "Salome with the 'ead of Samson!"

He reached up and drew back the sheet to reveal the lady who was as old as Benny's mum, sitting on a red cushion dressed in her briefs and holding a dinner plate with the head of an old shop window mannequin wearing a black wig. Apart from her briefs and a silly smile she was naked. The act of holding up the plate had raised one breast slightly whilst the other one drooped forlornly. Her skin was as white as my mum's, in contrast to the ruddy complexions of the men around me and my own spring-browned arms. There were several nasty bruises on her arms, and a large one on her thigh that she had tried unsuccessfully to disguise with make-up.

A sort of groan came from some voices in the audience, the curtain was hastily drawn over the proceedings and the barker announced, "Thangyew laydeez an' gennermen! And now we present the 'and maidens of Aphrodite!"

Once more he drew back the curtain and there sat the lady who looked as old as Benny's mum on an old gold-painted chair, the girl with the big nose holding a long handled fan, and the one I was in love with now sitting on the red cushion with her back to me. She held what looked suspiciously like a coal scuttle imploringly toward Aphrodite. I wondered if they were related; could that have been her mother she was facing? All three were topless, but I could not see the pretty one's charms from the position she held.

The barker closed the curtain once more and announced, "Thangyew laydeez an gennermen. And now we present 'The Birth of Venus'." He drew back the curtain and there was the same woman, this time wearing a huge wig which she held coyly in front of her privates whilst balancing on a dustbin lid, representing a shell.

The curtain was drawn back again and the barker bellowed, "Thangyew laydeez an' gennermen, and now we present 'The Toilet of Venus'."

"Oh fuck that," said a voice in front of me, "I suppose the old bird'll be sitting on the bog now!" and some of his friends laughed. The curtain was drawn back and there sat the lady who looked like Benny's mum with a different wig on. The pretty one was holding a mirror in hands that trembled slightly (I loved her more than ever for this) and the one with the big nose held a sort of comb to the older one's hair.

"They all look bloody silly if you ask me," an old geezer in front of me remarked, but I was transfixed by the young girl's figure. For the first time I could see her breasts. They were small and round and firm and I was dizzy with all sorts of emotions. The voices grew louder in my ears and the heat of the tent and the cigarette smoke swirled and the record player scratched on and the barker went, "Thangyew laydeez an' gennermen..."

Sweat poured from my forehead as the curtain swished closed again.

"An' finally the Three Graces thangyew!" With that, the torn curtain was pulled back to reveal the three of them, naked, in the pose of the famous statue. The one who was as old as Benny's mum faced the audience, a judicious crossing of her legs concealing the part that most had paid to see, and the one with the big nose and stubble armpits had her

head turned heavenward with a look of what I supposed was to represent divine inspiration but looked more like a mad woman to me.

I had eyes only for my love, who looked wistfully over one shoulder with a cardboard lute under one arm. I could just see one breast and her bottom and her pretty smile, and just before I passed out the curtain swung back and the barker shouted that the show had ended but we were welcome to call again.

I was almost carried outside in the rush to escape, and sat down on the grass in a state of shock and excitement. Men around me were grumbling and laughing but no-one seemed really to mind. I was slowly returning to reality; all I could see were the cadaverous white bodies with their thumb marks and bruises and the tatty surroundings and cheap props and torn drapes, then breasts and bottoms and pretty smiles. I was smitten.

"Look what fuckin' Benny's done !" Ronnie's voice was very loud in my ear. I turned round to see Bruce laughing silently as Ronnie pointed to his shirt which was covered with the contents of Benny's stomach.

"I couldn't 'elp it could I, it was all that banging about in the bumper cars weren' it?" said Benny with not much hint of contrition.

"Yeah but you could have turned the other way couldn't you? You twat," Ronnie added for good measure. I was glad to get up from my position and to laugh along with the others. Ronnie took off his t-shirt and his body was as skinny and white as the older men in shirt sleeves or vests, although the rest of us had the beginnings of tans as all the bits that poked out were getting brown. We strolled happily amongst the crowds until we found a standpipe amongst the trailers and caravans. Ronnie rinsed off most of the puke and we all had a swig of water, until a fearsome-looking old woman saw us and threatened to turn her dog on us.

"All right missus, keep your fuckin' 'air on," shouted Benny, and then he took off leaving the rest of us standing like idiots before following him, laughing our heads off.

Some way below us the racing had begun, but we took little notice. The crowd noise came to a crescendo as the horses reached the winning post. The sun continued to pour down on us all as I tried to digest what had happened to me and then suddenly I saw her. Not the object of my desire, but the old girl who had given me the job at the Mitcham Fair the previous year.

And there she was, a year on, in front of me and even in the hot

afternoon sun she still wore the same fawn-coloured overcoat she wore every day. Ominously there was no sign of the old man with his duck stall and I wondered if the cough had carried him off. Her skin was even greyer than I remembered it, and even from a distance I could see that her deep brown eyes had no life in them. As she wandered around the stall like a goldfish, her gaze stopped for a second in my direction. I thought that she had recognised me, but her eyes moved on to others in the crowd, each person viewed as a sixpence.

I drew a little closer, and there at the back of the stall was the same tea service with Bing Crosby written underneath. Now you could get a tiny plastic Barbie doll for Dale Evans, and on the floor scattered around the stall was the name Tab Hunter. I looked around for the others. Benny and Ronnie had made it up, Benny was eating another hot dog, and they were both laughing with Bruce, who had also recognised the old girl.

"Did she know you?" he asked.

"I didn't speak to her," I replied, and the four of us began the long walk back to the station. We all had a drag on Benny's last crumpled cigarette, and the journey back to Waddon Marsh Halt was altogether quieter than the outward one had been.

In my dreams the young stripper came to visit me and begged me to rescue her from her wicked mother, who owned a pick-a-straw factory where she was made to work long hours. She told me that she had seen me in the tent and had followed me home. She was prepared to live in our shed and to live off stolen breakfast cereals until we could find somewhere of our own, and to prove it she was about to let me do something with her, but we were already lost on an open common where we found a plate containing the head of Benny with a fixed leer on his face. I felt compelled to take it home with me and give it to his mum. I placed Benny's grinning head in a carrier bag and hurried across the open ground.

Suddenly I'm on my own, with Benny's head banging against my thigh uttering his prelude to speaking from inside the bag. "Gan gan gan…" it goes, in time to my step. Where has she gone? The sound of horses' hooves make me turn round to see her naked on the back of the leading horse. She is pursued by the barker and the one who looks as old as Benny's mum. As she draws level with me she leaps from the horse into my open arms and I am consumed by her softness and we fall to the ground.

We roll in each other's arms down the grassy bank and something is happening to me. Breasts the size of toffee apples float in my head, then hot dogs, and before the dream is consummated I awake with proof of my coming adolescence. I can see her still, though I couldn't tell you which horse won the Derby.

❧

wolf

One morning, it must have been in the winter holidays, the kids gathered on the street bars outside our flat. As usual, we talked and joked and woke up to the new day and thought about what we might do that morning. As we leaned on the bars, we noticed the shuffling walk of Teddy Wolf coming towards us.

He sidled up to the bars, stood there and pulled out a flattened cigarette from a packet of Player's that looked as though he had sat on them. As he struck the match we could see his hands shaking so much that he could barely line up the match with the end of the cigarette. He took down a huge drag and blew the combination of steamy breath and smoke out in an enormous cloud. Benny mimicked the action with an imaginary cigarette and a couple of the younger ones copied Benny. I was fascinated, though, as I had never seen anyone shake like this man was shaking.

Teddy was about twenty-two years old and therefore not really a contemporary of any of the kids who knocked about with the older brothers of our friends on the estate. The boys that Teddy would have known were either in one of the services, in prison, or else had married and moved away. Teddy had not grown up on the estate and his past was not known or much discussed. His hair stood up in a grown out crewcut and was

pushed back off his forehead, his skin was deathly pale, and he wore a thin 'Raindrop' fabric semi-Ted suit. His shirt was white and open at the neck and it was clear that he had no vest underneath. He finished his Player's and stubbed it out on the pavement, grinding it into the asphalt. Benny did the same with his imaginary dog-end.

"Anyone got a smoke?" asked Teddy without really looking at any of us. We felt flattered and grown-up to think that he might assume we could supply him with a fag. After a few seconds silence he pointedly looked at each of us, until Jimmy Wren offered to get one from his sister Jeannie.

"Go on then mate," said Teddy urgently, and lifting his empty hands to his lips blew steam through them. Benny copied him.

"You look like you're freezin'," observed Benny, "Ain't you got no coat?"

Teddy said nothing, and at that moment Jimmy returned with a cigarette with a filter tip that Teddy broke off before lighting it up with his trembling hands.

"I slept out last night," said Teddy Wolf, "in her shed."

"In 'er shed?" guffawed Benny, looking around at us with his eyebrows raised to share his incredulity.

I frowned at him to shut him up, and Teddy drew another deep drag on the cigarette before flicking it almost to the other side of the road.

"Where was I supposed to go?" he asked distractedly. "Where could I go? I ain't got nowhere I could go," and he swung round and looked pointedly at Benny. "Can I come round your house?" Benny looked embarrassed.

Teddy had not stopped shaking all the time he had stood with us. His collar was turned up on his jacket and his hands were pushed deep into his pockets. The suit would have provided a little style but no warmth at all. Shoulders hunched, eyes frightened and so alone you could feel it, Teddy Wolf *was* James Dean.

I looked as deep as I dared into Teddy's eyes and all I could see was desolation. There was this man with no-one to turn to except a bunch of little kids. We all stood silent watching him shake. Any moment now he has to stop, I thought, but the trembling persisted.

"Has anyone got another fag?" he asked.

Little Jimmy produced another Bristol that he had planned to smoke himself, but even at nine years old he realised that Teddy's need was greater than his own.

"Why did you sleep in 'er shed?" said Benny at last.

Another cloud of steam and smoke was exhaled across the road and Teddy replied, "I 'ad to leave and there weren't nowhere else to go."

"Where were you staying?" persisted Benny.

"With Poppy," said Teddy.

And then something happened. From the corners of both eyes, huge tears formed and splattered down his cheeks and splashed unchecked on to the freezing pavement. The strange little gathering looked at each other and wondered what could it be that would make a man cry? Benny at first grinned sheepishly and then even his expression gave way to one of concern.

There was no sound coming from Teddy as he stood there, just a slow rhythm of silent sobs shaking his torso against the faster shivering of the rest of his body. Without a word little Jimmy Wren climbed up on to the lower of the two bars to reach the shoulders of the crying man, and laid his hand on them. The effect of this was that a cry of such pain erupted from the throat of Teddy Wolf that it frightened us. A cry that tore the child's voice from within his grown-up body, his broken heart robbing him of the dignity of privacy. All the sadness spilled out on to the open street.

"Ain't anyone got an 'andkerchief?" asked someone, and we all instinctively looked at Benny, whose mum always made him carry one. Benny reluctantly half pulled it out of his trouser pocket and inspected it to see if it was still flexible, but his cousin Jimmy pulled it out the rest of the way and crammed it into Teddy's hand. Teddy absently started to use it.

"What can you do if you love someone and they kick you out? What are you going to do?" he sobbed. "I love 'er and that's it."

He blew his nose so violently that we all winced.

"Who is it you're talking about?" Benny wanted to know.

"Poppy, Poppy Spinner," said Teddy.

"Poppy Spinner, what, her who lives in Euston Crescent? Olly, Olly Voil?"

"Yeah, Poppy Spinner," he said, and then turning round again to focus on Benny, "what did you call her?"

"Nuffin'," said Benny, casting his eyes down.

Suddenly we all knew the cause of this broken heart, Olly, Olly Voil. Benny it was who invented nicknames for everybody, and with patience

you could work out the logic to their origination. For example, the old girl who lived diagonally opposite me on the other side of the road and the corresponding bars, was known to all the kids on the street as Shanny, or from Benny, "old Shannybags." She was a tough old bird who terrified us kids and used language that I for one had never heard coming from any woman before. She lived with her elderly and very infirm brother, who seldom ventured out beyond the front door.

We were convinced that she was a witch, and if a ball landed in Shannybags' garden that was where it stayed. It was Benny who detected her different accent and decided she was Irish and that her name was Annie. So she became 'Irish Annie' and later 'Shanny'. It took me years to work that one out.

Poppy Spinner was very tall and slim; she was about thirty-three and had two daughters. She was tidy and neat, and her little girls were plain but always spotlessly clean, as they had to be because they had two different fathers and Poppy had never been married. There was no particular stigma attached to unmarried motherhood on the estate; there were several that we all knew about, and just as many more who were being raised by Grandma and Granddad or even married aunts and uncles. It was just that Poppy kept herself to herself, managing all the while to keep her little ones looking as if they had a dad's wages coming in as well.

There were a number of rumours about the children, one of which suggested that it was a friend of her father who had made her pregnant first, and she dare not say for fear her old man would have killed them both. For me, this story elevated her to saintly proportions, heroically bearing her secret to protect her father from greater hurt.

For three years she never looked at another man, and then met a lad from a few streets away who swore he loved her. At length she gave in to his incessant pleading, only to find he had enlisted in the army and was killed out in Cyprus during the troubles with EOKA. Everyone knew this story, but it was never confirmed or denied by the relatives, who still lived on the estate.

Poppy was thin and wore glasses, and she had a retroussé nose; to Benny her name sounded like Popeye, so obviously she became Olly Voil!

Her downstairs flat was like a doll's house; you could almost smell the furniture polish as you walked past. Her windows were always sparkling clean and decorated with spotless nylon nets. The two little girls shared a bedroom with their mother, and this enabled Poppy to make her second

bedroom available to a single gentleman, for whom she would provide an evening meal.

This of course was all against the council regulations, but Poppy was otherwise a model tenant in every way, and no-one would have dreamed of grassing her up. Most of her gentlemen were older and just passing through, but somehow this time her system had broken down and she had taken pity on poor Teddy and allowed him to lodge with her.

Naturally people talked. Teddy was not from our area and he didn't know anyone; he didn't drink and all he wanted to do was stay in after his tea and watch a bit of TV with Poppy and the two children. Eventually Poppy told him to go down to the pub, just to get out for a bit. Reluctantly he did so, only to scurry back to his little nest on the crescent.

He started to do little jobs for her, like trimming her hedge, or putting the milk bottles out, occasionally washing up and sometimes buying a little box of sweets for the girls. People still talked, but it was warmer talk along the lines of, "So what if he is a bit younger than her, look at so and so, she was fifteen years older than him," or, "Ain't it wonderful how he looks after them girls. They think the world of him you know."

Whatever went wrong happened quickly. One day it was right; the next it had all changed.

We looked at the young man in the grey morning. It was still early and the watery winter sun was just piercing the clouds over the gasholder. The sunlight made him appear even more pathetic, as the redness of his eyelids and nostrils contrasted with his sallow complexion and the new day's stubble on his chin.

"What are you going to do?" I ventured at last.

"Dunno," came the eventual reply.

"Are you going to sleep out tonight?" I asked.

"I'll have to, ain't got nowhere else." He seemed to shiver harder at the thought of it.

Benny was looking bored and several of the younger ones were fidgety. They had been reverent to his distress but now there were things to be done, games to play, shtrews to catch, and the morning was getting to be warm enough to start all those juices flowing.

"We've got an old blanket in our shed if you want it," I offered.

Teddy said nothing and the kids began to peel away. I still felt I should stay and soon I was the only one at the bars.

"Have you got a fag mate?" he asked me.

"No, I'm sorry," I replied. He reached down to one he'd finished earlier and rolled the end in between his finger tips and got enough to light and pulled a few more drags down to the filter and beyond before flicking it away.

Then pulling the collar of his raindrop suit up, and without acknowledging any of us he uttered two words as one, "See-ya." He turned in towards the sunlight, thrust his hands deeper into empty trouser pockets, and walked off in the direction of Factory Lane.

Benny came up to me. "You won't see him again," he said, watching the figure move off away from us, and we never did. People talked like they do. Some said he topped himself by jumping in the water at the foot of the gasometer where a body would never have been discovered. Some said he moved to Brighton. Certainly Poppy and her little girls moved away and no word of explanation was ever uttered.

∿

puggy

Our home in Miller Road had a fireplace in which we were obliged to burn smokeless fuel. There was an irony to this, as all around us chimneys belched out a cocktail of obnoxious gases. From our front room window we could clearly see the main Croydon power station, a masterpiece of thirties brick architecture and a tribute to the skill of the old bricklayers. From our bedroom windows we could make out the chimneys of the B power station in Factory Lane.

Some Saturday mornings we would see a few kids coming back round the end of the road with prams full of coke. I asked the lads on the estate where they had bought it from, and they told me you could get it as a by-product of the power generation down on the Purley Way. We still had the wood barrow that Uncle Alf had made for us from our old pram, so the next week Bruce, Benny and I went down to get some fuel.

Whenever I see old Soviet Russian films glorifying industry, I think of this area of Croydon. All around us there was bustle and noise. At the bottom of our lane there were steam trains as well as electric services, and across Purley Way there were service steam engines delivering coal to the power station. As we walked down Factory Lane you could clearly see, through the shutters of the workshops, the gleaming turbines with polished copper pipes making energy. The hiss of the cooling towers and the

constant flow of trucks delivering garbage to the corporation dump was punctuated by factory horns and hooters, whilst down the street boys revved and tuned old motorbikes and screamed up and down showing off their machines. It was all such a contrast to the sedate Waldrons.

As we entered the gates of the power station and headed to the coke dispensary, huge machinery clanked and thundered on either side of us, cranes dealt out huge quantities of coal and diggers pushed it into place. Steam hissed and everyone had to shout to be heard as they delivered their order. They had a minimum of what they would sell, so we had to ration our visits.

Once we had the hang of lighting the fire, we had warmth none of us had ever experienced before. Our new living rooms were half the size of the ones we had come from and we were all as snug as bugs in rugs. Our bedrooms were still cold and damp, however.

One day in conversation Benny told us about Puggy Mearns. Benny was like that, he would let you make a mistake before telling you that he had seen it coming, or let you go one way and then tell you the way that you should have gone. After you had paid so much a pound for apples, he would tell you where they were cheaper.

"Ol' Puggy Mearns sells coal an' that," he said one day out of the blue.

"Puggy?"

"Ol' Puggy Mearns sells coal an' 'e ain't got no eyes an' 'e's deaf as a post."

Benny chuckled mysteriously.

"What was his name again?" I asked and Benny repeated it several times before I could understand what he was saying. For all I knew he was making it up; Benny was the creator of many of the nicknames on the estate, like 'Shannybags'. But this part of Croydon used many words that I have not come across since, and I knew by now that to 'pug something up' or 'pug it away' meant to hide something. Could Puggy have something to do with hidden things, I wondered? Benny either failed to catch my drift or was deliberately unforthcoming.

"Is he cheaper than down at the power station?" I asked.

"About the same but it's worth it just to look at 'im. 'E's only got white eyes, no middle bits like we 'ave, an' 'e's got an ol' woman what 'e shouts at all the time an' 'e shouts at everybody an' it ain't 'alf scary an' 'e's black like the bleedin' coal an' all."

Benny had done it again. He took a huge interest in everything around him, and once again had whetted our appetites to see this character. Blind Puggy Mearns. He sounded like some character out of Robert Louis Stevenson.

In fact, Puggy Mearns turned out to be real. He had a coal yard down on the Mitcham Road. You entered by two wooden gates into a cobbled yard. In front of you was a giant heap of coal that spilled out from under a slate roof into a covered area, from where old Puggy Mearns served his reverential customers. I say reverential, because usually when we queued up for anything there was a lot of banter and small talk among the clientele, but not in Puggy's yard.

I took my place at the back of the small line of people, and soon someone joined on the back of me, and to the background sounds of a shovel being scraped across cobbles and its contents being dropped into a metal pan, we slowly moved forward. As we neared the front of the queue I noticed that Benny was getting quite excited as he guessed what my reaction might be, and I could hear him trying to suppress nervous laughter. Every now and then I could hear an old, but not frail, voice bellow out, "That's a pahnd ain't it?" or "That's a ten bob right?"

We turned the corner and I could see the form of the old man as he bent to shovel up another load. By now I was bursting with curiosity to see what he looked like. From the back he seemed to be about five foot six. He had on the remains of an old suit jacket, and his ancient trousers were tucked into an enormous pair of wellington boots. On his head he wore a coalman's peaked cap, with a flap down the back to prevent the dust from going down his neck. He swung the shovel away from my direction on to an old scale, and to check if he had the right weight he touched the scoop with a black grimy hand to see if it was level.

As his customer handed him a note, Puggy Mearns leaned forward in the direction of the donor and bellowed, "It's a pahnd ain't it?"

"Yes," answered the customer.

"EH!?"

"Yes it's a pound," repeated the customer, a little louder.

"Go on then," said Puggy Mearns, "she'll give you yer change," and he motioned with his head in the direction of an old woman who sat at a small table with a cash box on it.

The sight of her made me jump and do a double take. She was as dirty as the old man and covered with a film of coal dust. Her fingers and nails

were black and her skin was pale and grey. As she doled out the change her husband pocketed the pound note and this seemed to be their way of handling the money: if you paid in coins you gave it to the old girl and if you paid with paper you gave it to the old man.

I shuffled forward a few feet, unable to wrest my gaze from the old lady. She reminded me of someone from my past and I couldn't think who it was. I turned back to express my incredulity at her appearance to Benny and as I did so I looked up to where Puggy Mearns had come into my eye line. In spite of all that Benny had said, I was not prepared for the sight that stood in front of me.

Puggy had swung around to confront his next customer.

"Yus?" he barked and I stood frozen to the spot.

There almost in front of me was the most terrifying individual I had ever clapped eyes on. He must have been all of eighty years old and weighed about ten stone. In spite of the coal dust, there was enough hair showing to indicate that whatever he had under the hat ought to have been white. His skin was pallid, with all the larger pores completely filled in with black. Around his mouth was coal dust set like mascara round an eyelid closed on an empty socket, for he had not a tooth in his head.

But his eyes, oh Christ, his eyes were awful. They were both completely covered by cataract. Each eye was as if someone had placed a sixpence in a saucer and poured a little milk over it. Just below the surface two pale irises, now as grey as the rest of his skin, stared unblinking and unseeing into the gloom of his shed from the sockets in his head. The dust had long since ceased to irritate the skin and there was no trace of redness to show any inflammation, whilst settled into the corner of each orb was a lump of coal grit big enough to throw on a fire.

Suddenly it was my turn to address him as I wheeled the old barrow up to the scales.

"Yus?" barked Puggy Mearns.

I don't know if it was terror that made me respond the way I did, or fear of being shouted at again. I was almost as tall as the old man and my wide eyes had not left his sightless ones. I leaned toward where his ear should have been and to my horror I saw that under his cap there was just a hole that led down some sooty passage into his head. As I recoiled from the orifice I hardly recognised the sound that came from my lips in a sort of strangulated yell.

"Half hundredweight of coal!" I screamed, and as a polite afterthought,

"please!"

The old man bent to his task without a flinch. Amongst the acrid smell of accumulated coal dust there was also the faint smell of urine. I stood back to allow him to expertly balance the scale and handed him the ten shilling note.

"Ten bob ain't it?" he bellowed.

"Yus!" I yelled back.

"She'll give you your change." He motioned to the old girl as he pocketed the note. As I wheeled the old barrow over to her I recognised her as the witch that jumped out of the wardrobe at me when we lived at The Waldrons, and a shiver went down my back as her cold grey hand plonked out the silver change.

"What'cha say?" hollered old Puggy Mearns at his next terrified customer. "Speak up why can't yer speak up like that last bloke what's the matter wiv everyone these days. You have to shout or I can't 'ear a bleedin' word. What'cha want?"

Once again the two sightless orbs instinctively rolled upwards as if to seek divine explanation.

As Benny and I wheeled the barrow out of the yard and into the thin sunshine outside, we grinned at each other. I couldn't think of anything to say for a while; it was like some miraculous escape from hell for me.

I kept thinking of old Puggy Mearns and his wife climbing out of their dusty bed from under their black sheets, eating crushed coal nuts instead of corn flakes off dusty plates, sprinkling coal dust on everything before they ate. I wondered if they ever bathed, or perhaps like summer birds they had dust baths and then sprinkled coal dust in places usually reserved for talcum powder. Had they ever made love? Perhaps they 'smoked' in bed! When he blew off perhaps he blew smoke rings from his bottom. How did he lose his teeth? Where did his ear go?

We had crossed the Mitcham Road before I could say anything at all, and then all I could manage was, "They were both filthy," and then, "those horrible eyes and no teeth."

"I bet 'e sucks raw eggs," said Benny inexplicably.

"I wonder what his sheets look like?"

"I wonder what 'is underpants look like?" said Benny, and we both guffawed.

"An' I wonder what 'er pants bleedin' look like?" said Benny, and suddenly we both wanted to change the subject.

"I suppose it doesn't matter to him if it's day or night," I thought out loud, "he can shovel away by moonlight and he wouldn't know. I wonder if he was always blind. Do you think he knows what she looks like?"

"I bet 'e don't know about washin' 'isself. An' she ain't goin' to tell 'im is she, 'cos that way the old girl don't need to go down the bag wash an' she saves money."

"Maybe he has a bath in the summer when the people don't need coal."

"Yeah," said Benny.

We rounded the corner into Miller Road.

"I told you 'e was bleedin' scary didn' I?" said Benny.

"Yeah, he certainly was horrible," I answered. "He wasn't stupid though. I mean he kept all the money didn't he?"

"Yeah," pondered Benny.

"Next time we'll take Bruce to see him."

"Yeah," said Benny as he peeled off to his house.

"See you."

"S-s-s-see ya," said Benny.

∾

old puggy mearns

Old Puggy Mearns was born in a coal mine
Damp dark noise level
Holler and shout
North south east
Without a pick or shovel
His teeth went west when he gnawed his way out

Old Puggy Mearns works in the coal hole
Cobble clatter shovel splatter
All night long
Sunshine moonlight
It really doesn't matter
If you can't see the present and the past's all gone

Old Puggy Mearns had a dad who was a sewer rat
Slimy slithery
His mother was a mole
Great big hands
With skin all leathery
Handy sort of grabs when you're shovelling coal

Old Puggy Mearns never has his klobbah washed
Squeak squelch rustle bustle
Smelly old clothes
When he sits down
Little clouds of dust'll
Rise from his collar and vanish up his nose

Old Puggy Mearns if you ever tried to bath him
Slop slurp fizz bubble
He's bound to have a fit
Wright's coal tar
Wouldn't get you out of trouble
Blocking up the plughole with his sludge and grit

Old Puggy Mearns has never ate an apple yet
Sucks on a lump of coal
Before he starts
Coal dust breakfast
Coke in the sugar bowl
Breath like an ashtray and smoky old farts

Old Puggy Mearns has got a dirty old woman
Sits in the corner
Smells like the drains
She has to look at him
He's never seen her
He keeps the pound notes she gives the change

Old Puggy Mearns ain't got a proper ear
Waxed up sooty little
Hole in his head
Deaf as a slag heap
Oil black dribble spittle
Burn him in the fireplace when he's dead

∾

PART FOUR

THE FACTS OF LIFE

facts

The effects of such episodes as Mr. Harvey's abuse in our last year at Howard Junior School are somewhat ameliorated by the realisation that there are girls in the world, and by the age of eleven I had been in sort of love with a dozen or so. It was usually centred on one particular feature that the girl possessed: her lips, her eyes or maybe her hair; the way she laughed or appeared not to notice me; her brashness or shyness. Or her changing shape.

Allison Rees had breasts at the age of ten, and by the time I left Howard School many of the girls were, as it were, sprouting. I asked the worldly-wise Chick Edgerton about girls changing shape as he had a sister, and somehow we got on to the subject of Miss Collet, who was very glamorous by our school's standards. She was young and very pretty, often wearing red which contrasted beautifully with her shortish blonde hair and dark brown eyes. She had the most pointed breasts we had ever seen, the points pricking provocatively at her red sweater.

Chick explained, "That's because she's got braziers *(sic)*." He wasn't sure exactly what they were but explained that they were principally invented for skiing. I have pondered this statement many times over the years and have come to the conclusion that her shape must have confused him and perhaps he was thinking of the Dolomites.

Originally I'd been offered a place at Archbishop Tennyson School, a secondary selective, and after my initial disappointment at not making it through to grammar school, I was content within myself that I would be able to handle what I supposed might be an easier level of work. This easing of the pressure meant that I passed the eleven-plus exam and Mum duly gave me the watch she had been given for passing the equivalent exam twenty-eight years earlier. I was extremely proud of the watch, although I did think after a while that it might have been more masculine in appearance.

When the letter came telling me that I had been awarded a place at John Ruskin Grammar School I was both thrilled and apprehensive.

One of the worst aspects for me in going there was the thought that there would be no girls at the school. I had to be content with dopey daydreams about pretty girls on the bus on their way to schools further up the road from our own.

It was in the first year at John Ruskin that I first heard the expression 'facts of life'. I became intrigued because amongst some kids these words always produced nudges and sly smiles. What did they know that I didn't?

One of the other schools in Croydon had decided to tell its pupils about the Facts, and I searched out one of the kids and asked him what they were. I don't think he properly understood or was really interested, and he just answered that it was "where babies are made." I suddenly realised that I had no idea how where or why babies were made—I just assumed that when you are married they arrived in due course. Some people were unable to have them because the lady had something wrong with her, and sometimes a lady had babies without being married because she had loved someone very much and it had happened without them getting married. I guess that was the closest I came to understanding.

I talked about it to my friends that had come up with me from Howard School: Vernon Burford, Michael Schwartz and Andrew Smith, but they could throw no light on the matter.

Help was at hand from an older boy called Cook. This lad was in the third year and was part of a pack of kids who were always grabbing other boys by the genitals. He befriended some of the first year boys; perhaps he was attracted to them in some way. He never interfered with them and seemed quite a kind and caring boy to me. He made it his business to

tell Michael Schwartz the whole story, and although we got all the technical information second-hand from Michael, it was pretty close to correct. On the way home on the bus that evening Michael told us the Facts.

I sat there open-mouthed. I was shocked, fascinated, sickened, excited, and had to say that I could not believe it. As the story unfolded, I found myself thinking about all the people I knew and tried to imagine them making love. It didn't add up. Try as I might, the thought of my grandparents doing it or my uncles and aunts was impossible to picture. I started to run through images of people in my street and the same incredulity hit me. Then I thought of some of the girls at school and got a funny feeling. I thought of Brigitte Bardot and hoped that it might be true, and then I had to change the subject or at least try to make us all laugh.

"It can't be true," I said. "Can you imagine my mum doing that?"

"Can you imagine *my* mum doing that?" asked Vernon, whose mum was a lot older than ours and almost crippled. None of us could possibly imagine Vernon's mum allowing anyone to do that to her.

"Well can you imagine my mum or dad doing it either?" asked Michael Schwartz and suddenly we all fell silent, because that's exactly what we could imagine Michael Schwartz's parents doing.

After a couple of seconds of non-confirmation from any of us Michael asked us, "What are you all thinking?"

Suddenly I burst out laughing and said, "What if it's true?"

We looked around the bus at the passengers. and began asking each other, "Do you think she does it? Do you think he does it? I bet he's never done it."

A fat man got on and we all said, "He couldn't do it even if he wanted to!"

Next morning as usual I saw Michael Schwartz on the bus with Andrew, and the look on Michael's face confirmed it.

"It's true," he said.

I looked at Andrew and Andrew nodded.

"My dad says that you do it on your honeymoon, and at first you don't but then you start to think that you would like to, and then you do it and it is a gift from God."

I started to think of Andrew's mother and father and I just could not picture them doing it. Then I thought of my own parents and I could sort of see my dad doing it but not my mum, and then I thought of Mr. and

Mrs. Schwartz doing it.

And then a pretty girl got on the bus and I *knew* that was how it was done.

Suddenly I understood why people tut-tutted when a girl had a baby when she was not married, and wondered where I might find one who might do it. What did it feel like to do it? All the films and jokes that were half understood before, I understood more fully and then another girl got on the bus and I wondered if she did it.

Derek Lester's sister was having a baby and she was only fifteen. So she'd done it!

I suppose most of my childhood ended right there on the 130 bus to New Addington.

In 1957 I had reached class 3U, which was the cramming stream for university entrance. It hadn't taken long to work out that I wasn't going to make the grade, and I'd decided to discharge myself. The only really surprising thing was that I had the courage to do it without consulting anyone. I just walked into the headmaster's office after break one morning and told him I had to leave, as I couldn't stand the pace of work or the commitment to the extra load that we were expected to cope with each evening.

The headmaster's name was Lowe and he reminded me a little of my Granddad in appearance; he was a dapper man with an air of calm authority. I suppose he could see the anxiety in my eyes, because he treated me very kindly as I told him my story; he even went so far as to tell me that I shouldn't have been put in the university stream as my second exam results were not quite up to it—I had come eleventh in my first exam and seventeenth in my second. I was a bit put out at this news, but soon realised it would soften the blow when I had to tell Mum.

Mr. Lowe asked me what I wanted to do when I left school, and without a hint of embarrassment I replied that I would like to be a missionary. He was taken aback slightly by this, as even in 1957 there was not much call for these people—at least not in the way that I saw the job. I had always been keen on religion, but at this time I was in the midst of a religious fervour: I'd joined the Scripture Union where I had to read the bible every day, and on Sundays, as described earlier, I was rushing around Croydon between Mint Walk Mission, Sunday School and St. Andrews Church Choir.

On top of this, my voices hadn't yet stopped, and above my bed at home I had assembled a number of religious artefacts including texts, pictures of Jesus, a crucifix and some beads—not altogether with my mother's approval, as she thought it smacked of Catholicism. I used to lie in bed and pray great long rambling prayers, which gave me comfort in my insecurity and darker moments.

Mr. Lowe handled my surprising answer with aplomb.

"Are you good at Latin?" he asked.

"Yes sir," I answered. I was indeed top of the form in that subject.

"Well, that should come in handy," he responded as he groped (and failed) for something further to say.

The result of the interview was that I was transferred down to form 2W.

Standing there nervously in front of the head, I was painfully aware of my distressed—as in, poor but honest—appearance. The first brand new clothes I'd ever had in my life should have been my school uniform, and I recall Mum sitting there in our damp basement looking at the list of items that we were supposed to buy from Horne's on Lower Crown Hill, and almost crying because there was no way we had money for any of that stuff. I wished I'd never passed the exam and was feeling thoroughly miserable and a little angry that the school would send this to someone like us.

Thankfully help was at hand, for at the bottom of the page was a list of part-worn items that were offered to help poor families like ours. When I entered the headmaster's office I was still wearing the same (secondhand) jacket I'd had in the first year; the badge which Mum had sewn on was now grey in the white bits between the shield, under which was written "Age Quod Agis"; and I was still squeezed into one of the two drip-dry shirts that we had bought to start my grammar school career. My shoes were a slightly more elaborate Teddy boy style than was properly sanctioned, and my trousers, well, they had a story all of their own…

When we lived at The Waldrons, the top floor flat was occupied by Mr. and Mrs. Clarke. Mrs. Clarke was the married sister of the Miss Dickinsons, who lived below her. She had congratulated me warmly when she'd heard that I passed the eleven-plus exam, and it was she that gave me the trousers, my first pair of long trousers. They had belonged to her

only son, who had been killed in the war as a navigator in a bomber plane. As she handed them over to my mother with this tale she burst into tears, and my mum said how much we appreciated the gift and that I would treasure them.

I was very moved by this experience. A boy's first long trousers are an important moment in his life; they are an affirmation of approaching manhood and a celebration of his departure from childhood. Mine, however, were an artefact of a dead eighteen-year-old hero and when I wore them I was conscious of bearing the mantle of his sacrifice. Although they were styled in the Oxford bag style of the thirties, made from the itchiest flannel known to man and were two inches too short for me, I had a duty to wear them. After all, what was my discomfort and embarrassment compared to his sacrifice? Mum had got round the problem of length by sewing false turnups into the bottoms, which she assured me no-one would ever notice. This assertion however proved false as they were noted by some bully the first day I wore them.

"What are you wearing brat?" he shouted. All first years were called "brats" and this was encouraged to some extent by a few teachers.

"They're my false turnups," I replied helpfully.

"False Turnups!" the bully exploded. "Oi come and look at this fellas! The brat's wearing False Turnups in his trousers, let's de-bag him!"

Fortunately for me the bell went for the end of break and I was spared the humiliation of having my pants pulled down by these older boys. I made a note of this particular one anyway, and some time later I sorted him out, which took a good deal of bravery on my part. I lived in fear of retribution for a whole term, but like most bullies he didn't bother me after I had faced up to him.

After I'd successfully negotiated myself down from form 3U to 2W, our school year decided to have a party, and our kindly form master Percy Wright asked us all if we could contribute a 'turn' or two for the entertainment. Enquiries amongst my contemporaries revealed that several boys in my class could or would play if we could get it together, so we formed a skiffle group, with Chris Ricketts and Derek Roach on uke and ukulele banjo and someone I've forgotten on tea chest bass. We submitted our idea to Mr. Wright, and he demanded an audition in his physics lab after school.

We were all as nervous as could be as he perched himself on the lab

desk and told us to commence. I am sure he was astonished at the volume we managed, but we certainly swung and he coloured up and was unable to stave off a grin although he tried turning toward the blackboard so that we should not see it. After racing through our first number he stopped us halfway through *Oh Boy* with a wave of his hand, and we waited until he said, "OK you can play," and then quietly, "Well done, boys. Go along then May, and take your band of tub thumpers with you."

We might as well have been handed a record contract, we felt so good. We met after school for smokes and rehearsal at Derek's place, where his father was warden of what was then known as a spastic centre. We had a great time practising and wheelchair racing; there were extensive grounds and even a tennis court (though I didn't play); and all the time Mr. Roach was keeping a weather eye on us and telling us about his cycle racing days, when racing bikes were fitted with wooden rims. He was a very kind man and he shared his Capstan Full Strength cigarettes with us. It was a matter of young male pride to smoke these fearsome tar-laden monsters without hiccuping or coughing, which we did. These days on Oakhill Road were some of the happiest at school for me.

The concert arrived, and although the other kids had to wear school uniform, we were allowed to dress more informally. With our plinky plonky sound, we were the undoubted hit of the evening. It was a wonderful feeling seeing our pals gyrating to our music, especially as we were standing on the same stage in the school hall from which our headmaster delivered his warnings, speeches, sermons and exhortations. We only played five tunes, but the evening belonged to us.

The next day it was back to normal and this would-be heartthrob was falling in love with another girl on top of the 130 bus to New Addington...

Tom Shaw joined form 2W shortly after I did. From the moment he walked into the class he stood out, with his almost film star good looks and his school badge sewn on to a double-breasted jacket. His hair did what he wanted it to do and he was already shaving at least part of his face. Tom was a year older than the rest of us. He had recently returned from America and spoke to no-one, which just added to his air of cool. He was seated in the desk in front of me and I was determined to make him my friend.

With his fingers deeply ingrained with nicotine from his American Chesterfield cigarettes, he was drawn into the smokers' group compris-

ing Les, Vernon and myself, and was the first boy I'd seen who could gently expel the smoke from his lips and inhale it gracefully up both nostrils. Tom didn't just inhale the smoke, he almost ate it. Each time he lit up he seemed to find a new trick to convey his deep satisfaction with the habit. Tom was an elegant smoker; each time he took out a cigarette he tapped it on the flat side of the box, so that a tiny rim of paper could be turned in to prevent strands of tobacco getting stuck on his lip.

He had a Ronson Variflame gas lighter which had a perfectly measured flame and always lit first time. On a still evening behind the bike sheds he could produce beautiful large smoke rings, and indoors he would make tiny rings by tapping his cheek gently with his finger. He would flick the ash off his cigarette any number of different ways, from gently removing it with his little finger or thumbnail to tapping lightly on the top of its length. Just before throwing it away he would sometimes grip the end between his bottom teeth and his lower lip and turn it into his mouth whilst the thing was still alight.

Tom's mother allowed him to smoke at home, and as if all this was not exotic enough, she was a divorcee. Divorce still carried a racy image in those days, and a bit of a stigma. Most unhappy couples just rubbed along in misery or, as in our family, one of the partners left home. The implication of divorce was adultery and this was quite exciting. The only other divorced person I had known was Mrs. Leisk but she could not be described as exotic, and anyway she had divorced her husband for his affair. I always wondered if it was Mrs. Shaw's own affair which caused them to part.

Tom's accent had no trace of Stateside twang, but there was a sophistication about him that went beyond his one year seniority, and maybe because of our similar parental circumstances we were soon good friends and joined the school army cadet force together. Neither of us had any interest at school outside of the army cadets but we did share a sense of humour. It was not long before Tom stayed over at my house and my mother, who found him very handsome, used to give him tea and put him up on the sofa. In those days all mums were addressed as "Mrs. —" and Tom was very polite and charming, which impressed my mother. It was a long time before I met Mrs. Shaw.

One day Tom's elder brother Roy, who was a young officer in the merchant navy, returned from sea and gave Tom a present that totally confirmed Tom's superiority. Somewhere in his travels Roy had acquired the first transistor radio that we had ever seen. By today's standards it was quite large, but in 1957 it seemed minute—battery-powered radios at that time were the size of small suitcases. As the kids gathered round to marvel at this gadget in the playground an idea was forming in my head.

It has to be said that form 2W was beginning to get a reputation (confirmed the following year in form 3D) of being one of the worst behaved classes in the school. I would prefer it to be described as mischievous, and the challenge we set ourselves—and I was one of the prime movers—was to make our misdemeanours as subtle as possible.

We were genuinely fond of many of the teachers we were able to fool. Mr. Neal was a very dark-haired man who dressed in a comfortable tweed jacket and corduroy trousers. He took the class for English and he had a warm mellifluous voice that often nearly lulled me to sleep. We decided it was to be him who would be amazed by this little wonder.

Our classrooms were quite modern and the blackboard occupied most of the wall we faced. To the right of the board was a switch which controlled the three radio stations on the BBC, with the loudspeaker high up on the wall. It was a bright morning as Mr. Neal breezed into the room, his gown flowing behind him.

"Good morning boys!" he said with that mixture of authority and confidence that today he was going to get through the lesson without it descending into noise and anarchy.

"Good morning sir," we chirped with unusual enthusiasm. He looked up suspiciously, alerted to the change from our usual desultory response, and I thought I could see just a hint of optimism that perhaps we had decided enough was enough and that we were all going to start to work like grammar school boys were supposed to. He turned and began to write something on the blackboard about clause analysis.

Tom switched on his radio at a very low volume so that you could just hear the sibilant sounds of voices through the tiny speaker. The class was eerily quiet as we waited to see the teacher's reaction. As his handwriting moved over to the right hand side of the board he put down the chalk, reached over to the radio switch and turned it one click. Tom responded

immediately by synchronising his off switch at the same time and the tinny noise stopped. No sooner was Mr. Neal back writing when on came the radio again.

"Somebody turn that thing off," said our teacher, and one of the boys got up and walked to the switch and pretended to turn it off. The pattern was set, and no sooner was the teacher's back turned than on came the radio. I still don't know if he had sussed exactly what was going on, but he must have been a little suspicious at the absence of talking, as we all strained in the quiet to enjoy his bafflement at the sounds which he presumed were coming from the speaker on the wall. Once the class work was set he sat down and looked at us all and especially those he knew to be ringleaders, but we buried our heads in our work—as much to disguise our sniggering as to avoid his search. Now the radio began its journey around the room being switched on and off by fingers under desks. The effect was perfect, and Mr. Neal duly obliged with all the range of expressions we would have asked for.

Annoyance gave way to curiosity, and when he asked plaintively, "Does it appear to anyone else that the sound is coming from all four corners of the room?", it was all too much for Les at the back who just exploded into one of his deep guffaws, and that started us all off.

"Just what is going on?" asked Mr. Neal as he stood up and wandered round the room with the radio following behind him, being passed from hand to hand and switched on and off in an aural game of hide and seek. Finally he swung round in the right direction just in time to catch Tom receiving the radio. He pounced and took it from him.

"What on earth is this?" he said in genuine astonishment, and instead of being angry he was totally amazed at the technology behind the prank. He could have confiscated it, but instead he asked to borrow it to take to the staffroom during the break.

Shortly after this incident Tom took me to his place, where I met his mother. She and Tom lived in an upstairs privately rented flat on the London Road in Norbury. Inside it was quite chaotic and I seldom stayed overnight there.

Mrs. Shaw had more than one man friend, and although Tom never talked about it I knew that he was a little embarrassed by her. I was intrigued because Mrs. Shaw was completely different to my mother. She was small, though putting on a little weight, and she wore glasses

with thick black rims. She never cooked anything, but she liked a drink, and she also liked men. My mum, on the other hand, cooked, hated drink and hardly ever went out with blokes—my brother and I only wished she would.

Tom's mum was a bit coy the first few times we called round, but she soon accepted my visits and didn't try to put on any airs, with her eyes swollen with sleep, a cigarette in her mouth and that sexy early morning rasp in the voice. She had a strong Liverpool accent and spoke in a whiny, sing-song sort of way. She wore a smart suit to work, but at home I never saw her wearing anything other than her nightie, and her thick black hair was always mussed up by sleep, or lack of it. She had an unmerciful cough and smoked all the time, and was often very seriously hung over when we made our late morning calls round at the flat.

Her latest beau was called Arthur. Working-class and worldly wise, he was smartly turned out in a way that suggested that, though he might not be actually involved in crime, he would definitely know a few strokes. He always wore a bow tie and his sideboards were longer than they ought to have been for a man in his late forties.

Mrs. Shaw was always saying that she was going to throw him out or chuck him in, but the truth is that Arthur kept her laughing, and although they were too old to be sexually exciting to a teenage boy, it was titillating to know that they were in a relationship for the pure fun of company, drink and sex, as opposed to the worthy obligation of keeping a home together solely for the purpose of raising children. Or living my mum's seemingly joyless, husbandless existence as she worked to feed us and dutifully see us through into the world.

Arthur belonged to a breed that I am not aware of any more. There was no doubt that he had been a bit of a lad in his time but he was sort of settled in his ways now although he'd never married. He might have admired younger women but one suspected he was perfectly happy with older ones, who were grateful for his attentions and made very few demands on his time.

They were an odd couple. Tom's mother would have been described as a handsome woman in Victorian times. From her appearance—the black hair and eyes, a slightly aquiline nose and full lips—I guessed that her origins were Mediterranean. Arthur looked so English as to be a caricature of one of the betting fraternity, with a centre parting, blazer and slacks. He smoked Senior Service and always obliged us two thirteen-

year-olds with smokes, and if he was waiting for Mrs. Shaw to go out he would talk to us about some of his escapades. I found these stories hilarious and daring, although I guess that Tom felt he might be trying to win him over by being nice. I didn't hear it as being patronising, as even at that young age I had seen enough to know that Arthur had absolutely no intention of ever getting permanently hitched to Tom's mum.

∾

ice

Mrs. Shaw was the catering manageress at Streatham Ice Rink. Her office was upstairs in the far right corner of the ballroom that most people attending the rink did not know existed. Behind this door was the catering area, and in the corner of this room was her inner sanctum, where she had access to a safe and a strongly locked cupboard where the spirits and cigarettes were stored. I often found myself staring longingly at the cupboard.

"It's a good job you haven't got X-ray eyes, Ralph. You'd burn your way right through that padlock," she would say to me. It was to this office that Tom and I were summoned one day, and Mrs. Shaw offered us both a job.

"We need some help clearing up the cups down on the rink," she said, "and there's some washing up and general cleaning in the kitchen there too, and there might be some weekend work doing weddings up here if all goes well. It'll pay ten shillings for Wednesday evenings and a pound for all day Saturday. And you can start this Saturday."

It must have taken me a hundredth of a second to say yes, but Tom strangely declined. I suppose it was the idea of being under his mum again, but that didn't bother me and I jumped at the opportunity.

"You are a lazy bugger, Tom," she moaned as she led us downstairs to

the rear of the rink to meet Alice the tea lady.

I liked Alice immediately. She deferred madly to Mrs. Shaw, screwing up her eyes and smiling ingratiatingly, but she had her pride all right. Slight and wiry, though stooped, with her hair parted neatly on the side and a kind of Esme Cannon twitter, she took tiny quick steps wherever she went, like someone who not only knows where they are going, but wants to get there quickly and get on with the next thing even quicker.

Alice worked in a continuum, each action leading to another. Even when it was time for a fag she would pick up a rag and start wiping the metal surfaces down, whilst running a bucket of water for me to wash down the floors—which we had to do at least once every skating session.

On weekdays outside of school holiday times she managed the tea bar on her own, but she was glad of my help and I was very happy working with her. She was one of the sweetest ladies I've ever worked with. Alice's patience was extraordinary as she taught me how to mop and wash floors properly, how to make the tea in the big pots and stack the shelves with bottles.

I learned how to carry crates of Pepsi-Cola by squeezing four bottles in two hands so that the bottles themselves gripped the wooden partitions that prevented them breaking against each other, and was soon able to stack them ten high using this method just like the delivery men. I loaded the fag machines and took out the empties and collected tea cups from all round the rink, and if it was quiet (which it seldom was) she would tell me to go for a skate. I even got quite proficient, given the horrendous condition of the wobbly-sided hacked-out things that passed for figure skates there.

I have loved skating rinks ever since those days, I think because they are romantic places for kids. There is a sense of fun, danger and sex in the freezing air, and flushed faces as kids learn the art of display and flirting, intrigues and spills. I quickly became aware of the culture of the rink and the wonderful diversity of characters there. Since moving from the comparative gentility of The Waldrons I had met some rough and ready people and was fast becoming a young man. Those closest around you hardly notice the changes going on, but as I entered the rink, I was fair game to the old girls at the tea bar. I was still taken aback, however, by old Mary and 'young' Margaret.

Mary was five foot tall and weighed about seventeen stone. She must

have been in her early to mid sixties. Her grey hair was probably quite long, but as soon as she had married she'd rolled it up in a loose bun to be practical, and there it remained. To denote rank she wore a blue and white striped overall with a whitish apron. Alice only ever wore white as did I, a usually ragged but clean starched jacket. Old Beatrice, the washer-up, wore menial green.

Beattie, as she was always known, could have passed for Alice's mother. She was about the same stature as Alice but even more stooped, and had one of those London accents that have all but disappeared. Sometimes you can hear it on old music hall artists' recordings of comic songs. The 'r' is rolled and the accent is far more animated than now. It was the only thing that was animated about Beattie; she moved incredibly slowly, but the other women liked her and probably kept her with them out of kindness. I think Beattie must have had the prototype National Health false teeth: they were as white as snow with bright red gums, and as she spoke there was a constant battle to keep them in place.

Because of the general jollity of the place there were a lot of smiles, and this too was a hazard for Beattie: several times I saw the top set fly out of her mouth into the washing up water, as something Mary or Alice had said made her chuckle. There would then follow a fairly frantic search among the cups and saucers before that which was lost was found, rinsed and returned, rejoicing, to join the other ill-fitting bottom row. It was a good job the punters didn't know.

Beattie was occasionally short with me, and when angry it sounded as if she had a marble clattering around in her mouth, as she battled to keep both sets in place whilst still sounding stern enough in her rebuke. Lip-reading would have been out of the question as her lips had become prehensile and were able to grasp under and over the two sets of teeth to stop them leaving her mouth altogether. Beattie would not have looked out of place in a hospital bed. She wore slippers and hardly ever came out of her still room area, except when I would bring her a cup of tea. She would pick it up and sip it then without a word walk over to the urn and tip it away and proceed to make a fresh pot.

"Never give a worker a stewed cuppa char," she would intone wisely.

Later Mary showed me how to make an individual cup of tea without a pot, for when one of the big bosses came down: take a big tea strainer and fill it up with tea, slowly dribble boiling water through the leaves so that the tea brews as it goes into the cup, then add just enough milk to

get it to the right colour.

From then on that's how I did Beattie's tea, and I think by the end she liked me, though she never got my name right, either deliberately or because she thought Ralph was too posh. I was sometimes Alf, and when it suited her the odd compromise Rilf was used.

Mary also always wore carpet slippers for work, with thick brown stockings. She had a huge bosom that she used to wave her hand in front of to show if she was working too hard, and she called everyone "darlin'". Mary was unwilling or unable to walk at anything faster than a slow sauntering shuffle, like Indian ladies in saris in summer, although she still made a slight breeze when she moved past you because of her density.

Mary's favourite adjective was "bleedin'" and away from the customers' ears she used it a lot. Mary had a great sense of humour and a sense of irony to go with it. She also learned very early on that it was easy to make me blush especially where sexual matters were concerned, and she never let an opportunity go by without trying it on.

"What's that in your pocket, darlin'?" she might say.

I would look down in all innocence and reply, "Nothing, why?"

"I thought you was trying to steal a bottle of Pepsi."

"Now come on Mary," I would say, "you know I wouldn't take anything without asking."

"Well what's that long thing I can see in your trousers? Perhaps it's a tube of Smarties. Let me have a feel to see if you're tellin' the truth."

By now of course I had sussed what was going on, and so had the others. Old Beattie would just grin and tut-tut, shaking her head without looking round, but Alice would giggle and put her hand to her mouth and give Mary a playful slap and tell her she was awful. If Mary saw me so much as put my hand in my pocket she would enquire after my 'thing'. I was a source of amusement to the old girls, but Margaret was a different matter.

Margaret was the sub-manageress in the tea bar and upstairs bar; she was unhappily married and always dressed to kill, with loads of make-up on. She was a tough south London girl in her early forties, and her only blemish was that she had lost a leg in a motorcycle accident when still a young girl.

The leg had been amputated just above the knee, but by wearing a

skirt that was a little longer than fashionable, she was able to disguise it until she had to walk any distance. The knee joint was operated by throwing her leg forward which, even when she was trying to be sexy, gave her a rather too military gait for most of her intended prey. However, Albie the dustman found her the most attractive woman in the world, and though I never actually saw him skate, he never missed showing up at any session that she was on.

I could see that Margaret had no intention of ever running away from her marriage, and though she often feigned irritability with Albie always hanging about, in reality she loved it. Albie was about twenty-eight and not terribly bright; his face had the appearance of being crushed in the tube train doors, as his features were sort of pushed together, but bone and muscle had got in the way and this had forced his eyes to jockey for position on his face. It resulted in a slightly crooked smile and eyes at different heights. The overall effect was that he looked both dangerous and puzzled at the same time.

Albie was still a Teddy boy; he wore a drape jacket and chukka boots, and his hair was his crowning glory in an elaborate Tony Curtis style. Once I had shown the proper respect and awe for him, he trusted me and I found him to be a simple but honourable friend. Albie was totally besotted by Margaret and he saw no imperfection even in her purposeful walk. Sometimes they would go for a drink together, but Albie wasn't really a drinker—he would have gone anywhere just to be near her. Drink helped Margaret to sin a little.

Mary was always telling Margaret she should oblige him, but somehow Margaret kept him at bay with hints and teases that he must have loved, for he stayed true to her all the time that I knew them both.

Mary also told Margaret that I was fair game and at fourteen quite a big boy for my age. To them I must have had 'innocent' written in huge letters across my forehead. Margaret joined in the fun, especially on Friday or Saturday nights when she often went up to the licensed bar and had just a little too much. She would come down to the tea bar looking a little flushed and send for me in the kitchen, then ask me to reach some item on the shelf behind her. As I raised my arm she would deliberately press herself up against me or let the back of her hand brush against my trousers, which always made me jump. This was a cause of much merriment as I fumbled or dropped whatever I was supposed to get down for her.

Another favourite stunt was to wait until I was on my hands and knees loading up shelves with bottles of Pepsi or lemonade and step over me so that my head was practically inside her skirt. For some reason this amused them the most, and whilst I was there, not daring to move in case I should see where Margaret's stump fitted into her false leg, they all believed I was scared to look up any further for other reasons. I suppose they were partly right, but my biggest fear was that Albie might see her doing this and kill me in a jealous rage. Margaret was delighted with the results of these little scenes and it didn't really trouble me, but I did wish I could control my blushes (which were the principal reason she played these games).

She and Mary were always thinking up new games for me to fall for. When Mary wanted me to mop the floors she would say, "Now darlin', go and get your big long thing and bring it out here!"

The mop lived in a special type of bucket which had a grille welded to the side that you could press the head on to squeeze the water out of the fibres. When I had filled it with water and bleach and brought it out to begin washing, she would instruct me thus:

"Now take your long thing and dip it into that hole [the open side of the bucket]. Now push it in and out slowly—not too quick or you'll spill all your stuff over the floor. That's right, in and out, ooh ain't he got a lovely twirl on that long thing of his."

Another time Mary asked me to go to the fridge and get the ham out to be cut. With no reason to expect anything unusual I opened the big wooden door and moved to pull out the ham. The sight that greeted me took me by surprise for at first I had no idea what I was supposed to be looking at. There in front of me sat two hams turned on their sides and stuck between the two was a Pepsi bottle. I turned round to look behind me where Margaret, Mary, reluctant Alice and old Beattie stood for a second as they burst out laughing, and then it dawned on me that this was an erotic catering sculpture of Pepsi penetration of female genitalia. As the back of my neck went a deep red so their merriment increased. I was rooted to the spot until Alice walked over to the fridge and, reaching over my shoulder, pulled out the bottle. Beattie's teeth had remained in place but Mary was crying with laughter and so was Margaret. For me it was embarrassing but in a strange way liberating. I wondered with trepidation if it really looked like that.

Some time afterward the first wedding reception took place at the

upstairs ballroom overlooking the front of the rink. It was a big do, with a sit down dinner before all the speeches. I was waiting at table, wearing a really good white coat and black cavalry twill trousers with black suede shoes. I was absolutely fascinated by the whole event; everyone was happy and jolly and all the catering staff came out to look at the couple as they sat eating their wedding supper. After the usual remarks about how pretty the bride looked and how handsome the groom, one of the waitresses remarked how well they were all tucking in to the food and drink, and Mary remarked, "Well I hope she saves some room because she'll be chewing on something else later!"

This remark brought peals of laughter from several of the women around but only bewilderment from me. What could it mean? Then I recalled a primitive drawing on the ceiling of the gent's toilet in the Duppas Hill recreation ground. I had to go and get a cold drink to calm myself down but the image stayed with me a long time. A photo of the happy couple was blown up and displayed in the foyer to promote the facility upstairs, and whenever I glanced at it I wondered if she did save some room.

I worked at the rink during school holidays as well as the weekends, and soon I was immersed into ice skating culture. On holiday morning sessions young middle-class kids had private instruction in figure skating circles and figures of eight, monotonously spinning slowly round and round, feet changing direction in the same place each time. Sometimes ice dancers would get the rink for themselves; I remember Diane Peach and an effeminate man called Peter, and although it was not something I would brag about to the boys I enjoyed watching them. All the girls who figure skated wore these little skirts that made their legs look lovely and long, especially when you added the height of the skate. It was often a different story when on the odd occasion you caught them in their normal dress, and the long-limbed glamorous dancer turned out to be a tiny little doll with a big bottom. Some of the girls' thighs were awesome.

The two different types of skates defined how hip you were. The ones available for hire were worn-out cheap figure skates with no support left in the sides, and all the beginners wore these. The hip boys only used hockey skates, which were altogether more macho and American-looking, and some boys had even acquired American high school jackets for wearing on the ice. Every afternoon they cleared the rink for the speed

skaters (mostly lads), and this was really exciting as they whizzed round the ice at breakneck speeds and impossible angles.

For these sessions the music stopped, which was a blessed relief. The sounds were provided by two blokes on organ and traps; no doubt they were competent musicians, but for kids in the fifties there could be little in the world more embarrassing than Buddy Holly tunes played on a Wurlitzer theatre organ. However, when I occasionally see a baseball game and hear the sound of organ and traps, I am transported through time back to the rink, and instead of nauseating me, the sound gives me a warm nostalgic glow.

After a while during these music-free speed sessions I found I could keep up with most of the hockey-booted lads on a pair of borrowed figure skates from the hire shop. There I had become acquainted with a strange bloke who first told me that it was possible to kill a man with a single blow from an oriental sport called 'karachi', and one day he would show me the dark secret if I was sworn to secrecy. He was one of those who like to work in dark holes in the ground, and in this case he must have also loved the smell of feet.

In those days the ice rink was painted in strange thirties abstracts in orange, dark greens and browns and there were couples in fumbling embraces and contorted positions in every corner. Rumours abounded of girls who would let you, and although it certainly looked as if they were, I doubt seriously if a couple could have actually got away with it. But there was certainly a sexiness to the place. My own favourite fantasies were two lovely south London girls, both pretty as a picture but tough too. They dressed the same with shoulder-length brown hair, matching high school jackets, tight blue jeans and white hockey boots. I think it was the white boots that did it. They were the sexiest things on the ice but they never saw me, even on the odd occasion they came up to the tea bar to order a couple of Pepsis.

"That'll be one and six please," I would say provocatively, only they didn't notice. They moved languidly about the ice, completely at home on it, and only quickened their pace to get out of the way of some of the blokes, whose main reason for being there was to speed up to a couple of girls and screech to a stop, spraying ice all over everyone.

Apart from the general kids' recreational skating, Streatham also had a professional ice-hockey team, cleverly named Streatham. They were mostly Canadians, but included a crowd favourite called Danny Wong,

whose feats were apparently the stuff of legend. Their arch rivals were the Paisley Pirates from Scotland. I only saw one match at the rink; most of the hockey games were on Wednesday nights, and from the tea bar they were not really visible. Anyway, team games failed to interest me until many years later, when I was too old to compete.

Boxing, however, was another matter.

In the middle of my time working at the rink, one of Britain's best boxers fought at Streatham. His name was Dave Charnley, and the atmosphere generated on those nights has lived with me ever since. I have never boxed myself, but my brother Bruce did a bit at school and my father was regimental champion at his weight. I did some sparring at the boys' club, but I was too unco-ordinated for the instructor to take me further, and truth to tell I was not unhappy. The sport, though, has fascinated me from about about the age of eight, when I got my *Freddie Mills Boxing Annual*, and I still love the old pictures of fighters on the walls of pubs and theatres.

The two fights I saw were towards the end of the 1950s. Rock'n'roll was established, teenagers had been invented, and the drab dark greens and browns of home decor were slowly being replaced by bright primary colours. Italian wallpaper had arrived, but the hangover of wartime austerity remained and a lot of working-class men were slow to adopt change. Dry-cleaning had been around for years, but few men ever had a suit dry-cleaned and many were the trousers that shone in the daylight from the accumulated dirt in the material. In the winter men wore big old overcoats, stored all summer in mothballed wardrobes, with scarves and caps or trilby hats, and all men smoked.

I cannot tell separate incidents from the two bouts I saw, but I do remember the totally different atmosphere in the rink as the crowds poured in for the event. The normal teenage babble, and kids' playground noises echoing off the ice and banging round the high ceiling and walls, was replaced by the animated but deeper rumble of men's voices. The ice was boarded over and the whole place was warmer than usual. The crowds grew, and as everyone lit up their cigarettes, the lights pierced the darkness like beacons searching for lost souls in the fog. Damp clothing warmed up and the smell of wet wool was added to tobacco and sweat. When at last Charnley entered the ring, the biggest shout I had ever heard in my life up to that point roared in my ears, and as I watched from the vantage

point of the tea bar, I soaked up every bit of the action like a dishcloth and revelled in the maleness of it all.

After the first fight, Margaret took the victorious Charnley some tea and a couple of Pepsis, but the boxing fraternity has just as many superstitions as showbiz people, and women are considered unlucky in a boxer's dressing room. Margaret was not allowed in and had to march back to the tea bar without sharing in the glory—no mean feat for a woman with one leg and all those stairs to climb. Charnley, it appeared, liked ice cream after a fight and she almost had to carry the whole lot back again, but of course I was sent for to take it. At the next fight I remembered his preference and I asked if I might be allowed to go up and deliver it. Margaret confirmed that she wasn't bleedin' well going up there again, so Mary gave me six tubs of assorted flavours (strawberry and vanilla!) and I trooped off upstairs to the changing room behind the bandstand.

Inside the tiny room, surrounded by some of the biggest men I had ever seen, sat the tiny champion. At fourteen I was already as big as him. As I was ushered into the room his back was toward me, and I saw that he was still suffering from teenage acne. He seemed so pale and vulnerable still in his shorts and boots, with these cigar-smoking camelhair-coated admirers around him. Through the thick tobacco haze you could still smell the rubbing liniment and wintergreen that the champ had been anointed with before his ritual.

At first they tried to take the ice cream off me, but I suddenly heard a voice asking if I might be allowed in. I was surprised to find it was my own.

Charnley must have heard my plea, and said, "Let the kid inside," so I got in and handed him the tubs of ice cream and told him how much I appreciated the fight. Not that I saw much, but that's how I got to meet him and it was a great moment for me.

At the first Streatham fight a boxer called Mancini was on the bill. I watched him get beaten on points, much to the disappointment of the crowd, as in spite of his name he seemed to be a local. As the next bout was to begin, the small group who had come to get teas dispersed, and I started clearing the cups away. An unshaven bloke appeared at the counter.

"Cup of tea, son," he said quietly.

I poured him a cup from the big teapot, and as I asked for his sixpence I looked closely at his face.

Blimey, he looks as if he's been in a punch up, I thought. There were contusions under both eyes and a couple of nicks above the left, but it was the look in his eyes that struck me most. It was a forlorn, lost look, and the pain expressed in it was not a physical one but more like a wound to the soul.

"Weren't you just in the ring?" I enquired hesitantly.

"That's right, son."

"You're Mr. Mancini, aren't you?"

"Yeah," he answered and moved to take the handle on the tea cup and lift it to his lips as his eyes looked down and away from me. Before he could raise it up to drink I grabbed it from him and poured it away, then using Mary's method I made him a fresh cup and handed it to him.

"That's on the house," I said magnanimously, and put a sixpence of my own into the till.

"Thanks son," was all he said as he raised his head in acknowledgement. But his eyes still looked into his cup and he slipped off into the shadows to drink it on his own. I never forgot that moment and the lesson it offered: if you lose your fight you have to buy your own tea!

Afterwards I told Mary about it and she said I'd done the right thing and made me take my sixpence back.

Towards the end of my time at the rink I was getting bored and a little lazy. This probably irritated Alice and Mary, who became a little more removed and stopped their constant teasing. It upset me a bit, but time was moving on and there were other things to do. I just did not have a clue what or where they were.

One day Tom's mum sent for me and asked if I'd like to work at Wembley in the car parks for the Cup Final. The job paid thirty shillings for the day, which was a ransom in those days and a third more than I made at the rink. She told me I'd got the job on her recommendation for my honesty. Tom too had a job there, and the two of us set off on the Saturday morning very early around 6 o'clock. Luckily, because it took us two hours to get there, arriving on time at eight. I let Tom do the map reading as I was not prepared to be the one to get us lost, so I didn't complain. It was good to have something on the person whose hair did what he wanted it to do.

At the stadium we were split up and I was assigned to the bicycle and car park, where I was met by Don, a miserable bloke with the skin on his

face and arms already brown from the early spring sunshine, like a deck-chair attendant. He was cockney and his bald head was as brown as his face, which surprised me as most of the time he wore a cap and a white coat.

I was surprised how many people came to the Cup Final on bikes, especially as it was the Rugby League Final and both teams were from up north.

"It's a fuckin' long bike ride from Sheffield!" observed my colleague, as he demonstrated the ticketing method I had to learn. Bikes cost six-pence for the day and motorbikes were a shilling. My mate was pissed off most of the day because he normally worked in the car park, where cars cost more to leave.

He had a little fiddle going, which he felt he had to let me in on. Each bike had two tickets issued when they paid their money over. One of them had glue on the back which enabled it to be stuck on to the bike. The other ticket was to be kept as proof that it was your bike.

"'ere's what you do," said Don. "When they pay you just give 'em one of the tickets and then you can keep the other ticket and sell it to the next geezer. That way you keep half the money you take for yourself. Easy ain't it?" He had a self-satisfied grin.

"Oh yeah?" I said, smiling nervously. Inside I was mortified; this was definitely stealing and I, who had never stolen so much as a glance up until now, was supposed to go along with such villainy.

"What if someone wants both tickets?" I queried.

"Nah, nobody's ever caught on, they're all too wound up for the game. They just take whatever you give 'em and piss off up to the entrance door. If someone starts to read what it says on the ticket you just ask sort of casual like, 'Whereabouts are you sitting mate?' Then they pull out their ticket and show you and then you tell them where to go to get in, they put their tickets both together for fear of losing them at the last minute and then they fuck off to the game," he explained.

I told him I didn't think I would be able to do it. This of course imme-diately made him suspicious, thinking that I might grass him up.

Desperate to reassure him that I had no intention of grassing, I groped around for an excuse and came out with, "I'm a deeply religious person," and when that didn't seem convincing, I added, "a catholic." I don't know where my conversion to Rome came from, but at that moment it seemed a convincing word to use.

"So am I a catholic, what's that got to fuckin' do with it? You'll learn son, you'll learn. Everyone's bent, you 'ave to nick a little bit 'ere an' there if you're goin' to get on. You'll learn. Fuckin' catholic—so fuckin' what!" he muttered as he walked over to a newly-arrived cyclist.

Eventually he was mollified and we were back on fairly friendly terms, although I knew he thought I was a bit odd. I offered to give him the other halves of my tickets, so that although I was an accessory to the crime I was innocent of profiting from it.

The incident was soon pushed into the background, for it was a beautiful sunny morning and soon there was a steady stream of customers for spaces. Then as the day wore on spectators began to arrive on foot or from buses. I was fascinated by these strange northern aliens with their broad accents and funny suits. Our Latin master, Mr. May, was from Sheffield so I knew the accent already, and everyone had heard Wilfred Pickles, but here were *thousands* of them. The disarming directness and openness of these strangers contrasted so much with the caution of the London men that I knew that I wondered if they were all a bit simple. Certainly none of them would have been a match for the sly bastard I was working with.

Not only that but they had such tiny feet compared to southern men— or at least that's how it looked to me. Most of these blokes were wearing what looked like a version of the demob suit, which was still fairly common in those days, except that for some reason the ends of their trousers were wider than the way we wore them in London. This may have accentuated my perception of the size of their feet, because for a long time afterwards I would confidently inform people that northern men had smaller feet than their southern brothers (strangely enough, years later I read an article which stated exactly that, though by this time I had stopped repeating my assertion).

At this time I had absolutely no idea about, or interest in, team sports and so the magnitude of the occasion was lost on me. I do however remember the roar of the crowd whenever the play picked up, and it was even bigger than that for Dave Charnley.

A couple of weeks later it was the FA Cup Final between Luton Town and Nottingham Forest, and back came all the suits and small shoes. Don trusted me enough to leave me to do the bikes on my own and went off drinking with some mates, but in the evening he reappeared and I was allowed into the central cashing up place, a small nondescript building

on the outside of the stadium. There queues of attendants stood in line waiting to hand over the cash for the day.

Because Don had not made any cash himself on the day, having been out having a drink, he let me take our pittance in to be weighed with the rest, and the sight that greeted me on the inside of the low building I will never forget. Several cashiers were behind a long table counting out the money as it was emptied from satchels and tipped on to the surface. The place was full of blokes smoking as if the sight of so much money made them all nervous; in a curious way it reminded me of the boxer's dressing room. Paperwork was filled in and forms signed and people whistled in and out at amazing speed. All I can remember is the piles of notes, mainly ten shilling ones but pounds as well, and mountains of florins and half crowns spilling almost on to the floor. My mouth must have been wide open as I gawped at all this treasure on show.

"Come on son," said an official, "if you're finished get your docket signed and get out, there's a good boy."

I got my docket signed and was duly paid my thirty bob. I said my goodbye to Don, who wondered if I'd be working there any more.

"By the way, who won the match?" he asked. I had no idea, but someone shouted, "Forest," and he perked up.

As we left the treasure house he leaned over and beerily informed me, "Well I'm a tenner up on the day, 'ow about you?"

"I done all right," I said, jangling my thirty bob inside my pocket and patronising his grammar at the same time.

"You're learnin' then," he chuckled. "Everyone's bent, they all learn in the end, fuckin' catholic or not."

∼

cadets

I joined the army cadet corps at school as soon as I was old enough, at the age of thirteen. By this time I'd discharged myself from class 3U, but my trousers were still making me an object of ridicule, as I had not yet grown out of even their extended life and length. It was hard enough as it was coming from Miller Road with all the mickey-taking; at that time I was the only boy in my road going to grammar school, and the conflict of cultures between the street and school was being won hands down by the street.

I loved my new surroundings, and I knew the idea of joining the army cadets would get around the estate and would temper the swot image I must have had already. We met every Friday after school and paraded in the school playground. Some boys brought their uniform to school in bags so that it would still be smart for inspection, but I wore mine all day as even the itchy flannel khaki was more comfortable than the false turnup trousers. I supposed it was partly my already gangly shape but I never really looked right, and try as I might I could never win the Best Turned Out Cadet prize. This was always won by my mate and smoking companion, Tom Shaw.

Tom seemed to get everything right: his beret fitted better and it suited him, his trousers were the right length, his gaiters always sat properly on

his beautifully polished boots, and his belt didn't sag like mine. We both spent hours pressing our uniforms with wet cloths and brown paper, but mine always looked a bit sad when it came to parade, whilst Tom's was immaculate. I did admire him but I was always jealous of his handsome appearance.

Our leaders were two teachers named Mr. Catchpole and Mr. Maggs. Mr. Maggs only had his left arm, having lost his right at the battle of Arnhem. This earned him a great deal of respect from the boys, and I for one was in awe of his small silver hook and scarred face. For one term he took us for Latin, but as the whole class were so bad at it we were forced to drop the subject en masse.

I was entertained and diverted by most of the activities of the cadets: marching, shooting in the .22 rifle range in the bike sheds, rifle drill and armoury training. I even enjoyed cleaning my kit, especially the leather boots. This was an amazing process: first you took an old spoon that you heated up in a flame, then you pressed this on to the toecaps and heels of the uppers, then you took lots of black boot polish (Kiwi, not Cherry Blossom) and smothered the tops and heels with this. You repeated the procedure until virtually all traces of the dimples in the leather had disappeared; then began the meditative process of polishing little fingerfuls of polish mixed with spit and water until a shine began to appear like glass on the toe caps of the boot. It was a slow laborious job, but it gave enormous satisfaction as the results started to appear.

I achieved marksman status with the .22 rifle and first class status with the .303. We all went away on camp and had a great time; I got to fire a Bren gun and I passed an armories course, and sometime later we went to Lulworth Cove where we got to fire two pound shells and a whole belt of machine gun bullets with tracers. I also learned to play the bugle and was made bugler for the school company. We went on school parades, church parades, and once marched through Guildford, the home of the Queen's Surrey Regiment. It was grand, and there was only one problem: Lieutenant Bisham.

Something I was to notice at many other times in my life, although I was not to work out its significance until much later, was that a disproportionate number of boys who were drawn to the cadets came from one parent families. Tom, like me, was raised by his mother, and there were other boys like me and Tom in the company; we were the ones Lt. Bisham came after. He was an unsightly man with huge pebble lenses in his glasses,

a very ruddy complexion and a hooked nose. He was dark-haired and a little stout and he couldn't pronounce the 'th' sound. He lived in Selsdon with his "muvver".

Lt. Bisham got to know all the boys in the company who didn't have fathers, and over the course of a few weeks he would call round to their houses and introduce himself to the harassed mums, who were only too glad to receive the interest of an avuncular older man who obviously had the welfare of their boys at heart. His chat line would be something like:

"Hello Mrs. May, my name is Lieutenant Bisham and I'm with the Queen's Surrey Army Cadet force. Since young Ralph has joined it has come to our notice that you are bringing up the boy on your own. We like to keep a bit of an eye on them as they enter teenage, to both their school work and their moral development."

His first visit was invariably in uniform, which gave him an air of authority and easy access to any home of this type. I know many of the mothers found him distasteful, but harassed as they were it never occurred to them that his motives were anything other than what he had stated.

Once indoors and after some small talk about school, he would ask the mother if he could have a word with the boy "on his own." She would readily comply, then when they were alone he would begin his interrogation.

"Well Ralph, how are you enjoying the cadets?"

"Very much sir, thank you."

"Are you getting on with your lessons as well?"

"Oh yes sir."

"Are you a good boy Ralph?"

"Yes sir I think so, I try to be sir."

"I mean, are you ever a naughty boy Ralph?" he smiled knowingly.

"What do you mean naughty sir?"

"You know Ralph, do you ever—"

He paused here for a moment.

"—touch yourself?"

Oh my God what did he mean? Had someone told him? Did anyone know?

"I don't know what you mean sir," I blushed.

"I think you do Ralph," he said, leaning forward in his chair. "Do you interfere with yourself, Ralph?"

"Oh no sir, I never do sir," I lied. "I know it's wrong sir, I would never do such a thing."

I had no need to feign shock as I was absolutely devastated by his questions. There was no way that I could tell my mother about it, and that's how it was for all of us miserable little sinners. Always the same questions asked several times a session, then he would say that he was glad that you were a good boy and try to tickle you on the ribs before taking his leave, making sure that he could call again.

We all knew this activity must be wrong, but none of us lads could see what he got out of it, and our Company Sergeant Major told us that one day we would understand. Camp was particularly harrowing, as he would pick on one boy after another, and these tickling games became little power battles; as long as we didn't fight back too vigorously he seemed satisfied and he never touched any of us in an intimate way. Even so, we all hated him but didn't know what to do about it.

Many years later I heard that he had overstepped the mark and was made to leave the cadet force. He was one of the slimiest bastards I have ever met, and although none of us were harmed in either an intimate or physical way, he got his kicks out of an exploitation of our weakened family status and he was part of our loss of innocence.

PART FIVE

I.J.L.B.

haircut

As much as I loved the cadets, I hated school. I slipped from near the top of my form to near the bottom in three years, and it slowly dawned on me that I would have to make some changes.

For some time I had been noticing adverts in the papers for boys' service in the army, and one day as I was slipping further down the ladder of failure I filled in a form and sent it off. My learning curve had all but vanished at school, and all I wanted to do was play practical jokes and have a laugh all the time. At one time Tom and my other best pal Les were also thinking of leaving with me, but in the end they both stayed.

After receiving a lot of paperwork from the army, it was not long before a recruiting sergeant called round to see me and my mother. I guess it was pretty routine for him calling on boys from council estates, but it all suddenly changed when he heard that I was at grammar school. At first he tried to convince me to attend the Welbeck College military school, but that just sounded like more of the same to me. Against his advice, I opted to join the Infantry Junior Leaders Battalion as a boy soldier in the Queen's Royal Surrey Regiment.

This decision was not made lightly, and in fairness to Mum she pressed me many times to make sure that I really wanted to go through with it. My mind was made up though, and anyhow hadn't my estranged dad

done the same thing, and hadn't Uncle Ray signed up at thirteen, and wasn't my younger brother Bruce trying to get into the Navy on the *Arethusa*? No, there was no turning back, although I did still have a few niggling doubts.

I enjoyed the next few weeks because suddenly I was someone different. I had made a decision to leave home and family and become a soldier. Some of my mates were still half talking about doing it, but I had actually gone through the whole bit except for the medical and swearing in.

The most memorable part of the medical was the eye test. After what was the most extensive examination I'd ever had, the doctor casually asked me what service I'd applied to join. When I told him that I planned to make the infantry my career he was surprised, as in all his twenty-odd years as a military doctor, he said, he had never come across any lad with better vision than mine. He wondered if the Air Force would have been a wiser choice. To me the RAF was still the 'Brylcreem brigade' and an upper-class service: this misapprehension was due to all the bloody war films I'd been subjected to as a kid, and I was quite surprised when I later met up with some airmen to find that they were as working-class as I was.

Anyway a compliment was a compliment, and I felt as if I'd somehow had something to do with it.

The swearing in was a different matter entirely. I was summoned to West Croydon recruiting office and there, in the company of two recruiting sergeants, I swore to be loyal to my Queen and Country and signed on for six years with the colours and two with the reserve.

Except that I hadn't. After I'd signed my name I noticed that instead of six years the sergeant had written *nine* and two with the reserve.

I immediately pointed out the error, expecting him to say that he was sorry and to amend the document, but instead he just smiled, pulled the paper away and said, "Don't worry about that son, you'll get paid more!"

And that was that. He gave me an old hat badge of the Queen's Surrey Regiment, which he said had belonged to him when he was doing his service, and wished me good luck.

I was now a soldier, and I slunk home with a very heavy heart indeed, the enormity of my decision slowly starting to sink in. Although deeply touched by the sergeant's gesture regarding the hat badge, I felt cheated. I would now be twenty-four by the time my service was up, and the two years on the reserve would make me twenty-six, but at least I would be

home then. Christ, I was already counting the days till I got out and I hadn't even arrived at the camp yet.

The next few days sped past and off I went to say my goodbyes to all my old school friends, most of whom I would never see again. Some of my teachers wished me good luck (and under their breath good riddance no doubt) but one of them, Mr. Field, just looked at me incredulously and said, "What! Why are you joining the army? You're certainly capable of eight O-levels."

"I don't think so, sir," I said.

"Nonsense May, of course you are! But if that's what you want to do, good luck to you." He shook his head in bewilderment.

My God, another compliment, why hadn't anyone said these things to me before? I felt even more wretched, and went through the school gates for the last time without a backward glance.

Friends in the street were used to boys leaving, and my friend Tony Potter from across the road had already gone off to join the Navy. I left to join the battalion on May 8th 1960 with a small bag of belongings including my boot polish, brushes, and a towel still clearly labelled in my mum's handwriting R. MAY, which had been prepared for my convalescence that never was after my road accident when I was five. After a manly but grinny handshake from my brother Bruce I turned to say goodbye to my mum. She gave me the first big hug I could ever remember and kissed me on the mouth.

"Take care of yourself, son, and don't forget to write," she said, looking quite tearful. I was so surprised by her reaction and this highly demonstrative show of affection that I nearly decided to stay.

As I left for Paddington up the garden path of 17a Miller Road I could almost hear the *Dam Busters March* being played on harmonicas. I looked to see if Amy Blair was watching me, but she must have been at school. I was fairly sure she liked me just from her glances, although we had not yet spoken as she lived so far away across the road. And now she would be even further away. My heart weighed twice as heavy as my bag.

The train journey from London to the west country is lovely and I am now very familiar with it. This was my first time, however, and although the countryside looked beautiful I was full of trepidation about what was in store for me once we arrived in Plymouth. For a long time I paced up and down the corridor and had cups of tea in the buffet till I couldn't drink any more.

Standing in the buffet car in a grey suit was a tall skinny lad with dark greased hair and brown eyes that sloped slightly upwards. He had a small mouth and a London accent.

"You joined up as well mate 'ave ya?"

"Yeah, that's right," I said, and told him who I was. "Are you going to Plymouth as well?"

"Yeah, I bin watchin' you moochin' up an' down so I thought I'd ask."

"What lot are you going in?" I asked him.

"I'm in the Middlesex Regiment," he announced.

"I'm in the Queen's Surreys," I said. "What's your name?"

"Brummel's the name," he replied, "but all my mates call me Beau."

"Oh. Why's that then?" I asked stupidly.

He gave me a quizzical look and said suspiciously, "Because of Beau Brummel, I suppose."

I wished the ground would swallow me. This was not the first impression I wanted to make; in the army I could be anyone I wanted to be, I could bring all my new-found street cred to my new situation and here I was making my first encounter with a fellow soldier and I'd failed to see the obvious connection with his famous namesake.

I could imagine him introducing me to other blokes, saying something like, "This is Ralph, he's from Croydon," then adding under his breath, "he's a bit slow on the uptake, but what can you expect from someone called Ralph who comes from Croydon."

I imagined everyone nodding sympathetically, and made up my mind that I would change my name to something more exotic and lie about my origins. Of course this was after I'd already told him my name was Ralph and that I hailed from Croydon. I also realised that I would probably have to stop saying my prayers at night and start swearing a lot.

The rest of the journey passed quite quickly and soon we were getting off the train at Plymouth. We had all been told we would be met, and so as the other passengers left the station a small unimpressive knot of skinny, nervous-looking young men grew on the platform. An old sergeant in the uniform of the London Irish Rifles arrived and called the roll. We had to answer "Here sir!" in a very loud voice.

"He looks old, I think he must be fuckin' deaf," said Beau, leaning into me.

"Not so deaf I missed that," uttered the sergeant. "What's your name lad?" he asked, looking directly at me.

"Me?" I asked incredulously.

"Yes you lad!" bellowed the sergeant to the red-faced lad on the platform of Plymouth railway station with the new recruits all looking at me, and now all the disembarking and embarking passengers staring as well.

"My name's May," I croaked.

"OK, Murray," sneered the sergeant, "I'll deal with you later," and he looked down his list. "Wait a minute," he said, "there's no-one down here called Murray."

"No sir, my name's May," I trembled. "M-A-Y." I spelt it out.

"That's not how you spell Murray boy," he seethed, "that's May."

"I know sir, that's my name."

"I hope you're not going to be a troublemaker May or Murray whatever your bloody name is boy, because you're in the army now lad and we have a way of dealing with smart arses like you!" As he uttered this chilling threat he wrote something down on his clipboard.

"Right you lot, form twos and follow me."

We half marched and half ambled out of the station and into a military coach that took us to Plummer Barracks at Crownhill. As we got off the lorry to view our new home the old sergeant leaned toward me and said, "All right Murray, I'll be watching you."

I looked over at my new friend Beau desperately, but he just grimaced and shrugged his shoulders in apology. We filed into the ground floor of Z Company barrack room and met the other lads who'd arrived at different times during the day.

"What a fucking great start!" I said to Beau. It felt great to say Fucking as well. It would be used a great deal over the coming months—and as it turned out it wasn't such a bad start after all.

I looked around at my new surroundings and noted the different types of boys there. We were all shapes and sizes, though there was no-one very overweight, and some looked far too small to have left home. Some wore glasses, one or two looked quite a bit older than the rest, a few had tattoos and several like me had Teddy boy haircuts.

We were all soon called outside and ordered to line up in loose military fashion. There was another roll call and we were introduced to our platoon sergeants. Mine was called Boon and the other one was called Roberts. They were the army's version of 'good cop bad cop'. Boon was short and wore a beret with a hackle in it. He spoke with a measured west country accent and was turned out immaculately. He had very light blue

eyes like my uncle Alf and seemed aware of the trepidation of his new charges.

Roberts's eyes on the other hand were completely hidden by his slashed peak cap. He was in the Welsh Guards and was even more immaculate than his partner. When he issued words of command his voice, devoid of any compassion, divided into two parts, one with the tone of a shovel being scraped along the ground and the other a screaming falsetto. He scared the life out of all of us, and was probably the sort of NCO who in time of war we would have followed anywhere.

As we made two ramshackle lines, the two sergeants moved down the line looking at us and occasionally shaking their heads in mock disbelief that they were expected to turn us into soldiers. In well-rehearsed moves the two of them looked at each other and clicked their tongues in despair. I half smiled to myself in congratulation that I had recognised this performance as a deception when suddenly Roberts rounded on me, and singling out two other lads as well, bellowed, "You you and you! Haircut! Now!"

I noticed all three of us had longish hair, but more importantly we had elaborate styles. Mine at the time was what was known as a drainpipe, which consisted of two rolls of hair turned into the middle and a DA at the back with a Boston. I was first up in the chair, and the barber leant toward my ear chattily, asking, "How would you like it sir?"

I naively replied, "Well, I suppose trim up the sides and take a little off the top."

I can still remember the horror I felt as my vanity shorn off me. His electric shears zoomed straight up the back of my head and I instinctively grabbed at my head as if it had been cut.

"Oh dear," he said, "it seems my hand slipped!" to nervous laughter from the other two lads who by now had been joined by one or two more. I told him to take it all down short, and although I hated the way it looked, I felt a certain bravado and in the next day or so we all looked the same. The rule, as explained to us, was that whatever was below the beret line, the army wanted, and we could keep whatever was left. One boy called Weller was so shocked by the sight of the first returnees from the barber that he decided to have it all off, and they duly obliged. He thought this very funny, and so did I as he had a big round face like a football, and shorn of his blond hair he looked like Charlie Brown. I got to know him straight away and we were soon friends; he was in the Royal West Kent

Regiment and his name was Robert, "but everyone calls me Sam."

"Why's that?" I asked.

"Because of Sam Weller," he explained. Beau was in earshot and I was sure he would later tell Sam that he had the same trouble with me and his nickname. When Sam asked me my name I was determined to have a nickname too, so I replied, "Ray." It was all I could think of.

"I thought you said your name was Ralph," said Beau.

"Yeah, Ray is sort of short for Ralph," I explained.

"Is it? I thought it was short for Raymond," said Sam.

"Yes, and Ralph as well," I said, and gambled, "I mean, how many Ralphs do you know?"

"None," they both responded.

"There you are then!" I said triumphantly, and from that moment on I was always Ray. The only trouble was that I didn't respond to it very well, so as well as being known as someone who was a bit slow on the uptake I was also thought to be a bit deaf as well.

That evening we were issued with underclothes and fatigues, two pairs of boots, socks, brown army plimsolls, knife, fork and spoon, and bed-clothes. We were ordered to bed and allowed to talk for a while before lights out. I lay there in the gloom and didn't sleep too well, as a feeling of foreboding crept over me.

The next day our training began in earnest. We were obviously undrilled, so to give us some sort of order we were bidden to run every-where at the double. We did PT rigorously and attended a rudimentary educational class, and it was here that I realised I was one of the few boys that was literate. I might have been bad at school but here there was no-one to touch me.

To be truthful I was horrified. There was nobody that I could talk to on more than a superficial level, and it was only really tolerable when I was joking with Sam. Some of the other boys had begun to realise that this was going to be tough and we found that most of us had signed on for nine years and two in the reserve. Then somebody pointed out that the two years we would serve as boy soldiers didn't count, and that in reality we were going to do eleven in uniform. In fact on the third day I went and spoke to Company Sergeant Boon, and all but broke down as the helplessness of my situation dawned on me.

He was, I think, a kind man in private, but here there was a strict

NCO relationship that was never allowed to develop into anything other than formal, and he was unable to comfort me in any way.

On the parade ground we were bullied and sworn at just like recruits always have been, but some of the oaths were appalling when used against these young boys, the idea being to break you down in order to build you up. Humiliating and physically demanding punishments were handed out, like running round the parade ground with your rifle held above your head, or standing to attention perfectly still for inordinate lengths of time.

We were not supposed to be hit, but on occasion we were. I was ridiculed for being unable to straighten my arms properly when marching, and whacked with a pace stick several times by the RSM before he realised I was unable to make them any different. I was also smashed across the knuckles for not having my thumbs pointing down the seams of my trousers. The physical torment was just about bearable, but the verbal abuse was awful. Sergeant Roberts's voice of command was awesome. He would walk up to the offending soldier, stand nose to nose and bellow at the top of his voice his favourite insult: "The best part of you, boy, ran down your mother's leg!" Or occasionally, "When you were born they must have thrown away the baby and kept the afterbirth!"

You invariably had to repeat it to the whole battalion. Once I was ordered to march out to the RSM and tell him that I had grass growing out of my hat badge. Most of the accusations were made up to keep us terrified, and though we all worked at our kit for at least an hour every night, it was never enough to satisfy our sergeants.

We were told that from now on the army would be our mother and father, and even then I realised the humiliation, the uniform, and the regimen were all designed to strip away our individuality and to mould us into a cohesive unit. Every opportunity was taken to humiliate us. There was a lot of excitement in the barracks when we were told that we were going for a run across Dartmoor, but that changed to embarrassment when we heard that we were to run in army boots. The sight of fifty to sixty lads dressed in baggy army shorts and red shirts with army woollen socks and hobnailed boots, clattering over pavements and rocks and moorland, lives with me still. The whole purpose of the exercise was to break in our 'best boots'. Henceforth these would only be worn for parades; our second pair would be worn every day and would be broken in gradually.

After that run many boys had to wear plimsolls until their blisters and ripped toes had healed up, and only the very serious cases ever got as far as the doctor. In any case, you had to convince your Company Sergeant that you were ill before he would let you report sick anyway.

Our uniforms were First World War type and very itchy; how I longed for the Clarke boy's Oxford bags. We had two service dresses, both identical, but we did not have to wear the puttees, thank God. The Army generously paid us, whether we were awake or asleep, threepence an hour, earning us about two pounds a week. Out of this, one pound was saved and the other spent mostly on cleaning equipment: boot polish, Brasso, Blanco, whitener for our SDs and yellow dusters for polishing. We all became good, eventually, at ironing and we all had to shave every day whether we had any whiskers or not.

Our barrack rooms were kept spotless (but not spotless enough for our sergeants), and the washrooms were scrubbed daily with bass brooms. We were expected to attend to our own cleanliness, but because we did PT most days we showered automatically. Some lads, however, were simply not used to bathing and had to be reminded by the others.

After three weeks of unbelievably hard training, we were to be allowed to visit the town for the first time. We were given strict instructions not to visit Union Street, and to keep up the process of humiliation we had to go out in military uniform, so that everyone in Plymouth would know that we were raw recruits. But not even this could dampen our eager anticipation for the weekend ahead.

∽

ANGEL LAUGHTER

town

For the last few days before being allowed into town, the talk was only about one thing: what we were going to do on our Saturday out. Boys' talk inevitably gets around to one thing and the lot in Z Company were no exception. I think most of us were virgins, but only one or two admitted to the fact, and it was obvious to anyone that we were inexperienced boys.

As fifteen-year-olds, we comprised all stages in male teenage development, from lads who looked as if they were wearing their first long trousers, with no facial hair and unbroken voices, to boys who shaved every day, spoke in deep manly tones and had muscular physiques. Not to mention those who had appalling complexions, terminal acne, halitosis, and who were suspected of perpetual masturbation. One Geordie lad was threatened with being put on a charge for the offence of having 'filthy flesh' and ordered to have instruction on how to remove blackheads with a key!

Inevitably all conversation turned toward sex, and the bedtime banter before lights out grew more and more lurid as boys would take it in turns to tell of their conquests, real or imagined. I suspect many tales were based on fact, but some were pure fantasy. One lad's story, however, had the ring of truth about it: his name was Malcolm Pringle and he was from Norfolk.

Malcolm had a picture of his girlfriend in his locker and he talked about her with genuine affection. I wanted to know all about her and he was willing to share details with me, albeit a little reluctantly—after all he was talking about the girl he loved. I was deeply envious of Malcolm as it became clear that he really did have a proper sexual relationship with this girl, for Malcolm himself was no oil painting. He had the biggest head in the platoon and had to have his beret specially ordered for him—and then it had to be stretched—and his SD hat had to be specially ordered too.

The other noticeable feature about him was his enormous feet; he took size fourteen, and the only thing the army had that would fit him were army issue brown plimsolls or 'pumps'. Poor Malcolm had to do all his early drill training in these soft shoes, which was faintly ridiculous as we had to bang our feet down with tremendous force when coming to attention. I am sure he must have damaged his spine before his two pairs of boots finally arrived.

Malcolm was odd in other ways too. For example, he thought that the army food was really good, and he always ate it all up and anyone else's leftovers as well. He was also one of three boys in my platoon who could neither read nor write. I was stunned by this fact, and it only served to make me more angry at the way I'd been conned into thinking that you had to pass an entrance exam to get into this mob. How the hell had these boys managed to get in?

Letters from home arrived for me on a regular basis and always moved me to tears as they were signed off "with fondest love, Mum." I also persuaded a friend from home to get me a pen friend so that I could pretend she was my girlfriend, and I loved getting her letters. As my friendship with Malcolm grew, he confided that he would like me to read him the couple of letters he had received from his girlfriend, and that's when I discovered that he was illiterate.

Malcolm's girl was called Pam. Her letters were written in big round shapes; they told of things back home but were quite short, although she always signed off that she missed him and sent her love. Malcolm then asked me to write his letters back. I was already writing for another lad called Rex to his mum, but Malcolm wanted me to write love letters!

This proved to be much harder than it sounds, because he could not dictate very well, so in the end I got him to tell me of his feelings and composed the letters myself, reading them back to him when they were

finished. This method had two effects: firstly Pam's letters got much longer and more passionate, and secondly Malcolm always broke down and sobbed after I had expressed his feelings for him. After no more than a couple of these intense missives I no longer felt able to continue this correspondence, as I'd started to look forward to her replies.

Another reason was that one day whilst Malcolm was talking to me, he confided that Pam was not the best shag he'd ever had—that distinction belonged to his sister. Malcolm obviously saw nothing wrong in this, or in the fact that his father was also having sex with her, and looked genuinely puzzled by my reaction. Even after he explained that she was quite happy with the situation it still didn't seem right to me. For a fleeting moment I considered asking Malcolm if she might accommodate me, but as I looked into his tiny eyes set into his huge head it occurred that she might look just like him, and I thought better of it.

At last our Saturday arrived. Rex, Beau, Sam, Malcolm and I filed into the guard room for final inspection and insults before being allowed out into the city of Plymouth for a few hours release. Naturally we headed for Union Street, where we found a tattoo parlour, and all of us resolved to get a tattoo next time out. Drink did not really interest us at this time, so we just wandered about soaking up the late spring sunshine in our itchy SDs admiring every female between thirteen and twenty. We puffed away on our fags and tried to look manly, worldly and cool all at the same time, as we slowly guffawed our way up to the Hoe overlooking the harbour.

Someone had a camera and we posed for photos. There were young couples walking hand in hand, a sprinkling of matelots and marines, and servicemen in civvies, easy to spot by their savage military haircuts, all milling about on the clipped grass on the promenade.

Late in the afternoon we noticed a group of three girls and the dare was on to go and chat them up. I think at this point it is important to say that, although I had lusted after Amy Blair and various other girls on the bus going to school, I had never actually spoken to a female of my own age since reaching puberty. The reasons were complex and common to thousands of young men, but of course you don't know that at the time, believing only that the pain is unique to yourself and the exquisite agony of sexual awakening is the punishment you have to bear for having such wicked thoughts. I had been led by my friend Tom Shaw to believe that the size of my nose would seriously undermine any attempt to pull a girl;

I also had a few spots on occasion and had resorted to crossing to the opposite side of the road whenever I saw a pretty girl coming toward me.

Suddenly all the bawdy barrack room talk vanished into the air as my mates found excuses not to intervene, and it was left for me to make a move on the three girls. Leaving my friends I sauntered over to them; strangely, they neither recoiled in terror, burst out laughing or pointed at my nose. On the contrary, they seemed quite coy and tickled that we were interested in them. It has to be said that they were not great lookers, but they were our age and they were female.

Sam had crept up to join me, and although I have no recollection of how the chat-up line went, Sam was most helpful when he removed his cap to reveal his largely bald head. His hair was growing but it was so fine and light in colour that it still appeared to be shaved. At first this made the girls scream, but then they laughed and that settled Sam's role in the proceedings: he was to be the comedian and I was to be the intense, cool and debonair one. It is of course not possible for an overexcited fifteen-year-old to be any of those things, let alone all at once, so I tried to gather all the information I had learned from the other lads' talk in the barracks (first of all you've got to split them up, next keep them laughing, feel their tits outside of their bra before you go inside it, blow smoke into their faces to make them want to shag you, and so on).

I decided to save the smoke-blowing for later, as it was windy up on the Hoe and rather public, but I did get mine away from the other two, and we went for a stroll. I learned that her name was Bev Winterburn and that she lived over the water in Turnchapel and that her last ferry was about to go. As I walked her down to the jetty she took my arm and I asked if she would come to the pictures with me on Wednesday. She said that she would and we arranged to meet outside of the Drake cinema at about two o'clock.

I kissed her on the mouth (almost), said goodbye and as soon as I was out of sight from where I'd left her I raced up to the Hoe to find my pals and tell them what had happened, that she was a dead cert and I was meeting her in the week. My mates looked pissed off, except Sam, who had decided to pretend he was a nutter and was making himself dribble and speaking loudly as if he had a hare lip and was desperately trying to be understood. This diverted attention from my good luck and we all finished up laughing our way back to barracks. The only other one of us to get a date was Malcolm.

For the next few days I was in a state of total sexual anticipation. In my mind this girl was metamorphosing into the most glorious creature who ever lived, with the darkest eyes, the brownest hair, and the most perfect breasts and lips, with a sexy Plymouth accent thrown in. By now, of course, my missed kiss had turned into a full scale grope, and I was able to compete on terms with the other lads as we discussed our erotic adventures.

Wednesday finally came; a big day because it was the first time we were to be allowed out in our own civilian clothes. I had black suede shoes and black cavalry twill tapered trousers, a white shirt with cutaway collars and a Slim Jim tie, and a black and grey striped Italian three button jacket. My hair had grown sufficiently to do something with it, I was shaved and aftershaved and with a bounce in my step and wings on my heels I made my way to the cinema to meet my girl.

When I got there I realised I hadn't bothered to find out what the film was, and as the couples met each other outside I tried to contain my anxiety that perhaps she wouldn't show up. My eyes scanned the people swarming around the cinema but there was no sign of my Bev, just a couple of sailor boys, a dumpy little thing in a yellow frock, two other girls who were soon met by two boys and another boy about my age.

Gradually everyone drifted into the cinema, and still no sign of my Bev. The two sailors flipped a coin and then went inside, the boy my own age was finally met by his girl and after giving out at her for being late, they too disappeared into the cinema. I was alone except for the dumpy little thing in the yellow dress, who was standing at the opposite side of the picture house entrance looking at me.

I was wondering if she had been stood up as well, when she suddenly smiled and said, "Hello Ray. I wasn't sure if it was you without your uniform."

I was stunned. Here was my Bev, totally transformed. When we had met a couple of days before, she had been wearing a dark green cardigan and skirt with very little make-up, her lovely brown hair loose over her shoulders. What stood before me now, tottering slightly in white high heels and a yellow frock, was a different person, a little dumpy thing whose newly-permed hair was set in tight curls. She was covered in make-up and I had completely failed to recognise her. She must have spent hours on this effect, but I was depressed. Where was the siren I had given my heart to, the country girl with flowing hair, laughing brown eyes and

huge tits? Gone, and in its place this travesty. She took hold of my arm and we went inside, where the film had already started.

As we sat down, her stiff petticoat bounced up on her lap and a little puff of talcum powder seemed to shoot out of her collar. Sitting there in the dark, I tried to remember the procedure for seduction as described by the various blokes in the barracks. The horror of her transformation was easier to bear in the cinema, and at last I managed to get my arm round the back of her seat in a nonchalant but unnatural move. Once there I was terrified about what to do next. Was I supposed to touch her hair or her arm? I knew there was a routine but it had escaped me in the heat of these moments.

Then I remembered: start at the top, hair first. Gingerly I raised my fingers to caress her curls, and as I did so I got another shock—the curls seemed to be made of wire. I had never heard of hair lacquer, and she had used about a tinful, which had made her hair feel as if she was wearing a crash helmet. I recoiled in fright and was left with my arm hanging over the back of her seat, too scared to move it and not quite knowing what to do next. Gradually my arm started to go to sleep and I lost all sensation of feeling in it as it was pressed against the back of her seat. Pins and needles began to set in and I was experiencing considerable discomfort, so I decided to withdraw the arm until it regained its blood supply and try again later.

Unfortunately my arm now felt like someone else's, and in attempting to haul it back over her seat to my side, it seemed to acquire a life of its own and thrashed about alarmingly, giving her a hard dig in her right ear. Mortified by this assault I apologised profusely, touching her shoulder and turning her face to mine, whereupon she lunged forward thinking I was about to embrace her. Our mouths met in a sickening crunch and we sprang back from each other to check our teeth.

Soon we were at it like every other couple in the dark and I prepared to make my next move toward the upper body, but this too resulted in confusion as she seemed to be entirely encased in sheet metal (I realise now that it must have been one of those bras that encircle the midriff to suppress undesirable bulges). She had metamorphosed into an armadillo.

At the end of the film we emerged mole-like and blinking into the warm spring evening, and my heart once again sank at the image before me. There was no doubt that our first encounter had been fairly passionate and promised more, but the truth was that I didn't fancy her any more.

The next day I wrote to her and made some excuse about not being able to meet her. When I next went into town I met another girl called Glenda, and we arranged to meet and go to the fair on the Hoe the next weekend. I wrote and told Bev that I was being sent to Oswestry as part of the advance party for our move to Parkhall Camp, but she saw me on one of the fairground rides with Glenda and wrote me a broken-hearted letter. I eventually realised what a sweet girl Bev really was, and that Glenda, who was so sexy, was actually going out with different blokes every day. She even got my name wrong on our last date before we moved camp. So now I'd had two girlfriends but no carnal knowledge—though none of my fellow boy soldiers knew that—and unbeknown to me there was some resentment growing.

౷

hard

Once we had passed out of Z Company and joined our training companies, we were bossed about by older boy soldiers, who were addressed as Junior Corporal or Junior Sergeant, and they tried with some success to be even worse than our senior NCOs. Fairness never came into it, and you were expected to put up with whatever prejudice the junior NCOs had. Complaint was a sign of weakness; it was your ability to take it that counted.

Junior Corporal Mostyn hated me on sight, and did his best to make my life even more miserable than it already was. I suspect it was because I was at least six inches taller than him. I suppose I should have read the other signs of resentment toward me and one or two of the other lads as we took our places with our training companies, but I didn't.

I was billeted next to an older, very capable lad called Derek, who was in the Dorset Regiment. We got on very well, and I just tried to carry on with a life that was making me more and more depressed. He realised that I was desperate to get out of service, but he also knew that my situation was hopeless. He managed to keep up my morale most of the time, and besides there were boys who were in a much worse position than I was.

Junior Private Bonney was from the intake before mine, but had been

in my company before being placed under arrest for self-mutilation. The poor kid was entirely unsuited to military service, and any psychiatrist would not have allowed him to join up. The trouble was that the army simply did not have the mechanism for dealing with this type of case. The story went that shortly after Bonney had passed out of his training company he'd started to behave oddly, at first by not getting out of bed in the morning in fear of the terrors that awaited him through the verbal abuse from the senior sergeants. It was only his neighbour who had saved him on numerous occasions by literally hauling him out of bed before the sergeant came into the room with the usual order, "Hands off cocks and on with socks."

Gradually Bonney failed even to respond to his fellow soldiers' pleas to get himself together. The next sign was that he started to drink Brasso, the cleaning fluid we used for our brass buttons and belt clips. Maybe he thought he would get drunk by doing this, but he just got sick and vomited. He then started to disobey orders and began slashing the soles of his feet with razor blades so that he wouldn't have to drill.

Finally someone found him trying to hang himself in the washrooms, and he was deemed a risk to himself. He was thrown in the guardhouse, charged with self-inflicted injury, and put on RPs (restricted privileges). His boot laces were removed and he was marched down to the canteen where he had to eat his meals with a provost sergeant and a corporal watching every move, in case he tried to smuggle a knife or other dangerous implement back to the cell.

Bonney was a sad character, a tussle of dark curly hair, sallow complexion, skinny as a rake and huge dark sad eyes, and the way he was treated was a crime of unbelievable cruelty. The sight of this sixteen-year-old boy shuffling down to eat in the mess with his army boots gaping laceless and his old fatigues, his eyes dead and hardly noticing his surroundings, was unspeakable. Everyone agreed that Bonney was a nutter and most of us felt pity for him, but I doubt many realised he was paraded nightly for our benefit.

One night I came into my bed space and was getting something out of my locker when Derek whispered to me, "Watch out Ray, they're coming for you. Don't look round, just listen to me, can you hear me?"

"Yes," I said, wondering what on earth he could mean.

"You're going to be charged and put in a kangaroo court. You'll get a

whacking and if you plead guilty that's probably all that will happen. They're going to do Alan as well."

"What are they charging me with?" I whispered as I began to shake.

"You're going to be charged with being a rookie and there's nothing you can say or do about it. So no more questions, just be ready."

I turned round to look at him but he would not look me in the eye; he was tight-lipped and grim faced and I noticed that he was putting on an odd combination of uniform. Our bed spaces were down at the far end of the barrack room and there was a lot of activity going on at the other end. I wanted to see what was happening but Derek, sensing this, shook his head to warn me against it.

Suddenly there was the order, "Attention. About turn. Quick march!" and the sound of two soldiers marching down the centre aisle grew louder and louder in my ears until they came to a stop at my bed.

"Junior Private May. Attention. Put your beret on and fall in with us." There was nothing to be done and, with one of the boys trying not to laugh, we marched like prisoner and escort back to the top of the room. Here two large tables had been set up, and seated behind them were three older boys dressed in a variety of strange bits of uniform and made up hat badges. In the middle sat the biggest bully in the company, a bastard in the East Anglia Regiment, and he was flanked by an Irish boy called Brady and another lad called Curry from one of the Lancashire regiments.

The East Anglian Bastard slapped a spoon on the table.

"This court is now in session!" he bellowed. "Junior Private May, what is your number?"

"23783801!" I shouted back.

"Two three seven eight three eight zero one Junior Private May you are charged with being a recruit. How do you plead?"

"You know that I'm a recruit," I said nervously. "What is all this about?"

The bastard leaped to his feet and pressed his face to mine.

"Shut your fuckin mouth you fuckin bastard May and just answer the fuckin question will you! I bin waiting for this you fuckin bastard, are you guilty or not guilty?"

"Guilty I suppose," I said.

"Guilty or not fuckin guilty you fuckin bastard!" he screamed and at the same time landed a tremendous blow to the side of my head with his fist.

"Guilty," I said.

At this admission my arms were taken and tied behind my back. They pushed me down between two beds, and my head was placed in the middle, held between the two steel frames that supported the springs. Then someone ripped open my shirt pulling most of the buttons off, and a box of Swan Vestas was produced. Without any instruction from anyone about a dozen matches were struck and whilst burning were stuck into my chest. I managed not to cry out because I was terrified about what other humiliations they had planned for me.

My chest now resembled a pin cushion, although I couldn't see this at the time and struggle was both futile and painful. As my head was held back at an acute angle I could not see who exactly my tormentors were, but it seemed that most of the platoon had been roped in. Suddenly I could feel my trousers being pulled down and I kicked out violently, only to be given a punch in the face by the East Anglian Bastard, and then I was aware of some liquid being poured over my genitals. This turned out to be the whitener that was commonly used to whiten our belts for our best SDs.

I was released from the bed's grip and turned over, and my shirt ripped from my back. They pretended to put a hot iron on my back as a brand mark; although they didn't actually plug it in, the coldness of it made me think I was being burnt. I was then turned over again. This time the East Anglian Bastard grabbed my hair and proceeded to hack off a four inch square right in the front above my forehead. That *really* hurt. He then gave me one more dig before I was dismissed and led back to the washrooms to try to clean myself up.

I felt completely desolate, and as I scrubbed away the whitener that had been used on me and saw in the mirror the extent of my tonsorial mutilation, the tears welled up and poured down my face. No-one came in to see me, and I had a few minutes to get myself together before I heard the same orders being bellowed from the barrack room, only this time they were coming for Alan, whose bed was across from mine.

In spite of what I'd just gone through, I went in to see what new tortures they had planned for him. Apart from blacking his balls with Kiwi boot polish, they cut his hair off just like mine, but instead of sticking lighted matches on his chest they gave him six lashes with a rifle strap before letting him go. All of this happened within half an hour and it all had a dreamlike quality to it. The whole room was involved in some

way and when it was over the place was eerily quiet and blokes didn't speak to each other. I started to go over to talk to Alan but was cautioned not to by Derek. I saw Alan's pain, and long after lights out and the others were asleep I could hear him crying quietly to himself.

For some time there had been rumours that the whole camp was to be moved to a new location. These were now confirmed and the destination was Oswestry, a small market town in Shropshire. I was still besotted with Glenda and needed an excuse not to go on an outward bound course on Dartmoor when Curry, who it transpired had done the intimate punishments on Alan and me, suggested a method by which I could report sick.

"Its called spooning," he explained. "All you have to do is wrap your hand up in a wet towel and then I hit you with a spoon and slowly your whole hand swells up and it looks like a fuckin' balloon and the doc doesn't know what it is and you get put on light duties."

I realised this was a ruse to get back on terms with me, but I was desperate to see Glenda again so I agreed to try the treatment. After applying the towel the spooning began. By Christ how it hurt. When Curry had exhausted himself another lad took over and after fifteen minutes I could bear it no longer and gave it up as a bad job. The pain was excruciating but the desired swelling had not occurred. I was resigned to going on the course after all and was standing at my locker with my door open when I felt a blinding pain across my arm. I fell down under the force of the blow delivered by the East Anglian Bastard who had crept up along side my bed space and swung the bass broom over his head and brought it down with all his weight on my skinny forearm.

"There you are May you fuckin' bastard that ought to get you out of goin'," he cackled.

Before my eyes my arm started to swell. Miraculously it wasn't broken, but the pain was unbelievable. I reported sick the next day and the doctor asked me how it happened.

"I fell down the stairs sir," was the response I'd been told to use.

"And who cut your hair?" he demanded.

"I did sir," I lied.

"I see," said the MO—and I'm sure he did—but he put my arm in a sling and I was put on light duties for a week. The rest of my platoon went off to Dartmoor and I got Wednesday in town to meet Glenda.

Needless to say, she wasn't where we arranged to meet, and my misery was complete when I saw her arm in arm with two regular sailors walking into a pub. On the bus back to the barracks I thought of Bev and felt bloody awful about what I'd done, but I managed to content myself with thoughts of the battalion's move to Shropshire. With some relief I noticed my arm was already feeling better and it would not be long before my first home leave was coming up. I decided I would ask Amy out and see if there was any way I could arrange to get some money together to buy my discharge.

There are two things I remember about the move: a senior officer had to sign for the train; and I saw my uncle George working laying track as we passed through my childhood holiday home of Banbury.

Parkhall Camp was not as austere looking as Crownhill, but it had been empty for some time and lacked the comforts of a more lived-in barracks. I was billeted next to an older boy called Spike. He was taller than me and had large teeth, but he was a good-natured bloke with a ready laugh and had been a keen cyclist before joining up. We got on fairly well, and with the aid of brushes and brooms and heavy use of the 'bumper', a weighted device that was swung vigorously back and forward across the floor to produce an unbelievable shine without polish, we soon had the place depressingly like our old home. By now we had been joined by a new intake of lads. I couldn't help thinking what a motley lot they looked and by comparison how soldierly we had become, but I still hated it and all my waking hours were becoming obsessed with how to get out.

In our company there were a few boys from the Irish Republic, where they were allowed to volunteer at fourteen. One of these boys, called Digby, was a very good hammer thrower and was being trained up to represent the army in his specialised sport. The other boy was from County Ofaly, and one night I heard him discussing his plans once he passed out from the IJLB. After a day or so I approached him and asked him about what he'd been saying.

"Are you really not coming back after leave?" I asked innocently.

"Who feckin told you that boy?" he wanted to know, his eyes narrowing and his fists clenching.

"Don't worry, I won't say anything," I said.

"You're feckin right there," he said, "if you do you'll have no feckin teeth left to say anythin at all wid."

"It's just that you said that once you're in the Republic they can't get you back here to England," I explained.

When he realised I was genuine, he became quite talkative and told me how, after getting his lance corporal stripes in England, he would automatically get one stripe in the free state army, and that I probably could do the same if that was what I wanted.

This was an impossibly long shot, but I was so desperate to get out that I thought I would try anything. I lacked the courage to pretend to be mad, unlike one of the new intake who had already begun talking to himself and had begun to cut his arms with his dinner knife. Another boy had cut his hair by himself to give him a crazed appearance, and was carefully mimicking all the symptoms of a brain tumour so convincingly that he was eventually discharged.

My day to day routine was getting harder and harder to cope with, and it was only the thought of summer leave which kept my spirits from disappearing altogether.

At last leave came and we were doled out our holiday pay and issued with travel warrants. In spite of my hatred of military life, it was still important to impress my friends at home, and in common with quite a few other boys I had made some slight modifications to my uniform. The peak of my cap had been slashed—the corners had their stitches removed and the peak tucked up so that it resembled a guard's hat, forcing one to look out at the world from underneath the peak—and I'd fixed collar dogs on my shirt collar points.

I took my best SD trousers and best boots carefully in a bag all the way home and changed into this dog uniform in the toilets at West Croydon. From there I marched all the way home and up Factory Lane hoping to catch a few admiring glances, but there was no-one about as I rang on the door of 17a Miller Road.

At least Bruce seemed to be impressed. I went outside and smoked a Park Drive on the bars and looked in the direction of Amy Blair's house. Soon I heard the babble and chatter of the girls coming home from the factories, but was overcome with shyness and went indoors. I sweated in my heavy army uniform until my mum came home and said it was nice to see me. Everything was as I left it, and family life attempted to carry on as it had up until that point, but actually nothing would ever be the same again.

The first thing I noticed was how slow everything had become. I was

full of energy and could barely saunter anymore; on the way to the Black Boy pub down Factory Lane I found myself striding ahead of the Marsden twins and then walking back again to rejoin the group.

It was the same when we went up to Mitcham Common on Sundays to watch football. I was never really that fascinated anyway, but it was something to do in the bleak afternoons after *Ray's a Laugh* on the radio; we'd sit in the café on the edge of the common and while away an hour or two over a cup of tea before going out to the pictures in the evening. I'd be pacing up and down the touchline as if I was really agitated by the state of play, rather than confused about my real plans to leave the army forever while at the same time pretending that I really liked it.

Pretty soon I plucked up the courage to ask Amy out, and she readily agreed. I guess I'd always known that she would say yes, and anyway I was considerably more experienced now than when I'd left. Amy was a very pretty girl with lovely brown eyes and a nice figure, but we found little to talk about, and although we had a few snogs in the dark I was shattered to find how quickly my long-held passion began to wane.

The most awful thing was that, terrible though army life was, the thought of knocking about with my old mates on the estate was almost as daunting; things were changing fast and I was having a job keeping up with them.

Back at the battalion I wrote to Amy a couple of times, and though I ached for letters back I can't say that they really fuelled my fantasies about girls, and my need for a girlfriend was starting to dominate my every waking moment.

On my first weekend leave in Oswestry I went out with a bunch of lads and cruised the town. It was a Sunday and there were drink laws that sent the Welsh pouring over the border in order to get a drink in England. Pubs didn't really interest me and anyway we were all under age; besides, I had other agenda to pursue.

As we ambled around the little market town I got separated from the others and found myself back at the railway station (maybe subconsciously I was still planning my escape), but there was no-one there—except the prettiest girl I'd seen all day. She was dark and slim with shortish brown hair, and was wearing a yellow frock with a blue jacket. Whether out of desperation, or confidence now that my mutilated hair had grown back, I can't say, but I found myself talking to her.

To my delight she talked back, and she was bright and she laughed at my attempts at being funny, and she wasn't fazed at my being in the army. I must have used this as the final test of our attraction, but she didn't even bat an eyelid when I told her.

She was waiting for the train to Llangollen, and I stood and waited with her. I knew we were hitting it off together, and rather than wait until her train arrived and I had run out of conversation, I suddenly blurted out, "Can I meet you next Saturday?"

"Yes, if you like," she answered.

"Where?" I enquired, my pulse beginning to race.

"What about here at the station, there's a train that gets in at ten past three on Saturday afternoon," she smiled.

I wanted to kiss her goodbye right there, but thought it might be a bit premature.

"I'll see you here then," I said. "Don't be late!"

"I won't," she said.

With that, I turned on my heels and with a forced air of casualness strolled out of the station. When I was sure that I was out of her eyeline I jumped in the air and ran all the way back to Parkhall Camp, feeling the happiest I had felt in the whole time I'd spent in the service. No-one had to tell me, I was definitely In Love.

The week seemed to drag by and I was constantly losing attention over petty things. On Friday morning I committed a minor infringement to do with my locker and was charged with some form of idleness, resulting in restricted privileges.

Saturday duly arrived and I got into my best grey Italian suit, spent ages disguising the cropped piece of hair in the front of my head, cleaned my teeth twice, shaved and aftershaved, and reported to the guardroom to check out for my longed-for Saturday tryst.

"Name?" shouted the sergeant.

"23783801 Junior Private May sir!" I yelled back. He looked down his clip board.

"There's no Murray here!" he shouted back at me.

"No, May, M-A-Y," I spelt out for him. There was a lengthy silence as he lip read the contents of his list. Finally he looked up.

"Who's been a naughty boy then?" he leered. "You're down for RPs. Report to the cookhouse at the double!"

"But sergeant—" I protested.

"At the double Murray, in fatigues Murray and any more talk laddie and I'll put you on a charge!"

There was nothing I could do. Perhaps if I got to the barrack room there would be someone to ask if they would convey a message, but when I got there only Sam was sat on his bed doing his boots, his moist lips even moister from spitting and polishing.

"Are you not going out?" he asked.

"No," I responded, "I've got kitchen RPs."

I trudged down to the cookhouse and wept great big soppy lad tears as I stood loading potatoes into the peeler and the first girl I loved slipped from my grip forever.

For years afterward I wondered if she ever turned up, and whichever way I viewed it, it broke my heart. If she had just been humouring me and had no intention of keeping our date it would have been bad enough, but what if she had turned up, all pretty and made up, and stood and waited and waited before catching the train back to Llangollen? I could not bear to think about it. Whenever I see that lovely Welsh name I think of her, but I'll never know what she was called and she will never know my nickname was Ray short for Ralph.

The cooks were regular soldiers from the Catering Corps. Some may have been conscripts, as it was the last year of national service, and they looked down on the boys with as much scorn as pity and had very little to do with our lot at all. I can only recall one of them, a corporal. He had a very white face with two tiny eyes that stared at certain boys with a look that made me feel a little unsure. Now here he was in front of me telling me what to do and fixing me with his beady little eyes; he always stared at me whenever he was aware that I was in his sight.

I think at that moment if he had made an advance toward me I would have stabbed him with my potato peeler, but I needn't have worried as the sight of my snotty nose and woebegone look seemed to put him off. Homosexuality was not evident in the barracks, although there were certainly some lads who were uncertain of their orientation. Sex was a solo affair for most boys, and obsessive masturbators were soon identified and the piss taken out of them by the rest, who were masturbating just as much but hadn't been caught in the act.

Its funny how you can sense something unusual is about to happen when the pressure builds up and a sort of unease spreads through the

rooms of the barracks. So it was this particular time, when in the afternoon on a hot spring day a diverting rumble ensued from the room across
the hall. Someone shouted "Fight!" in our room and we all rushed into
the next one to see what was happening. Right by the door a young lad
called Barker was being held down by four lads, and my first reaction was
that he was about to be branded or tortured in some way, but then through
the crowd of boys appeared Curry.

Someone ripped open Barker's trousers and Curry grabbed hold of
the poor lad's dick and began to masturbate him. Barker's face was a
strange mixture of fear, embarrassment and an odd sort of pleasure as
Curry manipulated the lad to an joyless climax. Suddenly all the boys got
up and left the kid on his own to clean himself up, and Brady the Irish
boy slipped Curry five Park Drive cigarettes.

I could not see the point of this action; I never worked out why it took
place or what was to be proved or disproved. At my school there was a
little homo activity that mostly consisted of grabbing of genitals and the
general argy-bargy that goes on in playgrounds everywhere, but this was
different and humiliating and scary and sad and dirty. For a long time
afterwards Barker was on his own and for a while so was Curry; the
difference was that Curry couldn't have cared less what anyone thought,
but Barker's eyes were often red from crying.

∾

needlework

Curry would do almost any thing for a smoke. His nickname was Twos Up, which translates as 'seconds'. For example, if you were using a broom to sweep your bed space and someone shouted "twos up" it meant that they had next call on the broom. Curry called twos up on everybody's cigarettes, and if someone already had a twos up on your fag, he would have twos up on your twos up. He was the first bloke I ever saw smoke a cigarette end fixed on a pin or between the prongs of a fork, so desperate was he for his nicotine.

Because of the lack of money and our age, drink did not play a large part in our activities. Cigarettes, on the other hand, were at a premium. I don't recall a boy who didn't smoke, and I was no exception. I had now settled on about ten a day; having delayed my first until after breakfast I could get through the day on four more, and smoke the other five during the evening.

Payday was on Wednesday, so everyone was desperate for fags on Tuesday when the money had run out. From very early in my life I had been taught the value of money and how to save, and this frugality enabled me to adapt very quickly to overcoming this problem. Just saving cigarettes till payday would not have helped, as anyone knowing you had them would simply take them off you. Even smoking one would be an embarrassment,

as you would be constantly asked for "twos ups". My way around this was to buy a packet of five Park Drive on Wednesday and hide them in the toilets above the cistern; then when I needed my last cigarette, I would creep in to the bog and smoke it. Nearly always someone would wander in and shout, "Twos up on your fag!" and I don't think I ever stubbed out a cigarette myself on a Tuesday. In retrospect it would have been easy to have become a 'baron' as the going rate for a whole snout on Tuesday was at least two on Wednesday, but I was only interested in feeding my own habit.

However, I did find another way of earning a few extra shillings. One evening I decided to taper a pair of jeans. No-one showed me, I just worked it out. First I turned them inside out, then when I had decided on the width I wanted to have at the bottom, I drew a line with a ball-point pen up to the knee and sewed up to it in tiny under and over stitches. The only problem area was where the inseam had to be oversewn, but I got around it and by skilful pressing (by now we were all experts) the effect was all right.

One lad had been watching intently while I was sewing. When I'd finished he admired the look and asked me to do a pair for him, offering me five bob. I was happy to oblige, and after a while I acquired a longer needle and the price had risen to seven and six. Even Brady wanted a pair done. I was getting behind with my cleaning and polishing, and to be honest I was getting pissed off with doing it, especially as Brady had not yet paid me for his.

I tried being a bit more forceful about asking him.

"I'll knock yer feckin teeth down yer troat," he said. I decided that being company tailor was not the life for me.

I had to wait a while to get my revenge, but the opportunity came when he promised me a quid if I would do another pair for him. Up to then I had always left the old material in place inside the jeans or trousers, but this time, knowing he would never pay me, I asked if he would like me to cut off the waste. He thought it would be a good idea, especially if I were to taper them right up to the crotch.

Taper them I did, only this time I made them almost skin tight. It was particularly difficult sewing round the crotch, as three seams meet there, and I was glad that he had agreed to let me cut out the spare material as it made it easier to stitch.

I finally completed the job and handed them over. I can see him now,

forcing the black jeans on with an anxious look in my direction as he pushed his large feet through the bottoms. They looked very uncomfortable round the privates, but to my relief he seemed to like his exaggerated profile. Norman Case from the Buffs Regiment was with me when Brady tried them on, and like me he had little time for this bully.

"They look really great," he enthused.

Brady looked at us both, but seeing no trace of a smirk, his own impression that he looked pretty snazzy was confirmed. He changed gingerly out of the garment, promising to pay me next week. Once we were sure he was well and truly out of earshot we burst out laughing at the thought of his appearance.

Between Norman, Sam, Rex, Beau and myself, we persuaded the other lads not to laugh at him when they saw him wearing them on the weekend. Somehow everyone managed to look the other way as Brady got dressed and left the barracks for town. Luckily, being an older boy he no longer needed to check out with the guardroom, or someone might have laughed and spoilt our enjoyment of this moment. From a distance he looked as if his bare legs had been painted black, and the tightness of the crotch was forcing him to walk in a very strange way. I was almost helpless with laughter and so were Sam and Norman.

"You want to watch it, Ray," said Rex, and my laughter suddenly stopped as the possible consequences dawned on me.

I didn't see Brady return to barracks but I heard from a couple of different sources the same story—unfortunately too late to prepare myself for my reward for his humiliation. I was queuing for breakfast when I heard my name called. I looked round and an awesome blow caught me full square in my face, making my nose bleed and eyes run. It was of course Brady, and as I washed myself down in the washroom afterward I was comforted to hear the tale of his undoing.

Brady had got into town all right, but his own discomfiture had been amplified by the stares of others; finally some girl had laughed at him and his embarrassment, which forced him riskily into a pub. Seating himself on a stool his bulging crotch had released itself from my sewing and so had half the stitching down one leg. An attempt to pin up the damage had resulted in a minor piercing injury, the inevitable unravelling began, and a drunk and dishevelled Brady crept back after dark with the remains of his trousers flapping in the night breeze.

No further punishment was enacted on me, and no-one ever asked me to tighten their jeans again. Sam once or twice told me to ask for my money, but I preferred to let that one go.

Once when I was at school I found a little drawing of a girl in a sarong with a palm tree in the background. I was so impressed with it that I kept it for a while, not just for its erotic content but because it was so well drawn. Whenever I found myself doodling I would attempt to reproduce it from memory. Not with any great success, but a stylised version of it began to emerge and could on occasion lead someone to believe that I could 'do drawing'.

At some point my little south sea island girl had been seen and I was approached by Nick, a lad from the Ox and Bucks Light Infantry, who asked me if it was true I could draw. With some modesty I replied that I could do a little bit. He asked to see some and when I showed him some doodles he was impressed enough to ask if I could do him a drawing of an anchor. He seemed happy with my effort and asked in a matter-of-fact way if I would tattoo it on him. At first I thought he must be joking, but he was deadly serious.

"But I can't do a tattoo," I said.

"Course you can, all you need is a darning needle and some Indian ink."

Now I have to confess that I'd always been fascinated by tattoos and on my first day out of barracks down in Plymouth had tried to get an appointment at Rex Zeta's establishment on Union Street. Unfortunately on the Wednesday I was to have been marked, a sailor lad had passed out in front of me and Mr. Zeta had cancelled the rest of the day's appointments as a precaution in case the lad had needed medical treatment. In those days an infected tattoo could be classified as self-inflicted injury, and the forces were actually against lads marking themselves, not realising that apart from giving themselves some individuality when the army tried to make everyone look the same, it was also a rite of passage.

As it transpired I was lucky to miss out, as in the world of tattoo artists Rex Zeta's work is not much admired. There were some lads in the company who had great work on their arms: a boy from Huddersfield in particular, who wore some beautifully drawn birds; and another cockney lad who had some work done by an artist on the Waterloo Road.

When I realised that this chap was serious, I picked the brains of all

the tattooed boys in the company as to how it was done. They were mostly unable to say except that it didn't hurt. This was hard to figure out as it became obvious that from all they said that it was necessary to draw blood, and it was the blood mixing with ink under the skin that made the mark. I began by practising on myself and the first thing I realised was that I could not decide what design to have but I did learn to minimise the pain and got to be able to prick the skin quite fast and soon I was ready to have a go. Wisely Nick had decided to forgo the large anchor on the forearm in favour of a smaller version on the second joint of his thumb.

On the appointed evening in front of a small crowd I laid out the tools of my new trade on the table that doubled as both writing and ironing table in the middle of the room: Indian ink, darning needle (jeans tapering, for the use of) which was a little blunt but a good size, a ball-point pen and a towel. After drawing the little anchor in biro I commenced tapping away with my blunt needle and ink. Luckily Nick bled easily and the job was soon done, the whole thing being the size of a thumbnail. As the scab peeled off it was clear that my dots weren't close enough together and another session was called for.

The end result was quite effective, and probably my best work. I was pressed to do more and thankfully most of my efforts were very small and were reasonably good as far as prison type tattoos go. There were however one or two minor exceptions, where what looked good on paper did not translate well to the flesh.

One bloke wanted my Hawaiian girl on his forearm, and in spite of my trying to talk him out of it, his mind was made up and reluctantly I had a go. I remember this for two reasons: (a) because it was so hard to draw blood from his arm—the needle was getting blunter and blunter—and (b) because the way he placed his arm on the table meant that when it was finished and his arm assumed its normal position, the island girl had a twisted appearance with more voluptuous hips than were intended.

Thankfully he never noticed it himself, for when he lifted his arm up to see it, the tattoo distorted itself back into its original state. He never had the face drawn in, though; I think he'd had enough after the hour or so it took to get the ink into his arm.

The tattoo I remember the best though was for poor redheaded Dennis, a lad in one of the Lancashire regiments. Dennis was incredibly thin and pale, a slow and serious boy with a continuous slight tremor that shook his body as if he was cold. I asked him about his shaking and he said that

he always had been like it. I wondered again at this army that was happy to take all of us misfits.

Dennis had decided to have a skull and crossbones with the words 'Death or Glory' written in a scroll underneath. The needle by this time had become almost too blunt to push through a piece of paper, but for some reason I had not thought to change it. To make it still more difficult, Dennis's arm was so thin that the crossbones had to be very small to fit on it, and the scroll had to start on the underside of his arm to get the words on so that they were legible.

As I banged away at his sad little stick-like arm with my head down, an extraordinary thing happened: when I started filling in the hollow eye sockets in the skull Dennis's voice began to trail off and he stopped shaking. I finally noticed this and looked up at him to ask if he was all right, but he could only nod through clenched teeth, and when I had finished the word 'Death' he suddenly shouted, "STOP!" unable to stand the pain any more.

Unfortunately I had also pricked a large vein on the underside of his arm, which decided not to stop bleeding for quite a while. It was all pretty gruesome and effectively stopped my career as a skin artist. It may have been the sight of Dennis bloody and tear-stained, or perhaps just my bad draughtsmanship, or even this half tattoo of a skull with the word 'Death' written underneath it. I didn't get around to drawing the crossbones, and as far as I know Dennis never added the 'or Glory' to the design.

&

out

In spite of what you might call these lighter moments, I found my situation increasingly desperate. The realisation grew that I would have to do something radical if I was to get out of the army.

In terms of female comfort, things were pretty grim too. Oswestry as a town was provincial but at the same time inured to squaddies, and some of a town's naiveté disappears as it becomes used to the exuberance and energy of young over-trained soldiers on the lookout for adventure and/ or sex.

Nevertheless, one rainy night I met Linda, a plain, slightly dumpy local girl. She was already going out with a lad from Wakefield who I knew vaguely by sight from B Company, though I didn't know this at the time. She had a lovely laugh and a pretty Welsh accent, and that first evening I walked her back to her place, which smelt of washing and ironing and clothes drying and made me think of home.

"This is Ray, Mam," she said.

"Hello," said her Mam, hardly looking at me.

It was late and I had to get back to barracks so I made my excuses and moved toward the door.

"Can I see you again?" I asked.

"If you like," she replied. "There's a dance on Saturday at the town

hall, we could go there."

We had a little kiss on the doorstep and off I went back to the camp.

The next weekend I met her and we went to the pictures. I don't remember the film but I was allowed to pay for her; in fact she never paid for anything during the time we went out together. On the way back to her house she suddenly asked, "How old are you, Ray?"

"Eighteen," I lied.

"Oh that's all right then, only I don't go out with boys who are younger than me see," she explained. Then—I don't know where the idea came from—I suddenly said, "I've already got a kid. Would you like to see a picture of him?"

She looked a little taken aback at this but managed a curious, "Yes, if you like."

In my jacket pocket I had a wallet that my father had made either when he was in the desert or when he was in prison, and in this wallet I had a picture of myself as a baby that I'd brought with me from home. I showed her the photo under a street lamp and she even said that he looked a bit like me. Then, taking hold of my arm, she said that she was going to break it off with the lad from Wakefield and go steady with me.

Linda was eighteen and had expensive tastes, as I found out when she ordered a milkshake that cost half a crown. However, I was flattered and on the way back to her house I joked about her soon to be ex-boyfriend, saying that he was a bit thick and that his eyes were too close together. I was full of confidence now that she had plumped for me, and by my little deception she would know that I had carnal knowledge and would eventually expect some consummation of our relationship. I was really on a promise, and there was only a little resistance when I felt her breasts as we kissed goodnight.

When I had joined up the track most played on the NAAFI jukebox was *Three Steps to Heaven* by Eddie Cochrane. Then it was *Cathy's Clown* by the Everly Brothers, and now it was *Only the Lonely* by Roy Orbison. I wonder if all teenage songs are as appropriate to each generation as they seem to have been for mine.

The Saturday hop was great and they played *Only the Lonely* at least half a dozen times which meant that I could hold her close and shuffle around the brightly lit room. I was definitely getting somewhere, I could feel it and even in my thick grey Italian suit pressed up against her so could she.

When I called for her on the Sunday her mother said, "She's gone out with Mick and she won't be seeing you no more."

I was stunned and just stood there with my mouth open.

"But why?" I asked, almost unable to believe my ears.

"She found out you were only fifteen and she don't go out with boys younger than her. I'm sorry Ray, but you shouldn't have told her lies. Don't worry, you'll soon find a girl of your own age," she added comfortingly.

After a miserable night back at the barracks I was standing in the breakfast queue when a sharp dig in the ribs made me swing around to confront Mick.

"Tha's bin sayin' I'm thick," he declared in a loud voice.

"No I haven't," I countered cleverly.

"Tha's bin sayin my eyes is too close together tha 'as," he added.

"No I haven't," I repeated. I just couldn't think of anything else to say and anyway I expected my life to end at any moment as I was sure I was about to be stabbed by him with his dinner knife and fork. Instead he just looked at me and appeared to be searching for something to say.

He finally managed, "Well tha doesn't fookin want to either or than eyes'll be too fookin close an all!"

And that was it. I turned away expecting to feel the eating irons to be thrust between my shoulder blades but they never came, and for all I know Mick and Linda went off to be a couple while I slipped gradually into a deep depression.

In my desperation I began to write home to my mother, telling her just how unhappy I was and more or less promising anything if she could get me out. At first her letters were homely assurances that things would probably pick up, and that it was normal to see the worst of things from time to time and so on. These letters only added to my frustration. I was becoming more panicky by the day with my inability to convey my desperation. Now the army was a prison from which I had to escape or go mad.

My letters became longer and more emphatic. A couple of them spanned more than eight pages, and the tone became increasingly hopeless as I tried to press my case more urgently. Whatever the cost I must get out.

In the end Mum turned to her brother (Uncle Ray) for advice. He

helpfully suggested she should leave me in to make a man of me. The poor bastard had joined the navy as a child of thirteen, and my brother Bruce had almost joined the navy training ship *Arethusa* but thankfully stayed at home.

My mate Sam had also been growing disaffected with military life, and when he realised that I was determined to leave, he embarked on a similar course—that of obtaining the then huge sum of fifty pounds to buy his discharge. I had as much chance of raising that sort of money as raising the Titanic, and again had to resort to begging Mum to try to get it for me, but only after I finally convinced her how essential it was for me to get out.

My life was falling apart; boys that I had previously got along with began to drift away from me, I stopped bathing regularly and lost interest in everything. All I could think of was escape. I smoked whenever I could and begged twos ups from the other blokes. Somehow I avoided getting put on a charge for generally being depressed and dirty, but one day Beau came into the washroom and said that some of the boys were about to organise a regimental scrubbing.

I don't know how this sort of information is passed down, but this particular punishment is also about humiliation. The victim is usually jumped by four or five others, stripped naked and thrown on to a table; buckets of cold water are thrown over him and then Vim or some other detergent, and then he is scrubbed with a bass broom. I had to discover who was behind this move and was upset to find that Rex was the proposer. I went to him and confronted him, telling him that I'd thought of him as a friend and threatening to get each and every one of them back if they were to carry out their plan. By the end of this speech I was in tears, but I knew that Rex could see that I was truly at the end of my tether. Although the proposed scrubbing never took place, my friendship with Rex and most of the others was at an end and would never be repaired.

Finally a letter arrived from my mother telling me that she had borrowed the money from her boss on the condition that I would return to school and attempt to get some O-levels, and that I would get a weekend job and pay off all the money in less than a year. I know that I have experienced happiness since that letter, but until that moment it was the biggest high I had ever felt. I rushed to tell Sam, who had also been promised money from home, and we danced about with glee.

I immediately wrote back to thank Mum and promised to comply with all the terms. Sam and I were placed on discharge fatigues as the army tried to humiliate us further, and we weren't allowed out until our papers were in order. One day when we were on garden fatigues, Sam gave lip to a sadistic Scottish sergeant, who struck Sam a fierce punch on the side of the head. Though we were sometimes pushed around or given the odd dig with a pace stick, I'd never before seen a boy physically abused by an adult sergeant.

As the pain took hold of Sam's emotions and tears streamed down his face he yelled, "Right you fuckin' bastard I'm reporting you for that I've got four witnesses and they'll back me won't you lads?" and he turned around to us for support.

"Yeah Sam, don't worry, we saw what happened," we agreed. Somewhere in barrack room mythology the idea had emerged that you needed four boy soldiers to charge one grown-up NCO. The sergeant looked at us all and very slowly turned round and went inside the sergeants' mess, returning a few seconds later with another sergeant.

"Did you see me strike this soldier, sergeant?" he enquired, not looking at his colleague but just eyeing us back and forth through narrowed eyelids.

"No sergeant, I certainly did not," was the deliberately delivered reply. The situation was hopeless and we knew it.

"Now get on with your work or you'll all be on a fuckin' charge!" he bellowed. The two of them grinned at each other, and we were left in no doubt that for a few more days the army still had the upper hand.

At last the day arrived and Sam and I were ordered to get into best civvies and report to the battalion commander's office. We were marched in one at a time, and the commander asked me my reason for leaving. I told him I had secured a place at Croydon Technical College, then he handed me a reference, my pittance of saved pay and a travel warrant, and I was dismissed and officially out.

I waited excitedly for Sam to emerge from his farewell interview and asked him what he had said when the CO had asked him what his future plans were.

"I told him I was going to get a good job working on the barges down at Gravesend!" laughed Sam. We said goodbye to a couple of lads that weren't otherwise engaged, and Norman Case asked for our addresses. I

gave him mine and he wrote once or twice, but I didn't bother to keep up with the correspondence as I had other agenda by then. Sam, who had little time for Norman, gave him a made-up address in Gravesend.

Now Sam and I were off out of the barrack gates and standing on the side of the road heading toward the railway station. It was overcast and there was a stiff breeze, but to me the sky had never been bluer or the air warmer. I looked back at the poor hapless bastards on guard duty, and already their brown uniforms were assuming the anonymity we give soldiers so as not to grieve for them as individuals. Birds were singing in the fields around Parkhall Camp, soon two beautiful blonde girls would pull up in a pink Cadillac and ask us where we wanted to go and did we want to have sex with them and we would say yes and they would have loads of money and I breathed great lungfuls of free Shropshire air and the taste of freedom is real I can swear to it.

What actually happened is that we hitched a lift on an open back lorry, and standing up behind the cab with the wind in our faces, we hollered and sang all the way to the station. I have felt freedom and exhilaration many times since, but never so strong and in equal measure as on that ride. We had cups of tea and biscuits on the train and talked excitedly all the way to Victoria station, where we were to go our separate ways.

We entered the busy station in the late afternoon. An announcement called the Gravesend train, and as Sam ran to catch it I suddenly realised I only had this imaginary address he had given Norman. I didn't know it then, but I wouldn't see him again for twenty years, by which time I would have a son named Sam and a new name.

~

postscript

Five years later I was travelling on a huge crane fitted with caterpillar tracks which was moving at about four miles per hour along the road from Thessalonika to Athens. I had been hitchhiking for hours and this piece of plant had passed me several times, offering me a lift that I had already declined. I had got a few lifts but my progress was slow.

As I saw its lumbering form coming my way once again I decided to clamber aboard. There, hidden amongst the machinery and curled up in a foetal position, was a young and totally spaced-out German called Wolfgang. He had been travelling for a few years and was as skinny as a rake with, shorter hair than was normal for that time. He wore a t-shirt and waistcoat, black trousers, sandals and a tiny hat like the ones the black guys wore at home.

Wolfie spoke English with a slight American accent and a trace of a lisp. Some of his adventures were incredible, but he told them with no attempt to impress; it was just his reality he was keen to share, and he seemed to be amazed and delighted by each new experience and acquaintance that came his way.

Today he was riding a crane, tomorrow it could be a Ferrari, and some weeks previously in Afghanistan it had been in an oven-like compartment on a steam train. He was unable to get out of this until the locomotive

stopped, which it mercifully did before he succumbed and was cooked alive. He was clearly not over this trauma yet, and every now and then he would leave his womb-like spot on the crane and we would both walk alongside the vehicle.

Wolfie earned his living on the road as a pavement artist, and apart from a tin whistle and a few items of clothing all he carried were his chalks. He also had one book with him that bore the stamp of a secondhand dealer in Rangoon: Brendan Behan's *Borstal Boy*. Wolfie insisted that I take it as a parting gift when I left his company to hitch to Istanbul. I tried not to accept, but sometimes on the road where friendships are struck that you know are not to become lifelong companionships, the taking or receiving of small gifts symbolises the transitory nature of the friendship between two people and eases both consciences as they part, probably never to meet again.

"Good luck, my friend, and may the road be good to you; and when you read this book you may think of me."

I still have the book, I loved reading it, and all I can say is that I would have swapped my time in the Army for a spell in Brendan's borstal any day.

✹